Please remember that this is a library book,
and that it belongs only temporarily to each
person who uses it. Be considerate. Do
not write in this, or any, library book.

Crime Is Not
the Problem

STUDIES IN CRIME AND PUBLIC POLICY
Michael Tonry and Norval Morris, *General Editors*

Police for the Future
David Bayley

Incapacitation: Penal Confinement and the Restraint of Crime
Franklin E. Zimring and Gordon Hawkins

The American Street Gang: Its Nature, Prevalence, and Control
Malcom W. Klein

Sentencing Matters
Michael Tonry

The Habits of Legality: Criminal Justice and the Rule of Law
Francis A. Allen

Chinatown Gangs: Extortion, Enterprise, and Ethnicity
Ko-lin Chin

Responding to Troubled Youth
Cheryl L. Maxson and Malcom W. Klein

Community Policing, Chicago Style
Wesley G. Skogan and Susan M. Hartnett

Crime and Drugs in Contemporary American Politics
Katherine Beckett

Crime Is Not the Problem: Lethal Violence in America
Franklin E. Zimring and Gordon Hawkins

Crime Is Not the Problem

——

Lethal Violence in America

Franklin E. Zimring
Gordon Hawkins

OXFORD UNIVERSITY PRESS
New York   Oxford

Oxford University Press

Oxford   New York
Athens   Auckland   Bangkok   Bogotá   Buenos Aires   Calcutta
Cape Town   Chennai   Dar es Salaam   Delhi   Florence   Hong Kong   Istanbul
Karachi   Kuala Lumpur   Madrid   Melbourne   Mexico City   Mumbai
Nairobi   Paris   São Paulo   Singapore   Taipei   Tokyo   Toronto   Warsaw

and associated companies in

Berlin   Ibadan

Copyright © 1997 by Oxford University Press

First published by Oxford University Press, Inc., 1997

First issued as an Oxford University Press paperback, 1999

Oxford is a registered trademark of Oxford University Press

Library of Congress Cataloging-in-Publication Data
Zimring, Franklin E.
Crime is not the problem : lethal violence in America /
Franklin E. Zimring and Gordon Hawkins.
p. cm. — (Studies in crime and public policy)
Includes bibliographical references and index.
ISBN 0-19-511065-X
ISBN 0-19513105-3 (Pbk.)
1.Violent crimes—United States. 2.Violence—United States.
3.Violent crimes—United States—Prevention.
I. Hawkins, Gordon, 1919–. II.Title. III. Series.
HV6789.Z55   1997   364.1—dc21   96-39538

1 3 5 7 9 10 8 6 4 2

Printed in the United States of America
on acid-free paper

To the memory of Hans Zeisel, unlikely mentor

Contents

Acknowledgments

The list of debts we incurred on the path to this volume is long and diverse. The book grows out of almost thirty years of empirical study of violent assault in U.S. cities by Franklin Zimring, an eccentric research project for an American legal academic to pursue. The late Hans W. Mattick suggested a scientific study of patterns of criminal homicide in Chicago in 1966, and his colleague Norval Morris supported the expansion of that study into a series of analyses of homicide, assault, and robbery.

The Earl Warren Legal Institute at the University of California at Berkeley devoted about half its energies and resources to this project for the three-year gestation of the research and the book. The more proximate supports to this project took a wide variety of forms. Financial support was provided by the Boalt Hall Fund at the University of California. The John Simon Guggenheim Foundation provided fellowship support to Franklin Zimring during 1995-1996.

A number of individuals and organizations provided data and data analysis that were of great importance to the venture. Roseanne Bonney of the New South Wales Bureau of Criminal Statistics provided many specific data analyses that were important to the venture. Pat Mayhew and P. H. White of the Home Office Research and Statistics Department provided British data, as well as referrals to helpful colleagues at the Metropolitan Police in London, who disaggregated data to facilitate the comparison in Chapter 3 and Appendix 2. Nicholas Crawford of the Metropolitan Police provided important data on burglary, robbery, and homicide patterns in London.

We also owe a critical debt to the researchers who conducted the transnational victim survey work mentioned in Chapter 1 and discussed at length in Chapter 3. The work reported in this book could not have been executed without primary research materials that have been assembled over the recent past, particularly the survey research efforts reported in Chapter 3.

Data collection and analysis at Berkeley was quite a cottage industry. Michelle Anderson, Sam Kamin, June Kim, William Nelson, and Johan van Vuren were the primary research staff. Karen Chin coordinated both the administration of the research venture and the preparation of the book manuscript. Lucia Hwang word-processed a major share of the book chapters.

Throughout the writing and rewriting process, we have benefited from the reactions of listeners and readers. Earlier drafts of chapters were the materials for a Murray Lecture at the University of Iowa and the Brainerd Currie Lecture at Duke University. Chapter 10 was presented at a faculty workshop at Fordham Law School. Norval Morris of the University of Chicago read and reacted to every chapter in this book and Deborah Leff of the Joyce Foundation read most of the draft chapters. Other readers of sections of the book included Francis Allen, Philip Cook, Meir Dan-Cohen, David Garland, James Jacobs, Pat Mayhew, Robert MacCoun, Helen McInnis, Albert Reiss, Edward Rubin, and Robert Weisberg. We know that the book was substantially improved by the suggestions of our preliminary readers. We hope the quality of the final product justifies the investment of the many people who provided assistance.

One final debt, reflected in the dedication, emerged as this volume took shape. The influence of Hans Zeisel on the comparative perspective and statistical analysis in this book is subtle, but quite substantial. Over the course of a quarter of a century, much more was taught, much more was learned than we would have supposed.

Introduction

The American understanding of criminal justice policy over the generation just past has been a peculiar mix of consensus and controversy. Everybody agrees that crime is a uniquely serious problem in the United States, a major threat to the quality of American life. Yet, there are serious disagreements about causes and about how government can best be used to reduce crime. Is the debilitatingly high crime rate in the United States a result of insufficient economic opportunity or insufficient prison capacity? Why does the public continue to be afraid when huge investments are made in crime control and criminal justice? Why indeed does public fear remain high even when rates of crime decline?

Two decades of unprecedented investment in crime control have produced no diminution in public fear in the United States; instead, in the debate over the 1994 federal crime control legislation, the contending parties agreed that crime policy had failed to produce acceptable levels of public safety. Why has policy failed? The ideological combatants in and out of Congress have a ready answer to that question. Each side tells us that the failure of current policy proves that its opponents cannot cure American crime.

The simple truth is that spreading our efforts and material resources over the entire range of criminal behaviors in the United States is fighting the wrong war. What citizens fear is not the theft of their property, but the prospect of lethal violence. It turns out that most developed countries have crime rates close to those experienced in the United States. But rates of lethal violence in these nations are a small fraction of those in the United States. Crime, under these circumstances, is a major annoyance, but no more than that in Western nations.

In the United States, the rates of death and life-threatening injury from intentional attacks are four to eighteen times as great as in other developed nations. Americans fear crime because they view these high rates of death and injury as a byproduct of high levels of crime and large numbers of criminals. They are wrong.

This study will demonstrate that lethal violence is a specific problem separate from general crime rates. The first five chapters of the book will present the available evidence on crime and lethal violence in the United States. The second part of the book will then examine how changing the subject from crime generally to lethal violence specifically can improve our understanding of the effects of factors such as guns, mass media, and drugs. A large part of the confusion that arises in discussions of the root causes of crime and violence can be avoided by focusing on the proximate causes of death and serious injury.

The third part of this book addresses the question of how governmental policies might be redesigned to reduce the volume of intentional injury and death in the United States. What can improve the criminal law as an instrument of public safety? What other governmental means can make the streets of America safer?

So the first segment of the book establishes the factual foundation for concluding that lethal violence is a central problem in contemporary American life. The second section shows some implications of the pattern established in Part I on our understanding of the causes of deadly violence. The third section then considers strategies of harm prevention.

The ambitions of this volume are high. We hope to change the subject, in both scholarly and policy analysis in the United States, from crime control to the control of lethal violence. In the cliché that emerged from the history of science, this study encourages a paradigm shift in describing the particular problem that sets Americans apart from the citizens of other nations and inhibits their enjoyment of civil society. Personal safety is the core concern of the anxious citizen; so too it should be the special focus of those who administer the machinery of state power.

Crime Is Not
the Problem

I

THE AMERICAN
DIFFERENCE

PART I OF THIS VOLUME provides a variety of statistical demonstrations that lethal violence rather than high rates of crime is the disabling problem that sets the United States apart from other developed countries in the 1990s. Chapter 1 compares crime volume in two sets of comparison cities, Sydney and Los Angeles, and New York City and London. After those city-level contrasts, national-level comparisons of homicide and general crime rates are presented, and some of the policy errors that result when violence problems are treated as crime problems are outlined.

Chapter 2 shows that property crime rates have increased dramatically in almost all developed nations over the last generation, while there has been no clear trend for lethal violence. Over time, it appears that neither the volume of crime nor the number of active criminals influence variations in the rate of lethal violence in most nations. In this context, changes in the level of property crime do not appear to be an important cause of homicide.

Chapter 3 compares crime and violence at the national level, using multinational victim surveys, official crime statistics, and health statistics on intentional homicide. The comparisons show that the rates of most offenses in the United States are not far removed from rates of crime victimization in other countries. Huge differences in homicide rates are not paralleled by large differences in rates of nonfatal violence or nonviolent property offenses. A series of specific comparisons of the death rates from property crime and assault in New York City and London show how enormous differences in death risk can be explained even when general crime patterns are similar. A preference for crimes of personal force and the willingness and ability to use guns in robbery make similar levels of property crime fifty-four times as deadly in New York City as in London.

Chapter 4 presents a detailed survey of violence in the United States. Patterns of homicide are explored in detail in the first part of the chapter. The second part of the chapter reports on the extent to which different types of crime risk the death of victims.

Chapter 5 applies the lessons of earlier chapters on the special importance of lethal violence to a reinterpretation of data on crime and violence among African-Americans. The chapter shows that among African-Americans as victims and offenders, life-threatening violence is far more concentrated when compared to white rates than is nonviolent crime. Just as it is dangerously inaccurate to think that America's major problem is crime rather than violence, the most serious problem by far in the African-American communities of the United States is not crime but lethal violence.

The aim of these five chapters is to change the topic of a recurrent American debate, to shift the subject from crime to life-threatening violence. Merely calling a problem by its correct name is not the equivalent of solving it, but the mislabeling of violence as a crime problem can only perpetuate a cycle of failure and frustration.

1

What Americans Fear

By LONGSTANDING HABIT, Americans use the terms "crime" and "violence" interchangeably. When expressing concern about urban conditions we commonly talk about "the crime problem" or "the violence problem" as if they were the same thing. When drive-by shootings create newspaper headlines, we demand that our elected officials do something about crime.

At the core of this interchangeable usage of crime and violence is the belief that crime and lethal violence are two aspects of the same problem. It is widely believed that there is much more crime of all kinds in the United States than in other developed countries. With so much crime and so many criminals, the high rates of lethal violence in the United States seem all but inevitable to many observers.

The mission of this chapter is to demonstrate that rates of crime are not greatly different in the United States from those in other developed nations and that our extremely high rates of lethal violence are a separate phenomenon, a distinct social problem that is the real source of fear and anger in American life. The chapter will provide a review of some objective conditions of crime and lethal violence in the United States and link these empirical patterns to the subjective dimensions of fear in urban America. The first section of this chapter will provide data on crime and lethal violence in international perspective. This section provides a preview of the extensive research findings that will be presented in Chapters 2 to 5.

The second section of this chapter presents a simple theory of why lethal violence is a major concern in developed nations as well as a problem of great importance in the United States. The third part of the chapter considers some complicating factors in the relationship between crime, violence, and citizen fears. We identify a process of categorical contagion that leads citizens to fear lethal violence in a broader variety of settings than those that carry any substantial risk to life and limb. To live in an environment where robbery presents a serious hazard to its victims seems to provoke citizens to fear for their lives even from particular forms of crime that do not place their victims at mortal risk.

The final section of this chapter shows that general crackdowns on crime are inefficient and potentially self-defeating methods of reducing the risks of lethal violence. It thus appears that one natural reaction to lethal violence, a heightened fear of all kinds of crime, may lead to ineffective responses to the life-threatening behavior that is the core concern of the fearful public. Citizen fears may systematically point public policy toward crime in the wrong direction.

Crime and Violence in International Perspective
Los Angeles and Sydney

Los Angeles is the second largest city in the United States with a 1992 population estimated at 3.6 million for its crime statistics reporting unit. It is a multiracial, multicultural city on the Pacific Coast with a crime rate that by most accounts is its most serious civic problem. Sydney, Australia, is also a city of 3.6 million located on the Pacific Coast of the continent. While multicultural by Australian standards, the ethnic and language mixture falls far short of that in Los Angeles. Crime in Sydney is a serious annoyance, but not a major threat to the continued viability of the city or to the health and welfare of its citizens.

Figure 1.1 compares the volume of four crimes reported by the police in Sydney and Los Angeles by expressing the number of offenses in Sydney as a percentage of the Los Angeles crime volume. Since the population of the two cities is the same, the crime volume comparison is also a crime rate comparison. The theft category reported at the far left of Figure 1.1 includes most forms of stealing that are unaggravated by elements that the law regards as increasing the gravity of the offense. This is the most common offense reported in all cities, and the two jurisdictions under review are no exception. Sydney reports just over 90,000 theft incidents, roughly three-quarters of the volume reported in Los Angeles.

Burglary is an aggravated form of theft where the offender breaks and enters private property in order to steal. The crime statistics for Sydney report the offense under two headings: breaking and entering a dwelling, and breaking and entering a building that is not a dwelling. The volume of such crimes in Sydney during 1992 exceeded 63,000, about 10 percent more than the number of burglaries reported in Los Angeles.

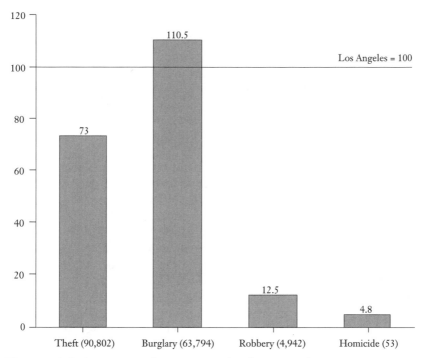

Figure 1.1. Sydney crime volume compared with Los Angeles, 1992. *Source:* U.S. Department of Justice, Federal Bureau of Investigation, 1992; New South Wales Bureau of Criminal Statistics 1992.

The pattern noted for burglary contrasts sharply with robbery, the other major category of aggravated property crime. Robbery is defined as the taking of property from the person of another by force or by the threat of force. In 1992 Los Angeles reported 39,508 robberies while Sydney reported 4,942, one-eighth the Los Angeles rate. The ratio of burglaries to robberies in Los Angeles is just under 3 to 2; the ratio of burglaries to robberies in Sydney is greater than 12 to 1.

The final crime category reported in Figure 1.1 is for homicides resulting from intentional injury. There were fifty-three such offenses reported by the police in Sydney during 1992, a crime volume equal to 5 percent of the 1,094 homicides reported by the Los Angeles police that same year. The difference between the two cities in rates of criminal homicide exceeds an order of magnitude. The citizens of Sydney can thus live with their high crime rate in relative comfort because they are not dying from it in large numbers.

The major statistical conclusion one draws from an inspection of Figure 1.1 is that the nature of the comparison between Sydney and Los Angeles depends on what is being compared. For theft and burglary the two cities are quite similar. For robbery and homicide they are vastly dissimilar.

The substantive conclusion to be drawn from this statistical pattern can be stated in two ways. It seems beyond dispute that what separates the two cities is not the amount of crime they experience, but the character of the crime they experience. But the point can be put more sharply than that: What is distinctive and threatening in Los Angeles is not a crime problem but a violence problem.

New York City and London

New York City is the largest city in the United States with a population at 7 million. London has a city population of 6.6 million. Figure 1.2 shows London crime rates per 100,000 using New York City rates as a standard for comparison. The statistical comparison in Figure 1.2 is even more surprising than that concerning Los Angeles and Sydney, and to the same effect. London has more theft than New York City and a rate of burglary 57 percent higher. But the robbery rate in London is less than one-fifth the robbery rate in New York City and the homicide rate in London is less than one-tenth the New York City figure.

The total number of offenses per 100,000 citizens in Figure 1.2 is higher in London than in New York City. If total crime rates were the problem,

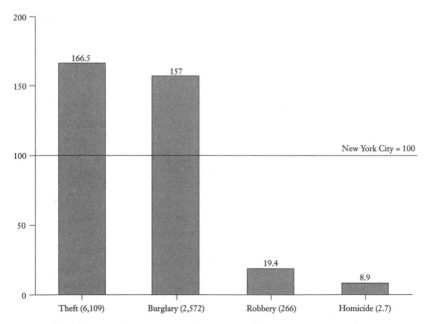

Figure 1.2. London crime rates (per 100,000) compared with New York City, 1990. *Source:* U.S. Department of Justice, Federal Bureau of Investigation, 1990; London Research Centre 1993.

Londoners should live in fear or New Yorkers in relative complacency. They have the same magnitude of crime. But with death rates eleven times as high as London, the population of New York City is far from comfortable. Lethal violence is New York City's distinctive problem, not crime, and lower rates of general theft are no consolation for huge death toll differences.

If readers are wondering whether these data are selective and misleading crime rates, or are numbers that are produced by the peculiarities of different reporting systems, the next set of comparisons should provide some reassurance that our city comparisons are part of a broad and consistent pattern.

Twenty Countries

We can show clearly that America's special problem is violence and not crime by comparing the results of a twenty-nation survey of citizens about the rate at which they were victims of crime with World Health Organization data on death from assaults for the same nations. Figure 1.3 (see p. 8) shows the violent death rates for each group of five nations with the highest crime levels, then the next two highest, and finally the lowest crime categories.

There are several indications that a country's crime rate is substantially independent of its rate of lethal violence. First, the variation in violent death rate is quite large within the separate crime rate categories. Within the group of highest crime nations, the homicide rates vary by a factor of eleven, in the next group by a factor of five, in the third group by a factor of three, and in the lowest crime group by a factor of eight. In contrast, the median homicide rates for the four different crime categories are clustered between 1.3 and 2.2. So knowing which crime rate category a country belongs in does not tell one anything much about what rate of violent death that country suffers.

And knowing a country's violent death rate does not predict much about its crime rate. The lowest death rate country (England) has a crime rate just over average. The next lowest violence nation is Japan, which has the lowest crime rate also. The third lowest death rate country is the Netherlands, in the highest crime rate group. The pattern is just as opaque at the top of the violence distribution. The most violent country, the United States, has a high crime rate as well. The next most violent country, Northern Ireland, is in the lowest crime rate group.

This data set provides a multinational example of the central point that lethal violence is the crucial problem in the United States. It shows the United States clustered with other industrial countries in crime rate, but head and shoulders above the rest in violent death.

It also suggests that lethal violence might be the best predictor of citizen fear on a transnational basis. Where would you rather live when exam-

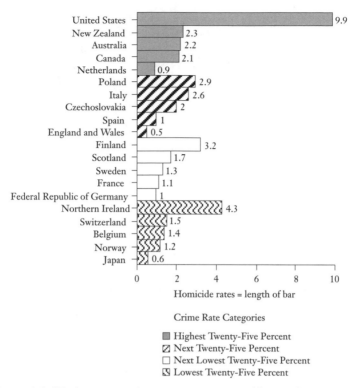

United States ———————————— 9.9
New Zealand — 2.3
Australia — 2.2
Canada — 2.1
Netherlands — 0.9
Poland — 2.9
Italy — 2.6
Czechoslovakia — 2
Spain — 1
England and Wales — 0.5
Finland — 3.2
Scotland — 1.7
Sweden — 1.3
France — 1.1
Federal Republic of Germany — 1
Northern Ireland — 4.3
Switzerland — 1.5
Belgium — 1.4
Norway — 1.2
Japan — 0.6

0   2   4   6   8   10

Homicide rates = length of bar

Crime Rate Categories

■ Highest Twenty-Five Percent
▨ Next Twenty-Five Percent
□ Next Lowest Twenty-Five Percent
▨ Lowest Twenty-Five Percent

Figure 1.3. Victim survey crime rate categories and homicide rates, twenty countries. *Source*: van Dijk and Mayhew 1993 (victim survey crime rates); World Health Organization 1990 (homicide rates).

ining the map of Figure 1.3? In England with its high crime rate and 0.5 deaths per 100,000 or in Northern Ireland with a much lower crime rate and nine times the death rate? Your money or your life?

Judging from Figure 1.3, the United States has about the same rate of crime and prevalence of criminality as the Netherlands and Australia. But ours is by far the most dangerous country to live in. We currently have a Netherlands-size crime problem and a king-size violence problem that threatens the social organization of our cities. Which problem is at the root of citizen fear in the United States? Which problem should we try to solve?

Three Dimensions of Fear

What types of loss from crime produce fear and anxiety among citizens? A common-sense calculus would emphasize three aspects of the types of criminal harms that are of the largest significance in provoking fear:

1. the importance of the interest threatened
2. the capacity of insurance and compensation schemes to restore the welfare of crime victims, and
3. the extent to which potential crime victims feel they can control their risks of loss by altering behavior.

For a mixture of obvious and nonobvious reasons, lethal violence is the most frightening threat in every modern industrial nation. The obvious reason why lethal violence is a priority concern is the importance people attach to personal survival. Physical survival, security from assault, freedom from the pain inflicted by serious intentional injuries are among the most basic interests citizens have. On this basis alone, we would expect life-threatening assault to be at the top of any citizen's fears about crime.

But the effectiveness of insurance and compensation schemes to ease the pain of property crime when compared with the impossibility of restoring life and health is an additional reason why serious violence is the central reason citizens fear predation. The security of property from criminal trespass can be achieved in the modern state by creating safe methods of preserving property interests and by facilitating insurance and other loss-spreading mechanisms to function when property is taken. Most economic assets cannot be taken by a thief in the age of the bank account and real estate title. Those chattels that remain at risk—the automobile, the home computer, and the bicycle—are usually the subject of automobile or household insurance. The percentage of gross national product that is redistributed by larceny and burglary in developed countries is quite small. When one of us asked a group of students, "What happens when someone steals your new BMW?" one student replied, "You get a better BMW," an arch response that nonetheless reflects social perceptions about automobile insurance with some accuracy. For most citizens, replacing one BMW with another comes quite close to making the crime victim whole; auto theft is amenable to a process we would call commensurate compensation.

By contrast, no amount of life insurance will give the insured back his life if he is killed in a street robbery. So even when programs are in place to deal with the financial costs of serious violence, the lack of commensurate compensation will make those criminal harms that cannot be reversed more worrisome to potential victims. In this sense, one natural byproduct of extensive insurance and property security is that citizens will concentrate their crime anxieties on those losses that cannot be effectively redressed. The special priority accorded to threats like homicide, forcible rape, and life-endangering injury will be more apparent in a system where most citizens have little to fear from standard forms of property crime.

The third dimension that we believe influences the level of fear expressed about particular criminal harms is the degree to which potential victims feel they can control the risks of becoming victims. The prospect of what the newspapers call "random violence" is particularly problematic because it suggests that there is no set of precautions a potential victim can take to reduce the personal risk of victimization. The more members of the public feel the risks of a particular harm are within their control, the more secure citizens will feel about their personal situation. But if potential victims feel there is no way they can take action to modify risks, this will heighten their anxiety about a particular risk. Later in the book, we will suggest that one reason citizens fear stranger violence more than they fear being killed by friends or family is because they feel more control over their choice of personal acquaintances, while the strangers they encounter are not as easy to choose or to reject.

If these three dimensions of risk are the significant factors in predicting citizen fear, two points of general applicability can be made about lethal violence as a crime control priority in developed nations. First, there is good reason to suppose that life-threatening violence is the most feared aspect of the threat of crime, even in countries where the rate of homicide is quite low. While an American observer might be amused to find fear of gunshot wounds is a focal concern in Japan, where there were thirty-two gun homicides in 1995 (Kristof 1996), the small chance of a major harm that cannot be effectively compensated or avoided might be more worrisome than less catastrophic injuries, even if these occur with much greater regularity. It may thus be rational for all of the countries covered in Figure 1.3 to hold lethal violence as the number one concern.

A second general point is that a special concern with lethal violence may be one consequence of successful social and economic development. The greater the success of a society in producing and distributing property, the larger the presence of insurance and compensation, the less average citizens will need to worry about their automobiles and their bicycles. This allows public concern about crime to return to bedrock worries about physical security. So the fact that lethal violence is a social control priority is not always a measure of social pathology. The greater the success of crime prevention and loss spreading, the more likely it will be that security of life and limb are the residual concerns of the citizenry.

So life-threatening violence should be a central concern in all developed nations, but nowhere in the Western world should lethal violence generate the level of attention it demands in the United States. Even if the rate of lethal violence is not relevant to whether such acts are the chief concern of law enforcement, the sheer amount of lethal violence is an important determinant of how much public concern is justified. A homicide rate five times the average of the developed nations and twice that of Northern Ireland in a time of troubles is an important cause of concern for the major developed nation in the modern world. Chronically high rates of lethal violence generate insecurities in the United States that are qualitatively different from those found in other advanced countries. Lethal violence is the most serious social control problem in every developed nation; it is by far a more serious problem in the United States than in any society with which we would care to compare ourselves.

Crime, Violence, and Citizen Fear

One sharp contrast between Sydney and Los Angeles invites us to consider the relationship between rates of life-threatening personal violence and public perceptions of the seriousness of crime as a problem. As measured by the political importance of crime as an election issue, or the degree to which fear of crime is mentioned as a major disorganizing influence on urban life, Sydney does not seem to have a significant crime problem. To be sure, housebreakers are not popular figures in New South Wales and complaints about crime are quite common, but terror is not.

Los Angeles is a city where fear of crime and of criminals is arguably the single most important social and political issue for the majority of citizens. Scientific surveys of public opinion reflect this difference to some degree, but they do not capture the palpable difference between crime as an annoyance in Australia and crime as a fundamental threat to social life in Los Angeles. The statewide Field polling organization in California finds crime to be the number one problem reported in the state; concern about policy toward criminals dominated the 1994 California elections to an extent that would be unthinkable at any level of government in Australia. The intensity of citizen concern in California is also reflected in the demand for substantial changes in criminal justice policy. The prison population in California grew 400 percent in the fifteen years prior to the 1994 elections, but California voters nevertheless overwhelmingly supported a referendum in 1994 that required a twenty-five years to life sentence for anyone convicted of a third felony if the offender's previous convictions had been as serious as housebreaking.

Since general levels of nonviolent crime in Sydney and Los Angeles are closely similar, why not conclude that it is levels of lethal violence rather than of crime generally that determine the degree of public fear? Why else would similar numbers of criminals and rates of crime lead to such a sharp cleavage in public response? The question is an important one, but far from easy to answer with confidence. Evidence regarding the relationship between rates of different types of crime and public attitudes is surprisingly sparse, and the specific question of the influence on attitudes of rates of violence, rather than rates of crime generally, has not been addressed systematically.

There are two different issues involved in determining the relationship between rates of violence and public fear: the salience of lethal violence as a focal point for citizen fear, and the influence of rates of violence on levels of public concern about violence. On the first issue the answer seems clear: when citizens are afraid of crime it is life-threatening, personal violence that dominates their attention. On the second issue, the evidence is far from clear. While the objective risks of violence undoubtedly influence the level of public fear, so also do many other variables. And the extent to which differential levels of public concern can be explained by differences in objective risk is not known.

To characterize concern about serious personal violence as the dominant image in public fear of crime may seem like an overstatement. Chapter 4 will document the relatively low levels of danger to life associated with residential burglary as a crime, but residential burglary is a crime that citizens greatly fear in California. Indeed, including residential burglary as a triggering felony in the California "three strikes" sentencing proposal was vigorously supported by the public even though it tripled the cost of the program (Zimring 1994). Is this not evidence that nonviolent threats are as salient to individuals as violent ones?

Probably not. Public fear of burglary is generated by images of the worst thing that could happen in the course of a housebreaking, rather that the kind of things that usually do happen when burglars appear. The majority of burglarized dwellings are unoccupied at the time of the invasion, but the image of burglary that provokes public fear is of the burglary of an occupied dwelling. The great majority of burglars would react nonviolently in any interaction with household members, but the image of burglary that produces high levels of citizen fear finds the victim defenseless in bed and at risk of murder. It is the worst-case burglar that provokes those citizens who express high levels of fear regarding residential burglary. This is an issue that could be explored by carefully constructed survey research. To date, however, the question of what images preoccupy citizens with high levels of fear regarding particular types of crime has not been investigated.

But fear of the worst-case burglar does not explain the contrast between Sydney and Los Angeles. Why would housebreakers provoke much more fear in Los Angeles than in Sydney? One reason might be the fact that many people have homogeneous images of "the criminal." That is to say that they do not think of robbers and burglars as different sorts of people, but rather imagine the criminal offender who threatens their sense of security as a composite of the personal characteristics of the criminal offenders they have heard about. If this homogeneity of image phenomenon is operative, citizens who live in environments where homicidal attacks are common will fear all kinds of contact with criminal offenders much more than citizens whose composite image of the criminal offender derives from a general environment that experiences less lethal violence.

In an urban environment where armed robbery frequently leads to the death of victims, the purse snatcher and the burglar will acquire much of the threatening character of the robber because the composite generalized image of the criminal that conditions public fear acquires the characteristics of the lethal armed robber. The fear generated by the kidnap and murder of Polly Klaas in California provokes long sentences for residential burglars because the burglar in the citizen's scenario has acquired the characteristics of Polly Klaas's killer.

High levels of interpersonal violence could thus generate a process we call categorical contagion. This is the agency whereby citizens come to fear many forms of criminal behavior because they imagine them all committed by extremely violent protagonists. Lower general levels of violence may be associated with less pressure toward categorical contagion because there is less in the way of frightening violence to condition the citizen's image of the criminal threat.

Processes of categorical contagion may operate in social life well beyond the frontiers of the criminal code. Just as personal safety and bodily security are the core concerns of fear of crime, concern about vulnerability to assault can produce fear of a wide variety of social encounters that include rudeness and incivility and even face-to-face contact with strangers in the streets if those strangers are seen as threatening. If a person carries profound feelings of physical vulnerability into a social setting, even ambiguous or innocuous behavior can produce substantial levels of anxiety.

It is also important to recognize that this process of categorical contagion may be a two-way street in which a high level of anxiety about strangers or face-to-face interaction may express itself as a fear of becoming a victim of a violent crime. Just as substantial anxieties about being robbed or attacked may make a person apprehensive about encountering strangers, an intense but nonspecific fear of strangers or foreigners or black people may produce more specific concerns that the subjects of our apprehension intend to assault us.

Some Social Causes of Fear

But what social circumstances predict variations in citizen concern about safety in a modern industrial society? This is a complicated question and one that has not been squarely addressed in the social science literature on the fear of crime. We would expect at least three major influences on the level of fear regarding serious crime: (1) the amount and seriousness of violent crime, (2) the level of fear-arousing social conditions in the immediate physical environment of the subject, and (3) the amount and perceived seriousness of fear-arousing cues in the mass media and the personal social universe of the subject.

How important are variations in actual risk in the mix of cues that produce levels of citizen fear of violence? We would expect variations in the risk of serious violence to be a major determinant of levels of fear that exert influence in a variety of ways. The higher the rate of serious violence, the larger the chance that the average citizen will have personal experience as a crime victim or be in some social relationship to a violence victim. The larger the risk of serious violence, the stronger the associations between fear of violence and various fear-arousing cues in the citizen's immediate social environment. The higher the number of people who get shot, stabbed, or mugged, the more fear-arousing will be citizen contact with boom boxes, broken windows, or threatening-looking strangers. Finally, we would expect that both the number of social cues and the amount of media attention to violence would be directly influenced by the rate and seriousness of violence, although we are more confident of this relationship in the contacts of the citizen than in the quantum of media cues about violence.

We would expect to find a positive association over time and cross-sectionally between risks of life-threatening violence and the mix of cues that determine levels of public fear. But variations in risk are by no means the only influences on levels of public consciousness in mass society. Processes of categorical contagion will link levels of public fear of violence to fluctuations in other social conditions that make people anxious and insecure. Further, to the extent that the character and quantity of media attention to violence is a variable that fluctuates independently of trends in risk, this will also influence levels of fear, particularly when citizens lack more direct experience. It thus seems probable that fear of violence in the 1990s is, to some extent, a media event independent of changes in other social conditions. We would also expect that variations in media coverage will be of larger importance in determining levels of concern and fear amongst groups that lack significant first- and second-hand experience of violence than among persons with more direct experience.

We do not know the maximum level of public fear that can be produced and sustained in an environment of general social anxiety, but low levels of lethal interpersonal violence. An attempt to import an American-style "law and order" campaign into English electoral politics would be a natural experiment to see whether fear of lethal violence can be induced and sustained at high levels without a high death rate from violence as a feature of the social environment.

A similar issue concerns the generality of fear induced by incivility and disorder. James Q. Wilson and George Kelling argued persuasively in their "Broken Windows" article that indications of incivility and disorder produce citizen fear and the demand for law enforcement and social control (Wilson and Kelling 1982). One reason such indications could arouse fear is that they convey to many persons the message that they are vulnerable to more direct and more violent predation. But will the level of fear produced by disorder and incivility be as great where rates of lethal violence are low as they will be where those rates are high? The context in which the broken-window argument was made was urban conditions with high rates of lethal violence. The extent to which fear of lethal violence and fear of concentrated threats to public order feed off each other should be a priority concern in the social psychology of crime fears. And the social psychology of citizen fears should be an important topic for scholarly research.

Crime Policy as Violence Policy

Life-threatening violence is, of course, against the public policy of the modern state in all but exceptional cases, but so are a wide variety of acts that range from larceny to illegal drug taking to sexual exploitation of the immature. What, if anything, is wrong with public policy that treats violence only as one of the many crime problems that are best addressed by police, prosecutors, and prisons?

This section outlines some of the difficulties associated with misdefining American violence as solely a crime problem. In pursuing this analysis, we do not deny that crime in the United States is destructive, costly, and disorganizing. Rather, we argue that it is the violent strain in American social life which causes the special destruction and disorganization produced by American crime.

Further, there are hazards associated with making general crime control policy the dominant governmental and social policy with respect to violence: the narrowness of a crime policy perspective, the failure to address noncriminal sources of potential violence, and the diffusion and loss of priority that result when violence is principally addressed as part of the U.S. crime problem. We will first provide a general outline of these objections, and then illustrate many of these problems from the historical record of recent American crime wars.

Three Objections

NARROWNESS OF PERSPECTIVE

The first problem we encounter when lethal violence is regarded as a crime problem is that it tends then to be regarded as only a crime problem properly to be addressed with the usual tools and processes of the criminal justice system. One difficulty with this narrow view of violence prevention is that current criminal justice processes do not seem to be very successful in combating any form of crime, so that limiting the campaign against violence to available anticrime mechanisms is not a promising emphasis.

Assuming that the rate and seriousness of our life-threatening violence is a natural outgrowth of a high volume of crime and criminals is also a false diagnosis of the problem. It is widely believed that the reason the United States suffers particularly from violent crime is that America has so many criminals. If lethal violence is a crime problem, the most natural and obvious cause is an excess supply of criminals and whatever social processes may be responsible for that surplus. The problem with this diagnosis is its demonstrable falsity. Recall the comparative incidence of theft, burglary, and robbery in Sydney and Los Angeles. For every ten theft offenses reported in Sydney, Los Angeles reports just over thirteen such offenses.

The supply of thieves in the two communities would seem to be at rough parity. The distribution of one form of aggravated theft, burglary, lends further support to the hypothesis of equivalent criminogenesis: For every ten burglaries reported in Sydney, Los Angeles counts nine. But for every ten robberies reported in Sydney there are eighty in Los Angeles. The significant contrast between the two cities will not concern the number of offenders any more than it will involve the number of offenses. It is only the kind of crime that differentiates the cities, so that searching for the causes of crime generally as an explanation of the particular problem in Los Angeles is barking up the wrong tree.

It is not helpful to respond that the reason other countries have similar crime rates and much lower rates of violence is that cities in the United States have different types of criminals and crime. This merely begs the question of why United States crime is so much more likely to include life-threatening violence. The central fact that regarding violence as principally a crime problem obscures is that rates of homicide and robbery cannot be implied, predicted, or explained as a consequence of our general level of crime or population of criminals.

THE FALLACY OF UNDERINCLUSION

A related problem is that searching for the sources of lethal violence only in the caseload of the criminal courts would be to miss many processes of great importance in generating violence. A propensity for violence is characteristic not only of American crime, but also of many other aspects of American social life. The reader will recall that for every homicide reported in Sydney, twenty bodies are added to the count in Los Angeles. Only a minority of Los Angeles homicides grow out of criminal encounters like robbery and rape. A far greater proportion of Los Angeles homicides grow out of arguments and other social encounters between acquaintances. Only those arguments that produce great injury and come to the attention of the police are regarded as criminal. Most of the processes that generate the risk of violence are not analyzed.

Why should arguments in Los Angeles lead to so much more loss of life than in Sydney? It is likely that the same social tendencies that make crime more dangerous in Los Angeles also make barroom fights and arguments among coworkers more likely to be life-threatening. The tendency toward violence in the United States is neither limited to a discrete criminal class nor confined to criminal patterns of behavior. The same social tendencies that predispose American offenders to robbery more often than their foreign counterparts also make arguments more lethal in California than in New South Wales.

DIFFUSION OF FOCUS

If violence in the United States is a much broader problem than crime, it is also the case that the range of criminal behavior in America is much broader than that of violence. Most offenses and most offenders are not violent. In Los Angeles for example, only 26 percent of index crimes in 1992 involved the use or threat of personal violence. When nonindex offenses such as drug sales and possession are added, the proportion of crimes involving violence declines to about 15 percent.

If this small portion of crime involves violence, the first concern with using a general anticrime policy to combat violence it that the policy will miss the target (if violence should be the target) 85 percent of the time. A related problem of diffuse focus is the lack of any explicit priority given to punishing and controlling violence. The best illustration of the practical impact of unfocused anticrime crusades is found in recent American history.

On the Paradoxical Impacts of Crime Wars

The dramatic increase in resources devoted to the punishment of crime in recent years provides a clinical case study of the impact of a general crackdown on crime on policy toward violent crime. The paradox of the crime crackdown is this: When penal resources are scarce, the priority given to more serious offenses means that life-threatening violence will receive a large share of the most serious punishments. No matter how small the prison, we tend to make room for Charles Manson and Willie Horton. But expanding punishment resources will have more effect on cases of marginal seriousness rather than those that provoke the greatest degree of citizen fear. The result is that when fear of lethal violence is translated into a general campaign against crime, the major share of extra resources will be directed at nonviolent behavior.

Serious crimes of violence result in prison sentences when offenders are apprehended under most criminal justice policies. Armed robbery, attempted murder, and offenses of equivalent magnitude are seriously punished even before special efforts to increase penal severity are introduced. This pattern of serious punishment means that there is less room left in the system to get tough with this sort of offense.

Instead, crime crackdowns have their most dramatic impact on less serious offenses that are close to the margin between incarceration and more lenient penal sanctions. This pattern of nonviolent offenses absorbing the overwhelming majority of resources in crime crackdowns can be clearly illustrated in the recent history of criminal justice policy in the United States. During the decade 1980-1990, for example, the state of California experienced what might be described as the mother of all crime crackdowns. In ten years, the number of persons imprisoned in California quadrupled, and the population of those incarcerated in the state's prison and jails increased by over 100,000.

Figure 1.4 shows the impact of this unparalleled "get tough" policy on the growth in the population confined in the California prison system as a result of conviction for the four offenses that were profiled in Figure 1.1. The relative growth in prison population for the two nonviolent offenses is greatly in excess of the growth experienced for robbery and homicide.

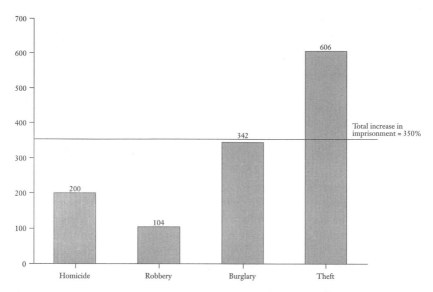

Figure 1.4. Percentage change in prisoners by offense of conviction, California, 1980–1990. *Source:* Zimring and Hawkins 1992a, Table 1, p. 39.

The relative growth of the number of burglars in prison was over three times that of the number of robbers, and the growth rate of prisoners convicted of theft was six times the rate for robbers.

The relatively modest impact of California's crime crackdown on violent offenders is not a result of lenient attitudes toward robbery and murder in California. Quite the opposite. Since robbery and murder were always seriously punished in California, there was a smaller number of leniently treated robbers and killers who had been spared by the previous regime and were thus available to be swept up by the crackdown.

This tendency for changes in criminal justice policy to have the most profound effect in marginal cases produced a sharp contrast in California's prison system over the decade of its unprecedented expansion. Sixty percent of all California prison inmates in 1980 had been committed for offenses of violence; but only 27 percent of the additional prison space added between 1980 and 1990 was used to increase the number of inmates who had been convicted of violent offenses. If one imagines that the efficiency of an anticrime policy as a way of combating violence can be measured by the proportion of offenders imprisoned for violent offenses, the prison resources available in 1980 could be given a 60 percent efficiency rating, while the additional resources committed to imprisonment during the 1980s were employed with 27 percent efficiency.

The national pattern is less pronounced, but also shows shrinking proportions of violent offenders as prison populations increase. In 1979, 46 percent of the 274,563 persons in state prisons had been convicted of a violent offense. But just under 35 percent of the 429,618 additional prisoners that were present in 1991 had been convicted of crimes of violence. This diminished overlap between imprisonment and violence is in large measure an inevitable consequence of substantial increases in the proportion of felony offenders sentenced to prison. It creates an enormous gap between the motive for crime crackdowns and their effects, a gap we will examine in chapter 10.

Bait and Switch

For those who wonder why both violence and the rate of imprisonment increased in the late 1980s, we present the parable of the bait-and-switch advertisement. The practitioner of "bait-and-switch" selling advertises a brand new vacuum cleaner with several attractive features for the unheard of price of $39.95. That advertised product is the "bait" designed to attract customers into the store. When consumers enter the shop, advertisement in hand, they are either told that the advertised special is no longer available or are shown an obviously defective piece of merchandise and actively discouraged from its purchase. The salesperson then attempts to "switch" consumers by interesting them in the $300 vacuum cleaner that the whole scheme was designed to promote.

The "bait-and-switch" character of anticrime crusades occurs in the contrast between the kind of crime that is featured in the appeals to "get tough" and the type of offender who is usually on the receiving end of the more severe sanctions. The "bait" for anticrime crusades is citizen fear of violent crime. Willie Horton is the poster boy in the usual law and order campaign. But the number of convicted violent predators who are not already sent to prison is rather small. In the language of "bait-and-switch" merchandising, the advertised special is unavailable when the customer arrives at the store. The only available targets for escalation in imprisonment policy are the marginal offenders and offense categories. If an increase in severity is to be accomplished, the target of the policy must be "switched." Nonviolent offenders go to prison and citizens wonder why rates of violence continue to increase.

Conclusion

Rates of common property crimes in the United States are comparable to those reported in many other Western industrial nations, but rates of lethal violence in the United States are much higher than can be found elsewhere in the developed nations. This penchant for violence cannot be a natural result of a high volume of either crime or criminals. If it were, other developed nations with high crime rates would share our higher rate of violence. The propensity toward life-threatening violence varies independently of general crime rates. That is why violence is not a crime problem.

The concluding part of this chapter discussed the inadequacies of "getting tough" on crime as an antiviolence strategy. If lethal violence is the priority target of governmental concern, the anticrime crackdown is inefficient, diffuse in focus, and misses the opportunity to look beyond the category of criminal behavior for the sources and control of violence. The inefficiency of anticrime crusades against violence recently has been demonstrated in the diffuse impact of the huge increase in penal confinement in the United States.

There is, however, one linkage between citizen fear and government policy that may systematically broaden anticrime efforts beyond lethal violence. The categorical contagion processes we mention may mean that a murder by robbers generates citizen fear that burglars will murder and is expressed in relation to a broad variety of crime that may involve little objective risk of violence. Unless some discipline is imposed on the policy-making process by analysts, the generality of fear of crime may render law enforcement less effective against the life-threatening acts that are the greatest cause of fear.

The two concluding chapters of this book will address in some detail the policy implications of a priority concern with lethal violence in the United States. The four remaining chapters in this section provide the factual foundation for that type of policy analysis. And the materials in Part II show how changing the subject from crime to lethal violence changes our conceptions of the causes of current problems.

2

Violence and the Growth of Crime

Some Lessons from Recent History

IS LETHAL VIOLENCE merely the most serious part of a larger crime problem or is it a distinct set of social behaviors only loosely connected to many other types of criminal behavior? This chapter will examine some historical evidence on trends in crime and homicide to address the linkage between rates of deadly violence and rates of crime. What can historical patterns tell us about the crime–violence connection? If the level of crime and the number of active criminals in a social setting is a good predictor of rates of lethal violence, then trends in crime over time should lead to similar trends in rates of lethal violence. If the volume of crime is not a good predictor of trends in homicide, then there is no good reason to regard a society's lethal violence as a byproduct of its crime rate.

The logic of historical comparison is straightforward. If general levels of crime determine the rate of lethal violence, then increases or decreases in crime should result in parallel increases or decreases in lethal violence. Even a high correlation between crime and violence cannot prove causation, of course, because some third force can be the cause of changes in both crime and lethal violence. If social disorganization or riots cause increases in both theft and murder, the correlation between theft and murder will be high, but the social disruption is the true cause of each.

On the other hand, if the patterns of change in crime and violence are not closely related, this would be evidence that lethal violence is substantially independent of crime. If steep increases or decreases in levels of criminal activity are not closely reflected in trends in death from intentional injury, then life-threatening violence should not be considered a byproduct of criminal activity.

The trend comparisons reported in this chapter attempt to compare trends in common crime and in homicide. We use homicide as an index of all acts of lethal violence. We use either crime indices or rates of theft as our index of nonviolent crime rates. Data are presented for three separate analyses. The first section compares crime and homicide trends in the United States. The second section presents yearly data over long periods of time for England and Australia. The third section compares theft and homicide trends in all of the Group of Seven (G7) nations, the largest industrial democracies in the period 1960–1990.

Is there a close relationship between crime rates and rates of lethal violence in the industrial nations? The best modern evidence suggests that crime and homicide vary independently. There has been one exception to this general pattern, however, and that is where our detailed analyses will start.

Some American History

Figure 2.1 shows the relationship between index crime rates in the United States and rates of homicide over the two decades 1961–1980. The "crime

Figure 2.1. Trends in U.S. homicide and other index crimes known to the police, 1961–1980. *Source:* U.S. Department of Justice, Federal Bureau of Investigation, 1961–1980.

index" is composed of seven crimes ranging from homicide to theft, but the bulk of the offenses in the rate are noncontact property crimes. The relationship between crime and lethal violence during this period is both clear and strong. As the rate of index crime tripled through the 1960s and 1970s, the rate of lethal violence, as measured by homicide, also increased sharply: from 4.8 per 100,000 in 1961 to 10.2 per 100,000 in 1980. This pattern of property crime closely tracking rates of lethal violence is consistent with trends in crime playing a major role in changing death rates from violence.

But while the trend relationship shown in Figure 2.1 is clear, the evidence it provides of the link between high-level violence and general trends in crime for this time period is less compelling than might first appear. The data in Figure 2.1 are for one country only and for a relatively short time period. Furthermore, this was a period of nearly uninterrupted growth in both crime and lethal violence. There were only two years in the 1960s and 1970s when the homicide rate declined from the previous year and there were no years of decline between 1963 and 1974.

The growth in index crime was almost as steep with only three declines in twenty observations. So while the statistical relationship of crime and violence was strong over this period, the statistical relationship of each with time was just as great. Further, the circumstances in which the relationship is tested are only those of high growth. Attempting to learn a great deal from this time period about the relationship between crime and lethal violence is like trying to become an expert on the stock market by confining one's attention exclusively to bull market periods without periods of price stability or contraction.

Some further postwar U.S. data are available to test the relationship between general crimes rates and lethal violence in earlier periods. And trends in this earlier time period cast doubt on a systematic relationship between crime and lethal violence in the United States. When we look at the same measures of homicide and index crime for 1947–1957 in Figure 2.2 (see p. 24), we find a different pattern. The year 1947 was chosen as a base year because it is a calendar year wholly outside the transition out of World War II. The year 1957 is the end point of the analysis because procedures for the Uniform Crime Reporting program were changed after that in ways that produced great increases that may be artifactual (see U.S. Department of Justice, Federal Bureau of Investigation, 1958:1–3). The relationship between crime and lethal violence for 1947–1957 is the opposite of the pattern recorded for 1961–1980. The volume of index crime other than homicide increases in all but three of the time periods set forth in the figure, while rates of homicide decline in eight of the ten year-to-year comparisons.

Is this evidence that increasing crime rates produce decreases in homicide? One reason to doubt this is the strong relationship between index crime rates and time—crime goes up as time goes on in both Figures 2.1

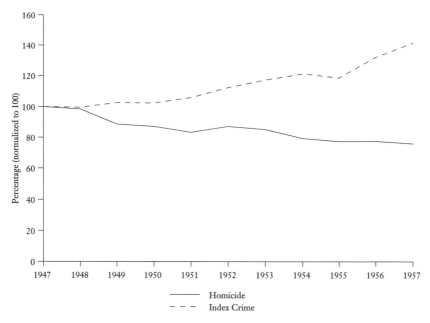

Figure 2.2. Trends in U.S. homicide and other index crimes known to the police, 1947–1957. *Source:* U.S. Department of Justice, Federal Bureau of Investigation, 1947–1957.

and 2.2. Homicide rates are also related to time in 1947-1957, but the temporal trend for them is downward in this eleven-year span. Both the positive and negative correlations between crime and homicide are probably artifacts of expanding crime rates over time.

So, the postwar experience of the United States does not provide definitive evidence of the linkage over time between crime and lethal violence. Two separate postwar time periods provide a sharp contrast in the crime–violence relationship and the best reading of both periods is that crime tends to expand over time while lethal violence had a downtrend in the first period and an uptrend in the second. The next step is to look outside the United States to find whether patterns can be discerned in historical trends.

England and Australia Over Time

Our search for reliable data on trends in crime and homicide produced two data sets of value in published research. Dane Archer and Rosemary Gartner collected unaudited data from a number of countries on various crime rates for their pioneering *Violence and Crime in Cross-National Perspective* (1984). Figure 2.3 shows trends in homicide and theft for England and Wales over the period 1950-1970. Theft is the most common

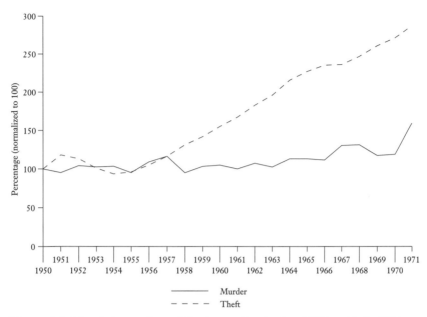

Figure 2.3. Trends in murder and theft rates, England and Wales, 1950–1971.
Source: Archer and Gartner 1984.

of the property crime categories and the best index of property crime generally. The data on theft are not audited, but the reputation of British crime statistics is good. The World Health Organization homicide data are also of good repute.

The theft offense profiled in Figure 2.3 is the most common property crime throughout the industrial West: the taking or attempted taking of another person's property without a threat of force that would aggravate the offense to robbery or a breaking and entering of premises that would aggravate the offense to burglary. Homicide is the intentional infliction of serious injury that leads to a death. The rate of offenses per 100,000 for each of these crimes is represented in the chart with value of 100 for 1950 so that the chart can more clearly illustrate trends in each offense without the visual distractions produced because the incidence of the theft offense is vastly greater than the incidence of homicide.

The rate of theft offenses in England and Wales is relatively flat for the first half of the 1950s and then begins an uninterrupted ascent that produces a rate in 1971 that is three times as high as the theft rate in 1955. The amount of change and the timing of change are quite different for homicide. Rates of homicide never increased by more than half over the more than two decades reported in the figure; and the trend for the first fifteen years after 1950 for homicide is extremely stable. For most of the period under scrutiny, the homicide rate fluctuates around a stable mean while the theft rate climbs steadily and inexorably.

What do these divergent trends tell us about the social processes that determine the rate of theft and those that determine criminal homicide? Certainly there are many changing social conditions that might have a similar influence on both homicide and nonviolent crime over time. Poverty, income inequality, levels of social conflict, family instability, and fluctuations in the young adult share of the total population are some examples of factors where a particular change might be expected to have the same kind of effect on rates of both homicide and theft. Yet the statistics for England and Wales show that homicide rates remained stable from 1955 to 1966 while the theft rate more than doubled. There were either twice as many property criminals active in England and Wales for every 100,000 members of the general population or else the same number of thieves must have become twice as active. In either event, the rate of theft in England and Wales more than doubled from 1950 to 1966 without any observable influence on the rate of criminal homicide.

Later sections in this chapter will show that the contrast between trends in property crime and life-threatening criminal violence is the apparent pattern in many developed countries in the past generation. As measured by official statistics, rates of property crime have expanded steadily with increasing material prosperity and female participation in the work force from Milan to Munich to Manchester. The temporal trend for property crime in postwar England and Wales was upward. The relative stability of homicide rates observed in England and Wales is not uncommon either.

Figure 2.4, showing year-to-year changes in homicide and larceny, is taken from a comprehensive study of crime and criminal justice data from the Commonwealth of Australia, compiled by Satyanshu Mukherjee (Mukherjee 1981). The larceny and homicide categories in this figure are the equivalent to the theft and homicide trends reviewed in Figure 2.3. In Australia, trends in larceny and homicide are different both in the magnitude of the changes noted during the period 1950–1976 and in the consistency of trend. The homicide rate in Australia during 1976 exceeded that of the 1950 base year by 31 percent, while the larceny rate grew by 142 percent over the same period. As these differences in total growth over the period might suggest, the tendency for larceny to increase on a year-to-year basis was much greater than for homicide. When controlled for population, larceny rates decreased on a year-to-year basis only six times in the twenty-six years following 1950, so that the general upward trend was reflected in the year-to-year comparisons about three-quarters of the time. In twenty-six year-to-year homicide comparisons after 1950, rates of homicide dropped fourteen times, and there was only one three-year period of consecutive increase in more than a quarter of a century.

The pattern in Australia parallels two key features found in the British and U.S. data already examined. First, there is a temporal trend of signifi-

Figure 2.4. Trends in homicide and larceny rates, Australia, 1950–1976.
Source: Mukherjee 1981.

cant increase in nonviolent property crime that is essentially uninterrupted over the quarter-century. Second, there is no parallel long-term temporal trend for homicide over the period. Instead, the fluctuations in homicide seem more cyclical throughout the period, with year-to-year fluctuations being much less predictable and no pronounced long-term trend.

A Multinational Trend Comparison

Are the British and Australian contrasts idiosyncratic or representative of industrial countries in recent decades? To construct a broad sample of nations, we collected unaudited reports of rates of theft for each of the G7 nations and homicide data from the World Health Organization for the period 1960–1990. The G7 is a collection of the largest non-Communist economic powers rather than an entity of any social or criminological significance. For that reason, it is an admirable sample of large nations to test the generality of the crime–violence pattern among major nations.

Table 2.1 shows changes in theft and homicide for each of the G7 nations. The aggregate contrast between theft and homicide trends is substantial over a generation. The median homicide rate of the G7 nations in 1960 was 1.4; in 1990 it had dropped to 1.1. But property crimes as measured by offenses reported to the police have registered steady and substantial increases in most of the industrialized world. The median theft

Table 2.1

Long-Range Trends in Per Capita Rates of Theft
and Homicide, G7 Countries, 1960–1990

Country	Theft (% change from 1960)	Homicide (% change from 1960)
France	+438	-35
England	+306	-17
Germany	+177	no change
Italy	+600	+85
Japan	+4	-40
Canada[a]	+208	+50
United States	+462	+110

[a] Theft rates for 1989.

Source: Data provided by Interpol 1960–1990 (theft); World Health Organization 1960–1990 (homicide).

rate reported by the G7 nations expanded over 300 percent during the 1960–1990 period.

Only Japan avoided substantial growth in theft over the period; every other nation reported theft rates from 2.77 to seven times the rates experienced in 1960. Homicide rates were stable in one country, fell in three others, and increased in three countries. While six of the seven G7 nations experienced theft increases greater than 150 percent, only the United States has a homicide rate that doubled. Theft rates expand on a different scale than that which measures variations in homicide. The fact that theft totals used in this analysis were not audited would be worrisome if the precise amount of a nation's theft increase were important. But the large jumps in six of the seven G7 nations make the key point without the necessity for any precise measure of the extent to which theft rates increase. The specific ranking of Italy, England, and France in rate of theft increase cannot be assessed with these data in any precise way. The general magnitude of the growth of theft, however, is beyond doubt.

The minimum lesson one learns from this kind of trend comparison is that many of the factors that have substantial influence on rates of property crime do not have similar influence on trends in lethal violence. It appears that every developed Western nation experienced enormous growth in property crime over the most recent generation, while the aggregate pattern for lethal violence among the G7 nations was trendless. This shows that different factors influenced rates of homicide and of theft. This thirty-year pattern is also strong evidence that expanding rates of property crime do not produce parallel expansion in homicide. The G7 nations average four times as much theft in 1990 as in 1960, but no more homicide. Whatever the factors are that are responsible for the growth of crime in the West have not produced a general increase in lethal violence.

This G7 finding might help us interpret the increases in property crime and homicide in the United States since 1960. It may well be that the increase in the total index crime rates that are dominated by theft in the United States was produced by the same changes in social conditions that produced increasing property crime trends in other developed nations. If so, the factors producing increased property crime rates in the United States can hardly be an explanation of the explosive increase in lethal violence observed in the United States since the mid-1950s because the sharp expansion in lethal violence was peculiar to the United States among the developed nations.

Responses to Crime

It should be possible to look for common themes in the responses to crime of a wide variety of Western nations over a thirty-year period since the rate of theft has more than tripled on average in every G7 nation except Japan. Of particular importance, given the perspective of this study, is examining responses to escalating levels of property crime in nations where rates of lethal violence have not increased markedly. What do citizens and governments do in France, Germany, and England when the level of theft increases relentlessly, but lethal violence does not? Or in Italy where the theft rates increase seven times as much as the homicide rate? Is there a general pattern or response notable in the developed nations with increasing theft?

Our answer to those questions must be a preliminary one. We lack the data and resources to do a detailed cross-national study of responses to the general escalation in property offenses and offenders over the past generation. The question deserves substantial attention for what it can tell us about the social importance of property crime as well as for the light it can shed on the different responses to changes in lethal violence and in theft.

The important findings about the impacts of general increases in theft levels that we would emphasize from our preliminary assessment are three negative conclusions. First, increases in theft rate do not seem closely associated with large increases in citizen fear over the past generation. Citizens are probably well aware of local risks in Northern Europe, Canada, and Australia, but burglary and theft are not producing the kind of fear and feelings of helplessness that strain the social fabric in many American cities. Home alarms, car alarms, and many other theft deterrent systems are on the increase all over the developed world. Further, there have been periods of citizen alarm about violence and public order in England and Germany. But these periods of alarm were in response to campaigns of life-threatening political violence. Epidemic levels of theft are a major annoyance, but no more than that, wherever they occur alone.

The second major negative finding is that large increases in theft do not seem to be associated with sustained social or economic declines. The period under study—1960 to 1990—was one of enormous economic growth throughout most the West, and the economic growth rates in nations with large increases in rates of theft was no lower than in Western nations with lower theft rate increases. Indeed, one element that may cause increasing property crime rates is increasing amounts of portable property worth stealing. To the extent that theft rates are a reflection of the opportunities for theft, general prosperity might produce an increase in theft rates in many circumstances. But not always, of course. We have the stupendous economic growth of Japan and her low and stable theft rate to deter us from mechanical theories about the influence of property ownership rates on theft rates.

The lack of association over time between growing national-level theft rates and economic declines illustrates the important distinction between factors that influence the distribution of crime within a society and factors that might influence the amount of crime at the national level. We would expect that poor and unemployed *persons* have much higher rates of theft in any particular setting—in New York City or London or Madrid. But that does not mean that the number of poor people is a good predictor of national-level theft rates either over time or cross-sectionally. This highly important contrast is discussed in Appendix 1.

The third major negative conclusion that comes from a brief survey of cross-national trends concerns the scale of the penal enterprise. There is no general tendency for penal systems to expand in proportion to general growth in the rate of crime. Table 2.2 shows trends in imprisonment for 1960-1990 where available. The overall conclusion best supported by inspection of Table 2.2 is trendlessness. Rates of imprisonment jump in the United States in singular fashion and increase substantially in the United Kingdom. Japan is at the other extreme with a rate of imprisonment half of its 1960 rate one generation later. The other four nations cluster closer to their 1960 rate of imprisonment. There is some pattern of regression toward the mean in the pattern for the six nations other than the United States. The three nations with the lowest 1960 rates show increases over the thirty-year period, while the three non-United States countries with the highest 1960 totals decline. The United States, with the highest 1960 total, has by far the largest proportional increase in imprisonment as well.

Overall, there is certainly no general trend in imprisonment parallel to increases in property crime. But the narrative dimensions of the table are much easier to provide than the substantive reasons why crime and imprisonment do not march in step. Crime rates are notoriously inefficient predictors of trends in imprisonment (Zimring and Hawkins 1991, at Chapter 5). But the data in Table 2.2 show this over an extremely long period of time in relation to very large upward movements in the incidence of theft. It may well be that the absence of citizen fear is part of the reason why

Table 2.2

Imprisonment Rates (per 100,000), G7 Countries, 1960 and 1990

	1960	*1990*	*Percentage Change*
United States	118	292	+148
United Kingdom	58	94	+62
France	59	82	+39
Canada	35	45	+29
Germany[a]	85	78	-8
Italy	79	57	-27
Japan	66	32	-51

[a] Data for March 1961.

Source: Home Office, 1961 and 1991 (United Kingdom); Istituto Nazionale di Statistica, 1961 and 1991 (Italy); Ministere de L'Economie et Des Finances, 1961 and 1991 (France); Statistics Bureau, 1961 and 1991 (Japan); Statistics Canada, 1961 and 1991 (Canada); Statistisches Bundesamt, 1962 and 1991 (Germany); U.S. Department of Justice, Federal Bureau of Investigation, 1961 and 1991 (United States); World Health Organization, 1961 and 1991 (all nations).

imprisonment does not rise to match the expanding incidence of crime. If so, we would expect a closer linkage between public fears and imprisonment policy over longer periods of times.

It appears that the growth of property crime has had its most substantial impact in citizen behavior in relation to the particular settings that generate the highest theft rates. We redesign our cars and also install metal theft-deterrence bars on steering wheels. Burglary alarm systems proliferate. Bicycle locks become ubiquitous. These are specific responses to specific theft risks. Provisions to reduce property crime risk grow most pronouncedly in the private sector rather than in government all over the developed world. Higher rates of theft change social life in many small ways, but no big ones.

Conclusion

This chapter has employed a new tactic in examining the connection between crime rates and lethal violence, the comparative study of trends in nonviolent offenses and trends in criminal homicide. Despite the large number of social forces that would be expected to produce a close relationship between crime trends and homicide trends, the weight of current evidence suggests that steadily increasing property crime rates in modern industrial nations do not produce and are not associated with any pronounced trends in rates of deadly violence.

The long-term movements discussed in this chapter should be distinguished from sudden societal breakdowns where crime and violence both increase because of the collapse of social control. If a large urban environment should lose its police force, for example, we would expect both lethal violence and property crime rates to increase substantially. There is some evidence available on such discrete failures of restraint (Zimring and Hawkins 1973:168–171). There may also be circumstances where a long-term erosion of formal mechanisms of social control is the major explanation for trends in crimes. The data reported in this chapter do not support that interpretation of developments in the G7 nations over the past generation.

Additional data from other nations and other periods will no doubt further illuminate the crime–violence relationship and we look forward to considering additional evidence as it develops. How broad is the trend toward expanding rates of property crime and how long has it been in progress? When, if ever, in the natural history of expanding rates of property crime does the acceleration stop? Are the decreases in crime in the United States noted during the early 1980s and again in the early 1990s signs that the uptrend has abated, and will this also happen in other developed nations?

Should we be surprised that homicide rates and theft rates are not closely correlated over time in Western nations? Why should they be closely correlated? The assumption that crime and violence are closely linked has usually been an intuitive feeling rather than an explicit theory. The implicit assumption may have been that the number of all criminal offenses is a function of the number of active criminals, but this has never been stated in any literature we have discovered.

If this is the theory of crime–violence linkage, would it also suggest that the level of burglary in a society should predict the relative prevalence of all types of crime, such as child molestation and drunk driving? To some extent, the degree of social organization and the cultural norms relating to obedience to law may be reflected in a general tendency in a society toward low or high crime rates. But the sharp contrast between crime trends and homicide trends in recent history is a basic datum of importance to this previously unstudied issue. Many nations experience significant growth in the volume of their crime, but do so without any larger threat to the physical safety of citizens. France in 1990 had five times as much theft as thirty years before, but one-third less homicide. We do not suggest that these divergent trends are the product of any particular public policies. Instead, the data indicate only that life-threatening violence is a specific set of behaviors that seem to respond to different factors than those that generate theft.

The national-level data discussed in this chapter are in aggregate form. When the focus shifts from time trends to cross-sectional comparisons, the amount of information available and the ability to obtain detailed portraits of patterns of crime increase, so the comparative materials in the following chapter will be set out in greater detail.

The comparison of crime and violence in different nations has problems of its own, of course. But the combination of historical and cross-national evidence makes a powerful case that crime is not an inherent threat to public safety in most countries.

3

Transnational Patterns

WHAT FEATURES OF AMERICAN LIFE account for its high rates of lethal violence? The most popular conventional explanation for the high rates of criminal homicide in the United States is the high rates of crime found in American cities and states. With so many criminals and so much crime, high rates of lethal violence seem to many observers almost inevitable. We have already cast doubt on that explanation by comparing general crime rates with homicide rates for a number of countries in Chapter 1. Many nations have high levels of crime without high homicide rates.

If a high crime rate does not provide a sufficient explanation for rates of lethal violence in the United States, what about a specific propensity toward violent crime as an explanation? The English and the Australians may have just as many burglars as are found in American cities, but not as many robbers. Are the higher death rates from American violence just the result of criminals in the United States preferring overt predation to stealth?

This chapter uses data from two multinational victim surveys and from detailed police statistics on crime victimization to subject these two common explanations for American lethal violence to sustained scrutiny. The pattern that emerges from existing cross-national data is sharply different from the conventional wisdom. The United States has a property crime rate at the high end of the international distribution for both crime rates and rates of violent crime. But neither property crimes nor crimes of violence are concentrated in the United States in anything like the pattern observed for homicides.

The first section of this chapter presents a detailed portrait of recent cross-national victim survey research on crime and violence. The second section presents official statistics for selected areas and augments that general statistical portrait with data obtained for London, New York City, Sydney, Australia, and Los Angeles. A concluding section discusses both the negative and positive findings of our comparison. Neither overall crime rates nor the rates of broadly measured and defined violent crime turn out to be good explanations for rates of lethal violence. The findings in this chapter suggest that a particular focus on the instruments that make violent crime more likely to kill and on the willingness to use them are more plausible explanations than either the quantity of crime in the United States or the willingness of criminals to use personal force.

A Survey Research Surprise

Figure 3.1 provides data on victim survey estimates of crime victimization for theft offenses not involving force against the person for eighteen of the

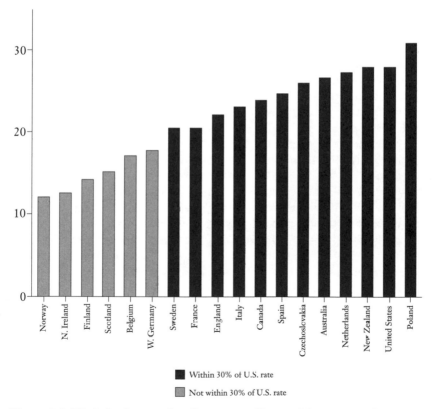

Figure 3.1. Victimization rate for all property offenses, eighteen countries, 1988–1991. *Source:* van Dijk and Mayhew 1992.

twenty nations that were surveyed in the late 1980s and early 1990 by United Nations-sponsored researchers using an identical telephone survey instrument in each country. Data on Switzerland and Japan have been omitted from the figure because rates were not available for one or more of the constituent crimes. When two surveys were conducted in a country, the rate provided in Figure 3.1 is an average. The darker bars show nations with a crime rate within 30 percent of the U.S. rate.

Once property offenses are aggregated, the United States rate of 28 percent is the second highest of the eighteen countries arrayed in Figure 3.1, slightly lower than Poland and slightly higher than a group of nations that includes New Zealand, the Netherlands, Australia, and Czechoslovakia. But the precise ranking in the survey is less important than it might otherwise be because of the nature of the distribution of property crime rates. The United States is bunched with five other countries at the top of the property offense distribution, with Czechoslovakia, Australia, the Netherlands, New Zealand, and Poland all reporting aggregate victimization rates within 10 percent of the U.S. rate. Three other countries— Canada, Spain, and Italy—are also quite close to the U.S. rate.

Under these circumstances, being found in the top half of this distribution seems to be a good deal more significant than the precise ranking within that group of nine nations. In this survey, there is a good deal of homogeneity in the victimization rates reported for the nations in the top two-thirds. Sweden with a reported victimization rate of 20 percent is well in the bottom half of the distribution reported in Figure 3.1. But its aggregate victimization rate is about two-thirds of that reported in Poland—the highest-rate nation.

By contrast, the distribution of victimization rates for all offenses of violence including robbery is not as tightly bunched as for reported property crime.

When all violent offenses are aggregated, the United States again displays the second highest rate of the eighteen countries. This time the top rate is reported by Australia. For violent offenses there are three other nations bunched within 10 percent of the United States rate—Canada, Poland, and New Zealand. For the five highest countries, the similarities in rate are much more important than the differences. This point is particularly to be emphasized because of the small national-level samples on which these estimates are based. But after the top five, the drop-off in violence victimization is more pronounced. Seven of the eighteen reporting nations generate violence victimization rates well under half that of Australia.

The major surprise for an American observer is the existence of reported rates of both violent and nonviolent crime in the United States that are quite close to those found in countries like Australia, Canada, and New Zealand. There is certainly little in Figure 3.2 that fits the average traveler's perception of danger or safety in the city streets of the reporting coun-

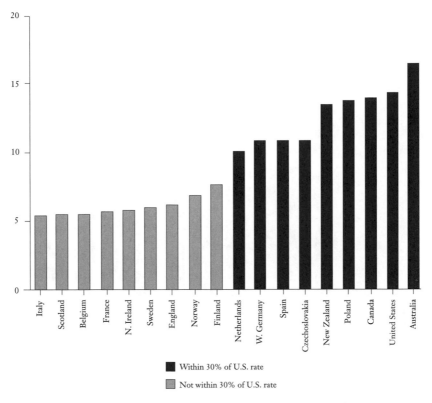

Figure 3.2. One-year victimization rate for all violent offenses, eighteen countries, 1988–1991. *Source:* van Dijk and Mayhew 1992.

tries. Indeed, there is no strong statistical correlation between rates of reported violent crime in these eighteen nations and the homicide rates for the same countries. For those countries, then, the rates of violent crime reported by citizens are not a very good predictor of their respective homicide rates.

Disaggregating the survey data on violent crime so that rates of robbery and assault are separately reported only continues the parade of surprising results. Figure 3.3 (see p. 38) provides data from the 1991 survey of robbery rates in thirteen countries arranged in the chart in ascending order. Figure 3.4 (see p. 39) provides parallel data for rates of assault with harm. In each case, the darker bars again indicates a rate within 30 percent of the U.S. rate. For robbery, the U.S. rate is second to that of Poland, but the U.S. rate is similar to those reported by Italy, Australia, Czechoslovakia, Canada, and England. Indeed, there is as large a gap between the United States and Poland in robbery rate as there is between the United States and Finland, which has the ninth highest total out of the thirteen nations.

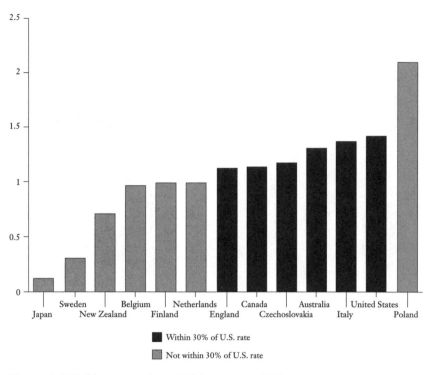

Figure 3.3. Robbery rates (per 1000) by country, 1991. *Source:* van Dijk and Mayhew 1992.

The robbery data contain another surprise. Despite the sharp difference in robbery rate between Los Angeles and Sydney that we noted in Chapter 1, the victim survey shows the United States and Australia to be similar in reported robbery victimization. On this measure, robbery victimization in the United States is not far removed from the rate reported for a number of European and Scandinavian countries.

The United Nations survey results for assault are even more surprising than the robbery findings. Of the countries in the 1991 survey that report assault, rates in the United States are lower than those found in Canada, New Zealand, and Australia, and are nearly identical to the rates reported for Finland, the Netherlands, and Poland. Of the five English-speaking nations in the survey, the United States reports the fourth highest rate of assault with harm!

The unexpected international patterns of assault and robbery are further complicated by the fact that the statistical relationship between these two violent crimes is not great. For the 1991 data the correlation between the robbery rate and the assault rate is 0.3 and is not significant. Thus, obtaining information from this survey on the rate of assault victimization

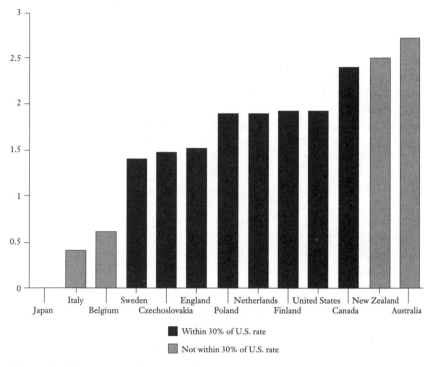

Figure 3.4. Assault rates (per 1000) by country, 1991. *Source:* van Dijk and Mayhew 1992.

in a particular country is not helpful in predicting that country's rate of robbery when compared with the other nations in the survey.

But the lack of relationship between robbery and assault rates is not the most important statistical gap to be discovered in this data set. The rate of fatal assault in the United States exceeds the rate of assault fatality in Canada, New Zealand, and Australia by at least a factor of four. Homicide rates in Poland, the Netherlands, and Finland are a tiny fraction of the U.S. rate; yet these low-homicide nations report assault rates equivalent to the United States.

The situation with regard to robbery is even more extreme. The Federal Bureau of Investigation's Supplementary Homicide Reports report 3,286 homicides in 1992 resulting from robbery: a rate of 1.3 per 100,000 for those cases alone in the United States. In England, by comparison, the total homicide rate *from all causes* for 1992 was about *half* that in the United States *from robbery alone*. A total of five robbery homicides were reported in London in that year, compared with 357 in New York City, a city only slightly larger than London. The number of police classified robbery killings in the United States for 1992 was about twice the total number of homicides from all causes in England, France, and Germany combined in 1990. With contrasts like these, it is not surprising that the correlation between victim survey rates and World Health Organization homicide rates for the reporting countries is a nonsignificant 0.37. The correlation between assault rates and homicide rates is 0.15; also nonsignificant. There is also no correlation between survey assault rates and survey robbery rates.

The unavoidable conclusion from these data is that victim survey rates of violent crime are not efficient predictors of rates of lethal violence in a country. There must be some overlap between assaults that carry a high risk of death and serious injury and other assaults in any society. But the less serious and far more frequent assaults not involving great risk to life seem to vary independently of rates of deadly assault and also dominate the total assault category. The same is apparently true for robbery. If lethal violence is a primary concern, currently available victim survey data relating to assault and robbery are not useful in estimating the magnitude of a nation's lethal violence problem.

Official Crime Statistics

Having reviewed the formidable difficulties confronted when using victim survey rates of violent crime as indices of variations in lethal violence, we now ask whether official statistics relating to the incidence of violent crime provide a better indication of how the risk of death and serious injury varies from country to country. The answer to this "yes or no" question is: Both yes and no. There are enormous difficulties in attempting to make international comparisons for crimes like robbery and assault. But they are different problems from those posed by sample surveys. And the availability of reliable data on intentional homicide for many nations provides a valuable guide to the interpretation of official statistics about other violent crimes.

Still, the emerging field of comparative criminal statistics remains a high-risk enterprise. Comparing aggregate data on crimes of violence in a number of different jurisdictions is impossible on a wholesale basis. Only carefully controlling official data on particular subcategories of crime can provide useful information about life-threatening violence that is not available from survey research.

Police crime statistics present two problems that the multinational surveys discussed in the last section do not encounter. The first problem with the international comparison of existing data derived from governmental sources is that crimes of violence are not defined in the same way in different countries and police also do not use the same thresholds of aggravation in the classification of violent offenses in different countries. While the telephone survey can give respondents in many different nations the same definition of what should be classified as an assault or a robbery, the individual countries that report to multinational agencies have considerable discretion regarding how they define particular offenses. The exception to this is intentional homicide as reported to the World Health Organization. Even where formal definitions in different nations are similar, different police systems may use different thresholds of what constitutes a serious assault or a robbery rather than a purse snatching. This can have huge consequences in the reported rates.

A second problem with multinational data on officially reported crime rates is that there is currently no auditing of the reports from individual countries to guarantee the veracity, reliability, or comparability of the crime statistics submitted by the different countries. The exception here again is homicide as reported by the World Health Organization. And that is one reason why the homicide statistics come so much closer to standard definition. Interpol, however, does not audit the crime classification and reporting procedures of its members. The function of the central agency that receives the reports is to open its mail and to transpose the data provided by the reporting nations into the multinational tables of data that it publishes.

The absence of auditing and the variations in classification and reporting procedures interact to produce very wide variations in reporting practice from country to country. Why, then, might the official reports that are produced under these twin handicaps be regarded as a necessary supplement to the victim survey data on assault and robbery? In one respect, official data on violent crime are superior to victim survey estimates in providing estimates of lethal violence. The same screening processes that cause official data on assault to vary from nation to nation will also reduce the proportion of nonserious cases of assault and robbery that so thoroughly dominate victim surveys. If methods can be found to estimate the degree to which different countries screen out less serious offenses, some international comparison of official data could provide a clearer indication of variations in life-threatening criminal acts.

There is one further advantage possessed by official statistics when compared with victim survey data. Reliable data on homicide are available in the statistical profile of all the industrialized nations. It is neither a truism nor a joke to propose that the best index of lethal violence in a particular country is that country's rate of criminal homicide. And reliable data on homicide can also be used to clarify the meanings and classifications used for other forms of violent crime.

Assault-to-Homicide Ratios

Figure 3.5 compares information for each of the G7 countries on the number of nonfatal assaults reported for each homicide. If a nation reports 1000 nonfatal assaults and ten intentional killings, the ratio between the two would be reported as 100 in the figure. This ratio provides important

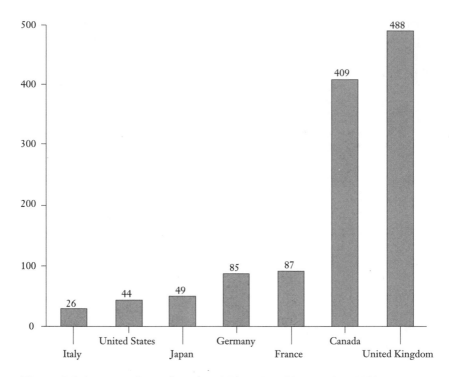

Figure 3.5. Aggravated assault-to-homicide ratios, G7 countries, 1990. *Source:*
Istituto Nazionale di Statistica 1991; Statistics Bureau 1991; Statistisches Bundesamt 1991;
Ministere de L'Economie et Des Finances 1991; Statistics Canada 1991; Home Office 1992
(aggravated assault); World Health Organization 1993 (homicide).

information regarding the kind of assaultive behavior each nation includes
in its criminal statistics on assault, and the extent to which officially
reported assault rates can be regarded as a good measure of life-threatening violence.

The assault-to-homicide ratios for the G7 nations range from twenty-
six assaults per killing in Italy to 488 assaults per killing in the United
Kingdom with little significant clustering in between. The U.S. ratio is
about twice as high as that for Italy and about the same as Japan. Germany
and France report ratios close to double the U.S. ratio. Canada and the
United Kingdom are ten times the U.S. ratio. Read literally, these statistics
would be telling us that a criminal attack in Italy is twenty times as likely to
result in death as an attack in the United Kingdom.

What might explain the enormous range in the ratio of assault-to-
homicide among the G7 nations? One obvious problem is that different
countries use different definitions of criminal assault and report different
official categories of behavior. The United States and Germany, for
instance, report aggravated assaults as a separate category; and the figure

given in the assault table is for the more serious subcategory. By contrast, the United Kingdom and Canada, the two extremely high-ratio nations, report only a general category of criminal assault.

But the announced differences definitions account for only a part of the large differences in assault-to-homicide ratios. Germany reports data on serious assaults only, while France says that it is reporting all criminal assaults. Yet the French ratio is almost identical to the German ratio (87 vs. 85), closer than to the assault ratio of any other country in the survey. Furthermore, the French "all assaults ratio" is one-fifth as high as the United Kingdom's "all assaults ratio" and less than one-fourth of the assault-to-homicide ratio reported by Canada.

The logical explanation for these enormous divergences in assault-to-homicide ratios is that official statistics on assaults report only a fraction of all intentional injury that occurs within a country's borders. The greater the injury associated with an assault, the more likely it is to be recorded as a crime. Different countries employ different formal and informal criteria to determine how far up the scale of seriousness an assault must be to be classified as criminal or to be upgraded to the aggravated criminal category. While the formal distinctions in the reporting system (battery vs. aggravated assault vs. assault) are reflected in the international reports, the less formal variations in the threshold of seriousness between reporting agencies can be discovered only by auditing procedures or exercises like assault-to-homicide ratio checks.

One other significant lesson to be learned from the range of ratios shown in Figure 3.5 is the overwhelming dominance of other than life-threatening assault in any aggregate category that combines serious and less serious events. If relatively small variations in police judgment about what should be classified as a criminal attack produce ratios as different as 87 to 1 in France, 409 to 1 in Canada, and 488 to 1 in the United Kingdom, many more potential assaults must be clustered at the low end of the seriousness scale in all three countries than at the high end. For this reason aggregate comparisons between nations that use crime categories that combine serious and nonserious assaults will not be sensitive measures of variations in life-threatening criminal attacks. So the general assault category in official statistics is an unreliable measure of rates of life-threatening violence.

But one implication of Figure 3.5 is that victim survey rates of assault are even less reliable as measures of life-threatening behavior than the most inclusive police statistics. The assault statistics from the United Kingdom may produce a ratio of attacks to killings which is twenty times as great as that reported by Italy, but the English police are probably still sampling only a fraction of all potentially criminal attacks when compiling their statistics. Victim survey responses to questions about assault with harm probably include many events that the police would screen out if they were ever brought to police attention. So that an assault-to-homicide ratio based on victim survey responses in the United Kingdom might well be 2000 or 3000 to 1. Using the estimated rates from the United Nations survey in England generates an assault-to-homicide ratio in that range.

Specific Comparisons

It is a small consolation that official statistics are a more reliable measure of lethal violence than victim surveys. It is by no means the equivalent of meeting the minimum threshold of scientific acceptability. Using homicide statistics to show the very different ratios of assaults to homicides alerts us to the problem that assault statistics from different countries are not comparable. But computing these ratios does not solve the problem. The best hope for using official crime statistics in cross-national comparisons is disaggregation: breaking up the heterogeneous collection of different types of assault that are lumped together into the general category of assault, so that the specific rates of different types of assault can be measured and made the subject of country-to-country comparisons.

This section reports on two such disaggregated offense analyses for the comparison of behavior that generates lethal violence in London and New York City. The first detailed analysis concerns the death rate from aggravated property felonies in London and New York City. The second concerns the death rate from assault by specific weapon used.

THE DEATH RATE FROM PROPERTY CRIME

Figure 3.6 shows the amount of robbery and burglary reported in New York City and in London and also reports the number of victim deaths generated by these crimes for each city. Two cities with approximately the same populations and the same number of combined robberies and burglaries in 1992 produced death rates from those crimes that were grossly different. New York City has a robbery and burglary volume lower than London, and a death toll from those crimes fifty-four times as great.

Two elements of the New York City situation produce the huge difference in death rates shown in Figure 3.6: the mix of crimes and the higher death rate from each type of crime. In both London and New York City, burglaries are much less likely to produce death than robberies. Robbery death rates are twenty-four times as high as burglary rates in London and twenty times as high in New York City. Nine times as many burglaries are reported in London in 1992 as robberies, while the mix in New York City is close to 50:50.

If New York City had experienced the same total number of robberies and burglaries but the mix had been in the London pattern of 90 percent burglary, the death toll from the two crimes in 1992 would have dropped from 378 to 112, or 70 percent if the death rate per each 1000 acts for burglary and robbery in New York City had remained constant.

But 112 deaths is still sixteen times the volume of homicide produced

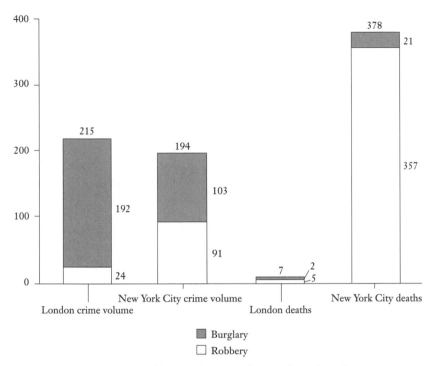

Figure 3.6. Burglary and robbery volume (in thousands) and resulting victim deaths, London and New York City, 1992. *Source:* Home Office 1992 (London); U.S. Department of Justice, Federal Bureau of Investigation, 1992 (New York City).

by robbery and burglary in London. So the New York City death rate from property crime would be vastly greater than London's even if the mix of robberies and burglaries in New York City were the same as London. The reason for this great gulf is that both robbery and burglary are much more deadly in New York City than in London. The death rate from burglary in New York City is a relatively small 0.2 per 1000 reported burglaries but this is eighteen times as high as the 0.012 per 1000 cases reported in London. The deaths per 1000 reported robberies in New York City is 3.9, more than thirteen times the 0.29 per 1000 cases found in London. For both robbery and burglary, a similar number of events produce a much higher death rate in New York City.

In order to investigate the factors that produced the high death rates from robbery in New York City, we obtained data on robberies and robbery killings by type of weapon used for the calendar year 1992. Guns are used in about 40 percent of New York City robberies and yet account for 85 percent of New York City robbery killings. The death rate per 1000 New York City gun robberies stands at 8.4, just under ten times as high as the death rate associated with all other robberies. And gun robberies are a major explanation for the total deaths from property crime. Gun robberies account for less than one-fifth of the aggravated New York City property crime, but produce more than four-fifths of all the fatalities from such crime.

Not all of the difference between the death rate from aggravated property crimes in London and New York City is the result of gun use. The death rate per 1000 nongun robberies in New York City is almost three times as high as the death rate from all robberies in London. Yet the significance of gun use in explaining the large differences between the two cities is extraordinary. If the mix of robberies and burglaries in New York City had remained at its 1992 rate but the 91,000 robberies had all generated deaths at the nongun rate of 0.86 per 1000, the number of homicides caused by New York City robbery would drop from the 357 that occurred in 1992 to 79. In this sense the use of guns in robbery in New York City alone seems to be responsible for more than three-quarters of all the deaths that result from robbery and burglary.

These comparisons assume that the death rate associated with gun robbery in New York City would not remain higher even if the guns were removed. The people who rob with guns in New York City may be more dangerous in any event than those who use other weapons or personal force. And the circumstances that are associated with gun robbery in New York City may also be more life-threatening independent of the weapon used. What this means is that even disaggregated crime statistics comparisons cannot produce a definitive estimate of the contributing causes to different death rates from violence in different cities.

But statistics such as those under discussion are more than suggestive of the significant differences that seem to account for the differential death rates from violence. Careful further disaggregation of representative samples of burglary and robbery events in London and New York City might take us even further toward estimating the significant variables that led to a 50-to-1 intercity difference in the death rate from property crime. But even if such comparisons took us only this far, the manipulation of case data from police agencies is a methodological tool of great value to a comparative criminology.

One of the significant lessons to be learned from the robbery and burglary comparisons concerns the way in which different risk factors in patterns of violent crime interact to escalate death rates. The fact that New York City offenders commit robbery almost as often as they commit burglary would greatly increase the death rate from property crimes even if guns were never used in New York City offenses. And the fact that 40 percent of all New York City robberies are committed with guns would greatly accelerate the death rate from property crime in New York City even if only 10 percent of New York City's aggravated property crimes were robberies. But the combination of a high propensity of robbers to use guns and a much higher proportion of offenders choosing to commit robbery compounds the death rate from New York City's property crime.

NEW YORK CITY AND LONDON ASSAULT

Assaults kill eleven times as many citizens in New York City as in London. Can an analysis of fatal and nonfatal attacks in the two cities tell us what factors generate this huge difference? We performed a preliminary comparison of assault and assaultive homicide in the two cities, which is reported in Appendix 2. Gun use was a major explanation for the gross difference in death rates, just as it was in robbery and burglary.

Three other factors also contribute to the rate differences. First, the reported assault rate is about 75 percent higher in New York City than in London. A second factor is that no weapon other than personal force is used in 81 percent of all police-reported assaults in London, compared with only 13 percent of the New York City serious assaults. Since personal force assaults generate a low death rate, this high concentration of no-weapon cases keeps the total death rate low in London. The final reason why London death rates are low is the absence of highly dangerous weapons in attacks. Guns are used in 26 percent of New York City assaults compared with 1 percent in London. Knives are used in 27 percent of New York City assaults compared to 6 percent in London.

Some Further Research

Two research opportunities deserve special emphasis in any discussion of cross-sectional comparison of violence. The first is further use of case-detail research. The second is expanding the sample of national experiences in comparative analysis.

While burglaries are relatively homogeneous events, robberies and assaults are heterogeneous. Assaults involve different types of offenders, victims, motives, weapons, and settings. Analysis based on aggregate data can break down events only into crude categories. Coding data on individual case events in comparative research offers the opportunity to make much more specific comparisons. What sorts of assaults result from arguments after traffic accidents in London and New York City and with what consequences? What is the pattern for taxicab robberies in the two cities? What weapons are used in reported domestic fights?

Rich case-level detail is often available in homicide cases in individual cities and could be used in intercity comparisons, but such detail is much harder to find in historical police records for assault and robbery cases. This problem can be overcome by prospectively collecting data on assaults and robberies (Zimring and Zuehl 1986). If lethal violence is the target of interest, official records are the sole source of data. This sort of careful comparative study should be a high priority for future research.

A second need is to expand the sample of societies where data on violence is available for transnational comparisons. A special problem is acquiring information on social settings outside the United States where rates of lethal violence are high. Study of developed countries gives us plenty of cases of high-crime nations, but only the United States is a high-violence case. Are most other high-violence societies also high-crime societies? Or are there low-crime, lethal violence cases?

Since high-violence areas other than the United States are not highly developed economies, the statistical systems in high-violence settings are typically not as good as in Western Europe and North America. But it is worth taking some risks with statistical quality to study a wider variety of settings, as long as those statistical risks are remembered when the data is interpreted.

General Conclusions

The materials we have assembled on New York City and London illustrate both the value and limits of the analysis of disaggregated official criminal statistics. This type of analysis can only be as good as the case detail that is available in official records of crime. And even the most detailed information falls short of providing the foundation for definitive statements about causation.

But the benefits to be gained from disaggregated data analyses are substantial. And even the limited information already discussed in this chapter provides a remarkably clear picture of American violence in international perspective. Very few detailed studies of crimes known to the police have yet been launched. Without doubt, such studies will increase knowledge about the special characteristics of lethal violence. But the general outline of the distribution of crime and violence in developed nations can be well described on the available data. And the conclusions that can be drawn from those data provide support for the central thesis of this study.

The data reported in this chapter suggest three general conclusions about the distribution of violence in the industrialized nations: First, surveys and police statistics show that many forms of assaultive behavior are spread rather evenly throughout the nations of the industrial West. With the exception of Japan where assault rates are quite low on both official and victim survey estimates, all the other G7 nations report rates of attack with harm over five per 1000 citizens per year. The assault reports from the 1991 United Nations survey show substantial similarity in the assault rates reported by citizens in many different European and former Commonwealth nations. With respect to robbery, the differences in reported rates are also less substantial in victim surveys than in national reputation. The rates reported by victims in many Western nations are quite close to those found in the United States.

Second, the major categories used by governments and survey organizations to report violent crime are dominated by less serious forms of assault and robbery. With the exception of homicide statistics, which are restricted to events in which loss of life occurs, official criminal statistics tend to mix life-threatening and nonlife-threatening events into a single category with the life-threatening subset of robberies and assault constituting a small and changing fraction of each nation's reported robbery and assault. Using official reports the ratio of assaults reported in G7 countries to homicides reported by those countries ranges from 26 to 1 in Italy to 488 to 1 in the United Kingdom.

But even in England, the dominance of low-severity assault is much greater in victim surveys than it is in police statistics. Instead of 488-to-1 assault-to-homicide ratios as found in official statistics, the United Nations survey suggests there were about 3000 reported assaults for every officially recorded homicide in England and Wales during 1990. So assaults known to the police constituted less than one-fifth of the estimated total assaults even in the country with the highest assault-to-homicide ratio in our analysis.

The dominance of relatively unthreatening robberies is quite pronounced in the international survey research. Nations like England, Canada, Australia, and Italy have reported robbery rates that are relatively close to the United States in survey research even though the robbery death rate in the United States is much higher than in those nations. The robbery death rate in the United States is over twice as high as the death rate for all types of homicide combined in England. And the number of deaths from robbery homicide in the United States is twice the volume of total homicides in Germany, France, and England combined. The inevitable conclusion is that general rates of robbery and assault are not sensitive measures of the risk of lethal violence.

Third, assaults and robberies that present special dangers to life are much more prevalent in the United States. Even those European and Commonwealth nations that report relatively high rates of violent crime have homicide rates that are a small fraction of those in the United States. The detailed comparisons of London and New York City isolate patterns of violence particularly associated with high death rates. First and foremost is the much greater proportionate use of guns in New York City assaults and robberies than in London assaults and robberies. Second is the tendency for persons committing property crimes to choose robbery almost as often as burglary in New York City, while the less dangerous burglaries outnumber robberies by 9 to 1 in London. The third element that makes New York City a more deadly environment than London is that the death rate from all major types of assault and all major types of robbery is higher in New York City than in London.

The higher death rate specific to attacks in New York City even when the comparison controlled for weapon use suggests that not all of the variance in death rates from assault and robbery has been explained successfully in the tables we have analyzed. Further detail in future research will no doubt explain more of the variation in death rates. Yet it is important to reiterate just how much of the variation in death rates between the two cities is associated with differences that our analysis has already identified. The higher proportion of gun use in assault and robbery and the larger proportion of robberies in the burglary and robbery mix account for in excess of 80 percent of all the difference in homicide rates from property crime found in the two cities.

The Sydney–Los Angeles comparison produced almost exactly the same list of explanations and the same proportion of the variations explained as we obtained for New York City and London. And the less detailed aggregate data that we have on Canada, Australia, and countries in Europe are consistent with explanations that lean heavily on gun use and the preference for gun robbery as explanatory variables.

The strategic aim of this chapter was to use comparative data from other countries in an attempt to gain perspective on the special problems generated by American violence. What separates the United States from the rest of the industrial Western world is not particularly high rates of crime generally or even much higher rates of the fist fights, purse snatchings, and street-level extortions that constitute the bulk of violent crime in most developed countries. The distinctive violence problem in the United States is the relatively small number of life-threatening attacks, usually shootings, and not infrequently attacks that occur in the course of armed robbery.

Yet it is not a proclivity toward violence that is distinctively American, but rather a willingness to engage in potentially lethal violence. The incidence of deadly violence is much less frequent than the incidence of criminal assault generally, or even of aggravated assault. But the frequency of acts that carry great risks of death is much higher than the annual homicide toll. What sets the United States apart from other developed nations is a thin layer of life-threatening violence that probably accounts for less than 1 percent of American crime and less than 10 percent of American violence.

4

American Lethal Violence
A Profile

THE PREVIOUS THREE CHAPTERS have demonstrated that the distinctive feature of violence in the United States is the high death rate from intentional attacks. Other industrial democracies have rates of crime comparable to those found in the United States. Even rates of violent crime in European and Commonwealth nations are closer to U.S. levels than had been thought. But the death rates from all forms of violence are many times greater in the United States than in other comparable nations. Lethal violence is the distinctive American problem.

This chapter provides a detailed profile of lethal violence in the United States. The first part provides an analysis of homicide rates in a variety of contexts including comparisons with other nations, comparisons with other forms of traumatic and nontraumatic death, trends over time, and demographic patterns. The second part explores the link between nonlethal violent crimes and the risk of death.

The distinctive feature of the analysis in this chapter is the focus on risk of death as an organizing principle for examining all forms of violent crime. On this dimension, assault is the most life-threatening of all American crimes, no more common in the United States than in other nations but much more deadly. Robbery is the other major killer among American crimes. Burglary and rape are much less dangerous.

Does the American reputation for violence survive this new type of statistical analysis? For the most part, yes. The singular reputation of the United States for violence is justified, but requires qualification in two important respects. The first qualification is that rates of life-threatening violence in the United States are much higher than those of other nations of comparable industrial and social development. They are, however, not much higher and in some cases they are lower than the rates of violence experienced in some less developed nations. What is striking about the quantity of lethal violence in the United States is that it is a third world phenomenon occurring in a first world nation.

The second major qualification is that the large difference between American rates of violence and those of other developed nations is most pronounced only in regard to the most serious forms of violence. Low-grade assaults, barroom brawls, the abusive disciplining of children, and the like are distributed broadly throughout the industrialized nations of the West. American rates of those behaviors place the United States at the higher end of the distribution for those events, but there is no pattern of singular predominance. It is for types of interpersonal violence likely to lead to death or serious bodily injury that the U.S. rate is four to ten times as high as other developed nations. That distinction between types of violence is a significant defining characteristic of the distinctively American violence problem.

Homicide: A Profile

Any survey of violent activity should give special emphasis to data on rates of intentional killing for two reasons. First, homicide is the most serious form of loss associated with violence, and by far the most serious crime that is prohibited chiefly because of its threat to the security of persons. Statistics relating to homicide are the natural starting point for the assessment of violent crime on grounds of seriousness alone.

Moreover, homicides are also the most reliably reported and recorded crimes: meticulously compiled both by the police and also in public health statistics. By contrast, most nonlethal categories of serious violence are neither reliably nor consistently reported. Substantial deficiencies in reporting are found in such traditional crime categories as robbery, serious assault, and rape as well as in physical child abuse and domestic violence among adults. Uneven and inaccurate reporting makes it very difficult to assess trends over time in many types of violence and to make cross-sectional comparisons. The more reliable data on homicide and on particular types of homicide, however, can be used as an index of related forms of violence that do not result in loss of life.

If statistics on the number of spouses who shoot and stab each other but do not kill are unreliable, the data on domestic homicides can be relied on. Trends in the lethal forms of domestic violence can be used as an index of trends in nonfatal forms of domestic violence. If carefully used, homicide statistics can both serve as independent evidence of trends in life-threatening violence and also provide a valuable way of checking the accuracy of official rates of nonfatal violence.

The objective in this section is to consider homicide as more than a crime statistic: to compare intentional killings in the United States with other countries, with other causes of death, and to compare trends in homicide with trends in other types of traumatic death such as suicide and accidents. For the reader bored by graphics and numbers, this section might seem heavy going. But these different contexts in which homicide is considered provide fresh and important insights. What all these charts lead to is a fuller account of what intentional homicide means in modern American life.

American Homicide in Context

Figure 4.1 provides data on rates of intentional killing for the United States and a wide assortment of other countries that report data to the World Health Organization. During 1990 the United States reported 23,438 criminal homicides, which represents a rate of 9.4 homicides per 100,000 citizens, or approximately one killing in that year for every 10,000 persons.

The American homicide rate is quite high by most international standards, but the relative position of the United States in terms of homicide

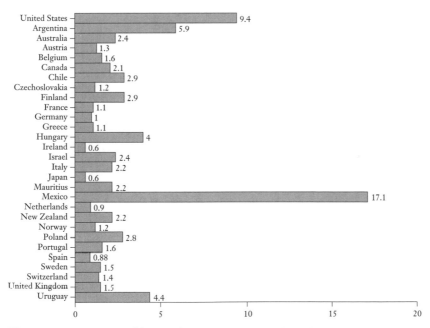

Figure 4.1. International homicide rates. *Source:* World Health Organization 1989.

varies substantially depending on the countries chosen for comparison. Homicide in the United States is greatly in excess of all the nations of Europe, averaging between three and ten times the homicide rates reported in Western European and more than three times the average homicide rates reported by the Eastern European nations as represented in Figure 4.1.

Rates of homicide in the United States appear less extraordinary when contrasted with the amount of homicide experienced in the rest of the Americas, but the World Health Organization statistics do not show this. The U.S. rate is significantly lower than the rates of homicide reported for Mexico in the World Health Organization statistics. A number of countries report homicide statistics to Interpol and the United Nations, but not the World Health Organization. These data are not audited and are not an integrated part of a death statistics reporting program. But the range of additional reporting countries in the Americas, Asia, and Africa justifies examining these data, even if they must be taken with more than a grain of salt.

Figure 4.2 presents data from the United Nations survey. A number of the nations that do not report to World Health Organization, such as Colombia, Ecuador, and Brazil, report rates higher than or equal to those U.S. rates in the police statistics reported to Interpol. United States homi-

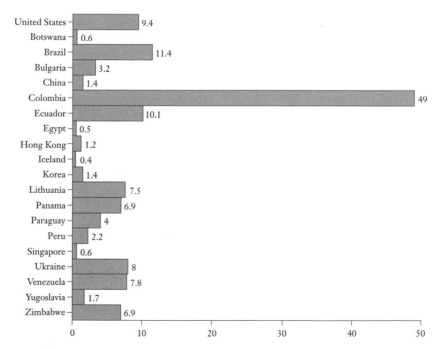

Figure 4.2. International homicide rates. *Source:* United Nations 1991.

cide is significantly greater than the rates reported for the rest of the nations of North and South America.

The limited number of Asian and African countries available for comparison in Figure 4.2 all reported homicide rates at much smaller frequencies than the United States, although the statistical picture for Africa is probably misleading. The major Asian nations report homicide rates smaller even than Western Europe. The rates of African nations reported in Figure 4.2 stand much lower than reported rates of homicide in the United States, but many African nations not included in Figure 4.2 have extremely high rates of criminal homicide, including South Africa, Uganda, and Kenya.

The moral to be drawn from international comparisons of lethal violence depends upon the standard of reference. When the comparison is made with nations of comparable social and economic development the contrast is dramatic. Figure 4.3 illustrates this by profiling rates of criminal homicide for the seven industrial and financial giants that constitute the Group of Seven (G7), the same sample of industrial nations used extensively in Chapter 2.

When the basis for comparison is broadened, the national experience of the United States, while still not typical of any region or stage of development, is nevertheless less extreme than in the G7 frame of reference. Its

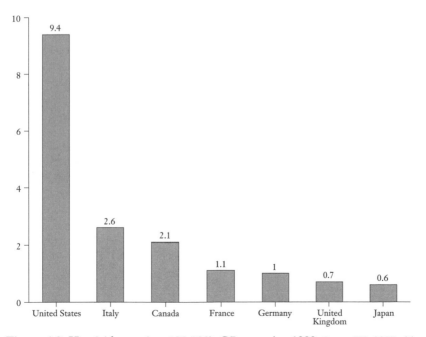

Figure 4.3. Homicide rate (per 100,000), G7 countries, 1990. *Source:* World Health Organization 1990.

current rates of intentional homicide place the United States in the upper third of the distribution of underdeveloped countries, but by no means at the top of that list.

Figure 4.4 begins the task of placing data on homicide in a public health context by showing the distribution of fatalities in the United States by cause of death for 1989. There are two common methods of indicating the relative magnitude of a particular cause of death: the rank of a particular means among the leading causes of death and the proportion of reported deaths that are attributable to a particular means. Intentional homicide is the tenth leading cause of death in Figure 4.4 and accounts for a total of 1.1 percent of all the deaths that occurred in the United States in 1990. When compared with the major fatal diseases, such as heart disease and cancer, the death toll from homicide appears modest. All forms of heart disease were responsible for about thirty times as many deaths in the United States as intentional homicide.

But two related characteristics of homicide deaths increased the social costs of homicide: intentional killing usually strikes down persons without any major disease, and it also produces, disproportionally, the deaths of younger victims. In this regard homicide is similar to fatal automobile accidents and different from the major categories of disease. The median age at death from all causes in the United States in 1989 was 78.9 (U.S.

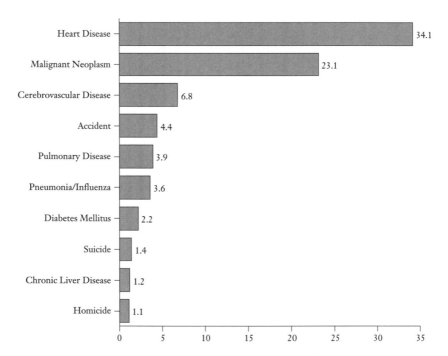

Figure 4.4. Causes of death, compared by percentage, 1989. *Source:* U.S. Department of Health and Human Services 1991.

Department of Health and Human Services 1991). The median age at death of those reported as victims of homicide was the group from twenty-five to twenty-nine. Youthful victims mean a reduction of life expectancy much greater than that just reflected in the number of deaths. Homicide cuts off about one-third as many years of life expectancy under age fifty-five in the United States as heart disease or cancer (Reiss and Roth 1993:67).

The net effect of this "potential life" measure is to emphasize the greater impact of traumas that typically claim younger victims. Even though it is one-thirtieth of the death rate due to heart disease, intentional homicide results in a gross under-sixty-five life expectancy reduction that is more than 40 percent of the total attributable to heart disease, and more than one third of the aggregate total attributable to all forms of cancer. By this measure, homicide and suicide together represent a loss of life expectancy that is 80 percent of the volume of life expectancy under sixty-five lost by heart disease and 70 percent of the aggregate total for cancer.

Trends Over Time

Figure 4.5 attempts to put homicide rates in long-term perspective by reporting trends in intentional homicide throughout the twentieth

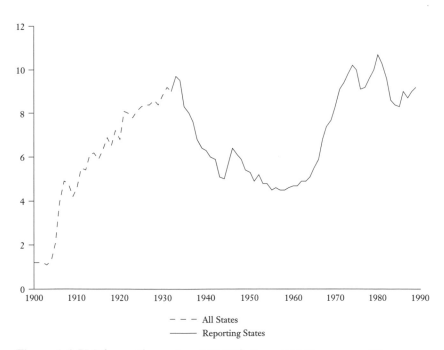

Figure 4.5. U.S. homicide rate (per 100,000). *Source:* U.S. Department of Commerce, Bureau of the Census, 1976; U.S. Department of Health and Human Services 1991.

century. This nine-decade range is not achieved without some sacrifice of the comparability and reliability of the data. Prior to 1933 the data on deaths in the United States are confined to a collection of death reporting states, while from 1933 onward the data are available for all states. Information provided after 1932 should thus be regarded as more representative of the country as a whole. Moreover the data for each year after 1932 should be regarded as more validly comparable with other post-1932 observations.

A long-range time series of homicide deaths in the United States produces some useful perspectives on recent trends. The first of these is the relatively narrow range within which criminal homicide rates have fluctuated. Putting aside the pattern for reporting states only from 1900–1909, rates of intentional homicide have fluctuated between a low of 4.5 per 100,000 population and a high of 10.7 per 100,000 over eight decades. Within this range, the death rate trended upward in the reporting states through the first third of the century, reached a peak in 1933—the first year of comprehensive reporting—and fell off gradually to the end of the Second World War.

Homicide rates then remained stable to the early 1960s. From 1964 to 1974 the national homicide rate doubled, fell off slightly in the middle of the decade, then rose to its century high of 10.7 per 100,000 population in 1980. Through the first half of the 1980s the homicide rate fell back, but it then moved up again from 1986 to 1991.

Viewed in this long-term perspective, there are three significant eras in American homicide since 1933: a long downward drift to the century's lowest sustained homicide rate in the 1950s and early 1960s; a sharp and sustained increase during the period 1964 to 1974; and variations around the new high levels ever since.

The long-term perspective is both reassuring and discouraging. It is reassuring to note that one reason why the increases of the 1960s and 1970s looked so dramatic is because they were starting from historically low homicide rates. It is also reassuring to know that recent American homicide rates have not increased significantly when compared with previous peak periods: 1933, 1974, and 1980.

The discouraging feature of the long-range perspective is the absence of any sustained downward trend over time during the past three decades. Also, even the lower rate periods since 1974 have involved consistently high rates of homicide by historic standards.

When trends in suicide rates are compared with those in homicide, two differences deserve attention. The first is that the range of values between the highest and lowest for suicide rates is narrower than even the homicide range. The low value for the period 1910–1991 is 9.8 per 100,000 in 1957. The highest value for that period was 17.4 in 1932, less then twice the 1957 low. The second contrast between suicide and homicide is that suicide rates trended downward through the 1940s and 1950s, but then have stayed close to the low end of the historic cycle levels while homicide rates increased.

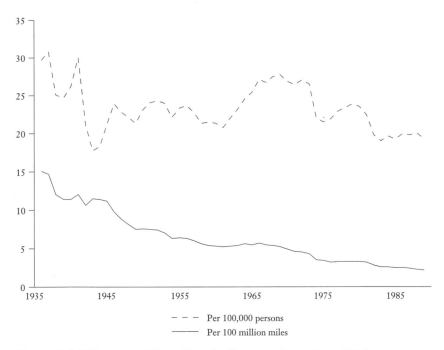

Figure 4.6. U.S. automobile accident fatality rates. *Source:* Federal Highway Administration 1990.

Figure 4.6 concerns trends over time in motor vehicle accident fatalities in the United States, another category of traumatic death that frequently involves young victims and large life expectancy losses.

The figure shows trends in automobile accident fatalities by two measures over the course of the twentieth century. The solid line reports fatalities per 100 million miles driven and represents nearly a century of uninterrupted progress. The dotted line reports trends in motor vehicle fatalities per 100,000 population. Rates of fatality per 100 million miles driven diminish substantially over the course of the reporting period and represent a small fraction of earlier risks per mile by the 1980s and 1990s. The pattern for the fatalities per 100,000 is more complicated. Automobile accident death rates per 100,000 persons escalate from 1.2 per 100,000 in 1909 to 30.8 per 100,000 in 1937 because the increases in miles driven overwhelms reductions in the death risk per 100 million miles.

The death rate per capita begins to drop in the late 1930s and falls to 17.7 per 100,000 in the war year of 1943 before turning up again with expanding mileage figures in the late 1940s. Through most of the 1950s increasing miles driven compensate for reducing levels of fatalities per 100 million miles to produce relative stability in the average citizen's risk of death. During the 1960s the death rate per 100,000 citizens increased with the explosive increase in miles driven and dropped somewhat in the aftermath of the oil crisis in 1973. After 1980, however, the risk of a citizen dying in a fatal automobile accident declined by 20 percent to just under 19 per 100,000.

Which of the two measures of Figure 4.6 is appropriate depends on which question the reader wishes to ask. If one is judging the relative safety of the automobile as a means of transport, the appropriate number for this purpose would be the death rate per miles driven—that is the best way of computing the risk of driving from home to the office or from New York City to Washington. If one is interested instead in computing the risk associated with the automobile as a social institution, the appropriate measure is the death rate per 100,000 citizens. Here one is asking, How costly is the automobile to the health of the population in the aggregate?

Long-term trends in traumatic death rates other than homicide may help us to understand the changing levels of social concern about homicide in the United States. In 1964 the death rate per 100,000 citizens produced by homicide, suicide, and automobile accidents was 40.4 deaths per 100,000 citizens. The homicide rate at 5.1 per 100,000 was 12.6 percent of that traumatic death total. Twenty-five years later in 1989 the joint death rate from automobile accidents, suicide, and homicide was 40.6 per 100,000. The stability in the overall death rate resulted from substantial decreases in the automobile fatality rate, compensating for a modest increase in suicide and a large increase in homicide.

But the homicide rate of 9.2 per 100,000 in 1989 accounted for 22.7 percent of the death rate from all three causes: an increase of 80 percent in the homicide share of traumatic deaths. This increasing share of traumatic death sharply increased anxiety about life-threatening violence and intentional homicide. The increase in homicide runs counter to social expectations of progress in public safety. The increased safety of the average citizen from fatal road accidents typifies and reinforces the kind of expectation of increasing safety that powerfully conditions social attitudes.

During the half-century between 1935 and 1985 the death rate for on-the-job accidents decreased by two-thirds in the United States, and the decline in death rate from home accidents was almost as substantial. These declines provide evidence of an expectational context that makes increasing homicide rates alarming when viewed against the substantial decline in the accidental death rate. The 13 percent increase in suicide risk over the period 1964–1989 seems like a regrettable upturn when measured against societal expectations of progress in public safety. But the 80 percent increase in the homicide rate over the same period could hardly be regarded as anything other than alarming.

The Circumstances and Demography of American Lethal Violence

Police statistics provide two types of information about the circumstances that produce homicide in the United States: descriptions of the apparent

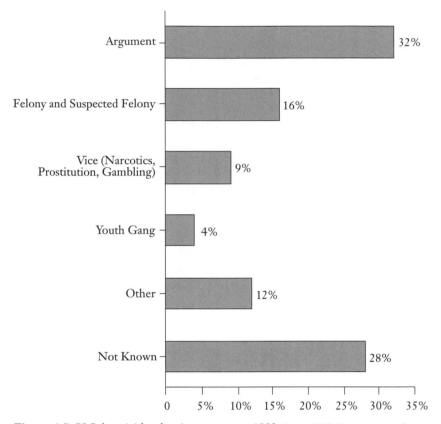

Figure 4.7. U.S. homicides, by circumstances, 1992. *Source:* U.S. Department of Justice, Federal Bureau of Investigation, 1994b.

motive and information about the prior relationship between the victim and the offender. Figure 4.7 provides the police classification of precipitating circumstances of homicide of the cases reported in the Supplementary Homicide Reports for 1992.

When the precipitating circumstances are known, the bulk of all homicides stem from conflicts that emerge from social relations. About 15 percent of the homicides are byproducts of collateral felonies where the homicide results from an interaction that began as a robbery, burglary, arson, or rape.

Does this mean that most homicides result from noncriminal social relations? In one sense, all attacks that result in criminal homicide are properly classified as criminal when the attack takes place. But the social processes that generate arguments that result in homicides are not distinctively criminal in most cases. Many of the same conflicts that produce non life-threatening outcomes in most cases also lead to homicides.

In one sense, then, social conflict is a cause of lethal violence. But this does not mean that the number of homicides that a society will experience will rise and fall with the gross amount of social conflict. Arguments over money, sexual jealousy, and male honor number in the millions in the United States, but also in every other industrial democracy. There is no reason to suppose that variations in the gross number of conflicts are a major explanation of variations in homicide. Our guess is that the rate of domestic argument is similar in England and in the United States, and that the rate of barroom arguments is as high in Sydney as in Los Angeles. The contingencies between conflict and lethal outcome are too numerous for predictions of homicidal behavior to be based on rates of conflict at either the individual or societal level. Indeed, the comparison of New York City and London crime outcomes in Chapter 3 shows that the volume of offenses is not an efficient predictor of lethal violence rates from burglary and robbery.

One other routinely reported dimension of homicide circumstance is the relationship between victim and offender, as shown in Figure 4.8.

The relationship between victim and offender can be specified by the police in six out of every ten cases when the Supplementary Homicide Reports are filed. Where the relationship is known, the offender and victim were acquainted in more than half the cases and were connected by family ties in an additional 15.3 percent of all homicides. The police judge

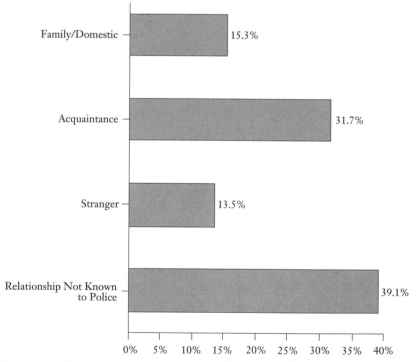

Figure 4.8. Victim-offender relationship in U.S. criminal homicide, 1992.

Source: U.S. Department of Justice, Federal Bureau of Investigation, 1994b.

that victim and offender were strangers in 13.5 percent of all cases or 23 percent of all cases where the police make a relationship classification.

What can we say from these data about the nature of victim–offender relationships in homicide? To estimate the total volume of stranger homicides in the United States as about 14 percent is certainly an undercount because the police report that they cannot identify the relationship between victim and offender in 39 percent of all homicides. But a controversy has emerged regarding how to treat the "relationship unknown" group of cases when estimating the total proportion of lethal violence that does not involve prior acquaintances.

One theory is that the police can usually specify the relationship in homicides involving domestic and romantic intimates. Since the "relationship unknown" category will involve few such intimate homicides, it is best to add all "relationship unknown" cases to the known stranger cases to estimate the true proportion of stranger cases. Such a procedure could produce an estimate that a majority of U.S. homicides involve strangers (Walinsky 1995; U.S. Department of Justice, Federal Bureau of Investigation, 1994b).

But the logical foundation on which this procedure rests is fallacious. There is no reason to doubt that killings by family members are not often included in the "relationship unknown" category of homicides. But to conclude that all unsolved killings are committed by strangers is unwarranted because the largest category of homicides in the United States is killing where there is some prior acquaintance between victim and offender, and there is no reason to suppose that homicides involving friends or conflicts between casual acquaintances are easy for police authorities to solve. Perhaps the best provisional estimate of stranger killings can be obtained by distributing the unknown relationship killings according to the proportions of the known relationship cases other than those involving family and domestic disturbances. This would produce an estimate of 25 percent stranger killings in the United States when the 13.5 percent of confirmed stranger cases are added to the estimated 12 percent of cases that probably involve strangers.

The Demography of Homicide

The preceding discussion of trends in violence over time presents data on total national rates of violence as the basis for comparison over time or between countries. But the national averages for rates of homicide or other serious acts of violence mask huge variations in rates of violence among different subgroups in the population.

This section is a preliminary attempt to mention and display some of the major variations in the risks of violence that lie behind the aggregate national averages. The consistent theme in our account of the demography of violence is that the most lethal subtypes of violence are also the

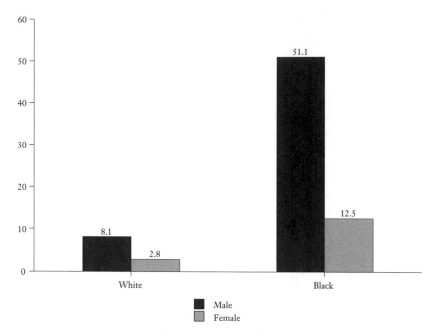

Figure 4.9. U.S. homicide risks by race and gender, 1989. *Source:* U.S. Department of Commerce, Bureau of the Census, 1990; U.S. Department of Justice, Federal Bureau of Investigation, 1994b.

most concentrated in pockets of social disadvantage, while the less lethal forms of violence are more evenly distributed. When the risk of violence is the topic the major demographic categories that must be examined include gender, race, ethnicity, age, community size, and socioeconomic status of neighborhood of residence.

Figure 4.9 begins the analysis by reporting rates of homicide separately by gender and race for Americans classified as white and black. Excluded from this analysis are some major racial and ethnic classifications, including Hispanic, Asian, and Pacific Islanders.

The aggregate homicide rate for the United States in 1989 was 9.4 per 100,000, but only one of the four groups represented in the figure has a rate close to that national average. Victimization rates for blacks are about five times those of whites, and victimization rates for males are about three times those of females. Thus the risks associated with being both black and male at 51 per 100,000 in 1989 are almost twenty times as great as the homicide experience of white women during the same years. Both gender and race are powerfully connected with the risk of homicide, but the predictive power of race appears to be slightly greater. Black women, the low-risk gender category within the high-risk racial group, have a 1989 homicide rate 50 percent higher than that of white males, the high-risk gender category within the low-risk racial group.

Racial and ethnic subcategories not reported have diverse risks of homicide. Native Americans and Hispanic-surname U.S. residents have rates of homicide much higher than whites but lower than U.S. blacks. Many other ethnic subcategories have homicide victimization experience lower than whites.

The relationship between victimization rates and offender rates for criminal homicide can be summed up in the proposition that a profile of homicide offenders will differ from the general population in the same way as will homicide victims, only more so. Thus the rate of homicide victimization is three and a half times as great among males as among females. But the rate of homicide offending is almost seven times greater for males than for females. Similarly, blacks are five times as likely to be homicide victims as whites, but eight times as likely to be arrested for homicide.

The data reported in Figure 4.9 also understate the diversity of American homicide experience because there are concentrations of homicide risk associated with age and location of residence not accounted for in the figure. In general, the risk of homicide is concentrated in the years of late adolescence and young adulthood with the median age of homicide death in the late twenties. Young children and middle-aged and older persons have much lower homicide rates. Again when considering age, the concentration of homicide offenders differs from the general population in the same way as for homicide victims only more so. A clear majority of all homicide offenders arrested are between the ages of fifteen and thirty.

The concentration of homicide in race, gender, and age clusters produces dramatic contrasts. Homicide is the tenth leading cause of death in the U.S. population as a whole, but among young black males in the United States intentional homicide is the leading cause of death, and the death rate for young black males ages fifteen to twenty-nine per 1000 population is over forty times as great as for white females of all ages (U.S. Department of Health and Human Services 1991).

Two other demographic factors associated with the risk of homicide, community type and neighborhood, have not been the subject of detailed national-level statistical comparison. But the statistical evidence that is available shows the great importance of both community size and neighborhood location.

Homicide is concentrated in the big cities of the United States, and in 1992 when the aggregate national homicide rate was 9.7 per 100,000, nineteen of the twenty largest cities had homicide rates that exceeded that figure with a median big city homicide rate of 27 per 100,000. Together, the twenty largest cities in the United States with 11.5 percent of the total population of the country had 34 percent of the criminal homicide reported to the police. As this concentration in the big cities implies, rates in the suburbs, towns, and rural areas are all lower than the aggregate national homicide rate—in many cases very much lower.

But discussing the risk of homicide as if the rates experienced at the city level were spread uniformly throughout the city is erroneous. Where people live within community areas has a dramatic effect on the nature and extent of the homicide they experience. Studies in Chicago of the geographical distribution of homicide show clearly an extreme concentration of reported homicide in heavily populated and highly disorganized black ghetto areas. The difference in homicide risk between high-risk and low-risk neighborhoods within each large city is much greater than the difference in homicide rate that is noted when big cities are compared with other population areas. New York City's aggregate homicide rate may be 27 per 100,000, but many residents of New York City live as safely on the borders of Central Park as do the residents of Sioux City, Iowa.

There is one further demographic detail that is necessary to complete even a sketchy portrait of the variation in the homicide risk: the influence of region. Homicide rates in the United States are highest in the South and lowest in the Northeast; the other two regions are in the middle of the distribution. The pronouncedly higher rate of homicide in the South, together with some statistical evidence that homicide rates in other areas are influenced by the percentage of residents who migrated there from the South, have led to a lively debate on the influence of "southernness" on rates of violence (see Hackney 1969; Gastil 1971; Loftin and Hill 1974).

While the various demographic factors that influence the risk of homicide can each be discussed separately, the interaction and overlap of such factors in American society are considerable. Homicide rates are highest in the slum neighborhoods of big cities that exclusively house the black poor. The race of the residents, the socioeconomic status of the neighborhood, and city size are all associated with elevated rates of homicide victimization.

Distinguishing the individual influence of a particular risk factor may be impossible when such interactive patterns are almost universal in high-risk homicide areas. Yet the major social and demographic risk factors for homicide almost never occur singly in United States cities. This means that we may know more about the social impact of a combination of characteristics than we do about the impact of individual factors such as race or type of neighborhood on the homicide victimization risk.

Violent Crime as a Cause of Death

This section will explore the link between different types of violent crime in the United States and the risk of homicide resulting from each form of violent act: While there is novelty in using the risk of death as a primary organizing principle in considering the entire range of crimes of violence, this strategy emerges naturally from the study's special emphasis on lethal violence. What types of violent conduct produce the distinctively high rates of U.S. homicide? What forms of criminal activity are most dangerous to their victims?

The Deadliness of Crime: An Overview

There are two different ways of measuring the death risk of particular types of crime: one focuses on the aggregate impact of a particular crime on homicide generally and the second measures the risk that an individual act will produce a victim's death. For highway driving, an aggregate analysis would measure the total death toll from auto crashes as a percentage of total deaths. An analysis of the death risk of drivers would measure the chances of being killed on an average 300-mile trip or per 100 million miles driven, perhaps comparing the death risk in auto travel with the death risk for traveling by private or commercial plane or by bus.

Figure 4.10 is a measure of aggregate death toll, estimating the number of criminal homicides generated by five crime categories in the United States in 1992 according to the Federal Bureau of Investigation's Supplementary Homicide Reports for that year.

The crime categories generate three very different levels of aggregate death toll. The general assault category is a residual that includes all attacks not associated with other forms of crime. It accounts for more than

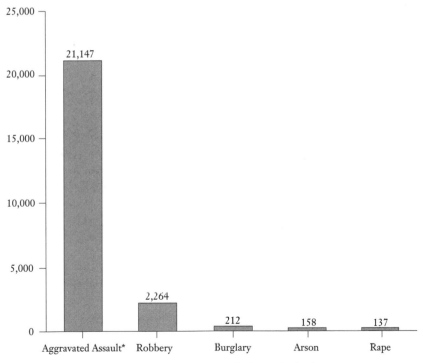

*Deaths not reported in other categories are assumed to be assault related.

Figure 4.10. U.S. deaths resulting from selected felonies, 1992. *Source:* U.S. Department of Justice, Federal Bureau of Investigation, 1994b.

85 percent of all homicides in the United States, about ten times the volume of killings the police attribute to robbery events in the Supplementary Homicide Report totals. The robbery death toll in turn is about ten times as great as the total number of deaths associated with burglary and more than fifteen times the death toll from arson and rape.

These estimates cannot be precise measures because there is a substantial group of homicides for which no clear motive is determined. But the existing data provide clear instruction on the relative risks associated with different activities. Of the 15 percent or so of U.S. homicides that are classified as felony murders, the vast majority are the result of robbery. Four times as many Americans are killed in robberies each year as are killed in burglary, arson, and rape combined. For this reason, even though women are far less likely than men to die in robbery (Zimring and Zuehl 1986), more than twice as many women die as a result of robbery than are victims of rape murder (324 vs. 127). The dominance of robbery in the felony murder statistics also makes the reduction of death from robbery a clear public health priority. A 1 percent reduction in robbery killings saves ten times as many lives as a 1 percent reduction in burglary killings. Using the estimates in Figure 4.10, a 10 percent decrease in robbery killings would save more lives in the United States in 1992 than eliminating arson or rape as a cause of death.

This enormous leverage for robbery is not an artifact of faulty reporting. The undercount in robbery killings is probably at least as great in percentage terms as in other forms of felony-related killings (Zimring and Zuehl 1986). And the death toll from robbery was more than ten times the number of all classified homicides involving fire.

While the data in Figure 4.10 tell the citizen which crime categories generate the largest number of deaths, they do not provide information on the risk of death per 1000 crimes committed. Statistics are available to estimate total offense rates in the United States for all of the crimes reported in Figure 4.10 except arson. Using the total number of offenses reported for 1992, Figure 4.11 shows the death rate per 1000 events for the four Part I offenses with significant death rates in 1992.

The data on assault, the highest death risk reported in Figure 4.11, are also the least reliable. The rate of 184 per 10,000 attacks is derived by assuming that the assaults that kill would all have been classified as aggravated assault by police if the victim had survived. If the denominator used to estimate the death risk for attacks without a collateral felony involvement were all assaults reported to the police, the death rate per 1,000 attacks would drop substantially, but then the assault category would be a mixture of life-threatening and less serious attacks with divergent death rates. Adding the less serious assaults does not move us closer to a true death rate estimate for life-threatening attacks. This problem was discussed in Chapter 3.

Whether the correct estimate is 184 per 10,000 or somewhat lower, the

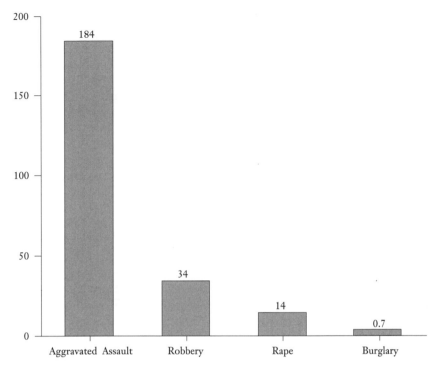

Figure 4.11. U.S. death rate (per 10,000 offenses), 1992. *Source:* U.S. Department of Justice, Federal Bureau of Investigation, 1992 (offenses); U.S. Department of Justice, Federal Bureau of Investigation, 1994b (homicides).

risk associated with an aggravated assault is much greater than that generated by other crimes because the intention to injure is present in most cases. In robbery, there is no unconditional intention to injure a victim, and the force that must be applied for rape to occur need not be life-threatening in most cases to achieve the offender's sexual objective. In crimes like robbery and burglary, life-threatening attacks most frequently occur when the interaction between victim and offender veers out of the offender's exclusive control.

The "safest" crime in the law's standard list of forcible felonies is burglary, for the obvious reason that the offender wishes to avoid contact with his victims. The burglar wants to get in and get out without human contact. Burglary has a death rate of less than one per 10,000 events. Only a very high volume of burglaries can generate any significant number of victim deaths. Rape, by contrast, is associated with 14 victim deaths per 10,000 crimes, a much higher victimization rate than burglary, which is offset by the much lower volume of reported rapes.

Robbery is a high-volume crime with a high death rate of 34 per 10,000. The combination of high volume and high rate produces an aggregate death toll from robbery that exceeds the homicide rate per 100,000 from all circumstances for many developed nations.

The major predictor of differential death rate from robbery is weapon use. Chapter 3 showed this for New York City. The national data for 1992 shows guns involved in 71 percent of all robbery killings, but 40 percent of all robberies. The death rate is about six per 1000 gun robberies, four times as high as the rate from all other robberies (U.S. Department of Justice, Federal Bureau of Investigation, 1994a).

Arson killings and rape killings are two subclasses of homicide where firearms are not the dominant cause of death. For this reason, the death rate from the offenses should be closer to rates observed in other developed countries to the extent that gun use is a major factor in high death rates in the United States for other crimes.

Heterogeneity and Differential Deadliness

The average death rate per 10,000 violent crimes reported in Figure 4.11 is useful information, but may also be misleading. To know that the average for all reported robberies is thirty-four victim deaths per 10,000 robberies can help us compare the death risk from robbery with the death risk from burglary and assault. But dealing only in aggregate averages masks two of the most important characteristics of violent offenses in the United States—heterogeneity and differential deadliness.

Appendix 3 provides demographic and circumstantial data on assault, rape, and robbery in the United States. For assault and robbery, the official definitions of the crime category are so broad that many different types of behavior carrying different degrees of danger to victims are reported under the same heading. Aggravated assaults can range from threatening gestures with dangerous weapons to multiwound shootings. Robberies include schoolyard extortions, unarmed muggings, many different types of street robbery, and loaded-gun invasions of commercial premises. Most robberies and assaults are clustered in the less serious categories. But the most dangerous forms of assault and robbery are the behaviors that cause most of the victim deaths.

With respect to sexual violence, the recent emphasis on victim survey data and the expansion of police attention into unsuccessful assaults and acquaintance cases has meant that many categories of sexual violence are also much more heterogeneous. As discussed in Appendix 3, the more serious forms of sexual assault are more concentrated among blacks than uncompleted assaults. This parallels the findings on assault where attacks that lead to death are more prevalent among blacks than nonfatal assaults.

Different forms of assault and robbery have very much different risks of death to their victims. A relatively small proportion of all assaults may account for the majority of all deaths from assault. That is one very plausible inference from the fact that general rates of assault do not differ greatly from country to country in survey research on assault rates (see Chapter 3). Much of the violence in the United States does not differ importantly from assault and robbery in other developed counties, but those are the assaults and robberies of the low end of the seriousness scale. The more dangerous the particular form of attack or robbery, the more likely that the prevalence of the behavior is concentrated in the minority neighborhoods of big American cities.

Conclusion: The Multiple Levels of U.S. Violence

The data presented in this chapter and in Appendix 3 show that American violence is a multiple-level phenomenon, an admixture of different kinds of behaviors that should be examined separately before coming to conclusions about causation or prevention. This point is sufficiently important and sufficiently novel to merit special mention by way of conclusion.

Much of the violent behavior present in the United States does not differ significantly from the patterns of violence found elsewhere in the industrial Western world. Most assaults in the United States grow out of conflicts of social life present in the United Kingdom, Western Europe, or in Australia: barroom fights, the battery of sexual intimates, the violent maltreatment of children, schoolyard extortions, and the like. These are chronic problems in most countries, and while the rates of many of these behaviors might be somewhat higher in the United States, there is a good deal of continuity between the kind of violence that makes up the bulk of reported assaults in the United States and the kind of conduct that observers find in other countries.

Using the broad categories developed in sample surveys of crime victimization, many, even most, of the violent acts reported in the United States resemble similar categories in other countries. But there are separate strands of high-death-risk violence present in the United States in much larger concentrations than in other countries, and these acts of high-death-risk violence are distributed among the U.S. population in patterns that are quite different from other types of violence.

There is a distinct layer of violent assaults in the United States involving woundings with deadly weapons and much higher levels of lethal outcome that are more likely than other assaults to involve blacks and males in cities. The high rates of life-threatening robbery in the United States also occur most frequently in the same urban settings and among the urban male population. The most serious forms of sexual assault—completed rapes—are also concentrated among black victims and involve the same offender populations.

Much, but not all, of the higher death rate produced by American violence occurs in the demographic clusters where the most lethal strands of violence are visibly concentrated. It is at least plausible that much of the rest of the difference in death rates from American violence could be attributable to separate layers of lethal violence involving white male offenders in noncore city environments, but this separate layer may be difficult to distinguish from the less dangerous varieties of assaultive behavior attributable to the same population.

Unfortunately, it is far from easy to distinguish lethal strains of violence when analyzing data relating to heterogeneous categories like assault and robbery. For assault, the most promising method of separately identifying lethal attacks is to focus on cases involving the infliction of wounds with knives or guns. This strategy should be distinguished from a special focus on all gun and knife assaults reported in surveys because more than three-quarters of all gun assaults in the surveys of crime victimization do not involve woundings.

All types of American violence deserve more scientific and scholarly attention than they have yet received. But special priority should be accorded to that layer of American violence most concentrated among minority males and most likely to cause death. Identifying methods that focus specifically on those highly dangerous attacks is neither simple nor easy to accomplish, but it is essential to understanding the special status and the special problems of violence in the United States.

5

New Perspectives on African-American Violence

No aspect of the demography of violence in the United States is more dramatic than the concentration of lethal violence among African-American males. While the statistics on the distribution of violence are clear, however, the significance of those patterns is anything but self-evident.

Every aspect of serious violence in the United States is linked with statistical and policy questions involving race. And very few of the important aspects of race relations are not connected to concerns about violence: its incidence, its consequences, and attitudes toward it. One cannot be concerned about relations between blacks and whites in the United States without also being concerned about African-American violence. One cannot be seriously concerned about violence in the United States without encountering a large number of questions that arise because of the substantial share of American violence that is black violence.

The subjects considered in this chapter fall far short of a comprehensive treatment of African-American violence. It provides only a descriptive statistical analysis of current conditions. No attempt is made to outline a history of, or offer a theory or set of theories regarding, black violence. Nor is there any discussion of, or prescription for, political intervention. Instead, it is the objective of this chapter to apply the information and perspectives that have been developed in the first four chapters to the statistics and issues relating to African-American violence.

The organizational strategy of the chapter is to focus first upon two generalizations about violence and race, which are disproved by the statistical data on violence in the United States. A second section supplements the national statistics on arrests by briefly analyzing data on arrests by race in five large American cities. The third section shows the pattern of victimization by race for nonviolent crime, violent crime, and lethal violence, with the concentration increasing with each level of severity. The consideration of African-American violence in the particular context of the previous chapters is a much narrower undertaking than more open-ended enquiries about the nature and distribution of black violence. But this special focus provides a novel and useful way of making sense of the statistical patterns.

Two False Inferences

One helpful way to organize a review of the data about violence, race, and crime is to discuss two propositions that are disproved by the existing data about violence among African-Americans:

1. that black violence is just a part of a general tendency for blacks to commit large numbers of criminal offenses, both violent and nonviolent; and
2. that rates of violence in the United States are disproportionately higher than those of other industrial countries only because of the high rates of violence among African-Americans.

Not a Crime Problem

Just as the high rates of American violence are falsely assumed to be a byproduct of high rates of American crime, there is also a common but false assumption that high rates of African-American violence are simply a byproduct of high crime rates among African-Americans.

Morris and Tonry, for example, write of the "disproportionate black criminality" that is represented by "the black contribution to the totality of crime." And they list the serious crimes in respect of which blacks "are overrepresented" as "rape and robbery, murder and mayhem, burglary and battery" (Morris and Tonry 1984:281–284). Similarly, Wilson and Herrnstein say that "even allowing for the existence of discrimination in the criminal justice system the higher rates of crime among black Americans cannot be denied." In relation to "the higher average crime rates of blacks," they say that "the preponderance of evidence—arrest data, victim surveys, and homicide statistics—confirms the higher rate of most kinds of common crimes among blacks than among whites" (Wilson and Herrnstein 1985:461, 466).

Once black violence is seen as simply a part of "the black contribution to the totality of crime," it is also seen as explicable in the same way as crime in general is explained. Thus, according to Morris and Tonry, the fact that blacks "disproportionately amass serious criminal records" can be

accounted for in terms of such things as the "agglomeration of social dis-
advantages that beset the black areas" and "the long history of cultural
adversity and its impact on the black family." In short, "disproportionate
black criminality . . . results from the social history of blacks in America"
(Morris and Tonry 1984:284).

By contrast, Wilson and Herrnstein list "four major theories of black
crime" to explain the "higher black crime rates." They do not endorse any
particular theory but say that it is "probably true to say that each theory is
partially correct." The four theories are: (1) "there are important constitu-
tional factors at work"; (2) "net economic disadvantage is a cause"; (3)
"there is a pattern of cultural pathology rooted in familial experiences";
and (4) "black rage at accumulated injustice is the cause of black crime."
There are, they say, "facts and arguments that support each of [these] theories of black crime, but there is not enough systematic evidence to evaluate their claims carefully" (Wilson and Herrnstein 1985:485–486).

What is significant here is not that the explanations suggested by Morris and Tonry and Wilson and Herrnstein are different from each other.
It is rather the fact that in both cases those different explanations are
advanced as dealing with the same unitary phenomenon. In both cases,
they offer what Wilson and Herrnstein call "theories of black crime" (Wilson and Herrnstein 1985:468) to explain "the higher average crime rates
of blacks" (Wilson and Herrnstein 1985:461), or "disproportionate black
criminality" (Morris and Tonry 1984:281).

John DiIulio of Princeton has produced the most flamboyant compound generalization in this regard—"America does not have a crime
problem; inner city America does"—at once defining crime as the problem
and the inner city as its sole location (DiIulio 1994:3).

The evidence presented in support of such unitary views of black crime
is that the arrest rates of black men for index crimes are higher than the
rates of arrest of white men for the same offenses. But a careful examina-
tion of the gross aggregate arrest rates that are usually cited suggests that
the degree to which black arrest rates exceed those of whites is anything
but a unitary phenomenon. Figure 5.1 (see p. 76) compares arrest rates for
black males with rates for white males for the seven index offenses in the
United States in 1992. Since the black–white ratios are the subject of
analysis, the black arrest rate is expressed as a whole number that is produced when the white rate of arrest for each offense is restated as 100.

The concentration of arrests among black offenders across the seven
index felonies is similar in only one respect: the arrest rates for blacks
exceed the arrest rates for whites for all index offenses. But the variation by
type of crime in black white arrest ratios is both substantial and patterned.
Arrest rates for burglary and theft are almost three times as high for black
men as for white men, while the black arrest rate is more than five times
the white rate for rape, more than eight times as large as the white rate for
homicide and almost eleven times the white rate for robbery. The differ-

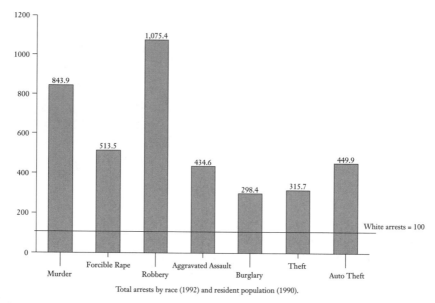

Total arrests by race (1992) and resident population (1990).

Figure 5.1. Comparison of black and white arrest rates. *Source:* U.S. Department of Commerce, Bureau of the Census, 1990 (resident population); U.S. Department of Justice, Federal Bureau of Investigation, 1992 (race).

ence between the concentration ratio for burglary and that for robbery is larger than the difference between the black rates of arrest and white rates of arrest for burglary.

The notable pattern in Figure 5.1 is that the highest ratios of black-to-white arrests are found for violent offenses and not property offenses. Of the four offenses of violence, three of them report a higher concentration among blacks by far than any of the index property offenses. The only overlap between violent and nonviolent offenses occurs because the racial concentration for aggravated assault arrests is slightly lower than the racial concentration for one of the three nonviolent offenses: automobile theft.

Even this is a false impression because the most dangerous forms of assault are more concentrated among black offenders than assaults generally. The ratio of black-to-white arrests rates for the three property offenses is 3.5 to 1, showing that white men are less than one-third as likely to be arrested for property offenses as black men. But the average concentration of violence arrests among black offenders is more than twice as high as the concentration in nonviolent offenses. Blacks are more than seven times as likely as whites to be arrested for offenses of violence.

Yet even this 7-to-1 ratio understates the extent of black offenses of violence. The aggregate national arrest picture tells us that blacks are slightly more than four times as likely as whites to be arrested for serious assault, but more than eight times as likely to be arrested for killing someone. Fig-

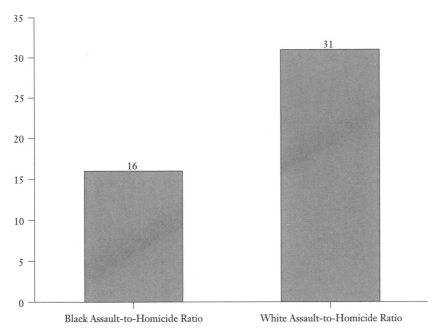

Figure 5.2. Ratio of aggravated assault arrests to homicide arrests, by race, 1992.

Source: U.S. Department of Justice, Federal Bureau of Investigation, 1992.

ure 5.2 shows one implication of these contrasting rates: the extent to which police-reported attacks by blacks have a much higher death rate than assaults, known to the police, by white offenders.

For every fatal attack that results in a black arrest, sixteen nonfatal attacks produce arrests of black suspects. The rate for whites is twice as high, so that there are thirty-one arrests for nonfatal assault for every arrest of a white for criminal homicide. The assaults reported in Figure 5.1 for black offenders are twice as likely to result in a killing as an assault attributed by the police to white offenders. This means that the rate of life-threatening assaults among blacks is probably closer to the 8-to-1 homicide ratio than to the 4-to-1 assault ratio. It also means that for offenses with a high death rate, the concentration among black males for arrest is probably about three times greater than the differential rate of commission of property offenses. The concentration of serious violence among blacks is so much greater than the concentration of other criminal offenses that a observer is on notice that two different patterns are operative.

One more arithmetic exercise can demonstrate how different the distribution of serious violence among blacks is from the pattern of nonviolent criminal offenses. If we assume that white rates of commission of all offenses remain stable at 1992 levels, what would be the impact if black rates of homicide were concentrated at the same level that Figure 5.1 reports for burglary arrests? Under these conditions the black arrest rate for homicide and presumably also the black offense rate would be 2.98 times the white rate rather than 8.44 times the white rate. At 2.98 times the white rate, the homicide rate for blacks in the United States would be 65 percent less than the current homicide rate and the total homicide rate in the United States would be reduced by 35 percent.

A similar numerical thought experiment can be performed by comparing the racial concentration of arrest for robbery and burglary. If rates of white arrests were stable and the concentration of robbery arrests among blacks was 2.98 times the white rate, as was the case in respect of burglary, the total robbery rate among blacks would fall by 72 percent, and the total robbery rate in the United States would fall by 44 percent. So the concentrations of violent offenses among blacks are much larger than the concentration of criminal offenses generally. If robbery and homicide were not more concentrated among black offenders than property offenses, the United States would be a much safer country.

This raises the same sorts of question discussed in earlier chapters. Robbery and burglary are two sorts of aggravated property offenses. Why are black offenders many times more concentrated in the robbery category than the burglary category? Most of the circumstances that generate homicide are not property crimes involving strangers, but arguments among acquaintances that nobody would regard as distinctively criminal until the attack began. Why are the life-threatening manifestations of these sorts of events eight times as concentrated among blacks as among whites?

Each of the statistical comparisons just mentioned illustrates a significant impediment to looking for a single cause for black crime and violence. The different robbery and burglary arrest patterns found for whites and blacks signal that no unitary theory of crime causation can explain the significant difference in choice between violent and nonviolent means of stealing property. The extraordinary difference in homicide offenses—most of them unrelated to criminal offenses other than assault—are a warning that no plausible explanation of black homicide will be principally concerned with explaining black participation in crime. It is far more likely that the influences that generate grossly disproportionate African-American homicide rates are broadly present in the social structure and behavior of the communities where rates are high. It is the propensity to resolve conflict with maximum personal force rather than any specific commitment to crime that is the precursor to high rates of conflict-motivated homicide.

There are two significant caveats that must be added to our previous remarks when using data on arrests by race to show that violence is not solely a crime problem. First, there is no reason to believe that all the different varieties of violent crime have either the same causes or the same concentrations among blacks. Thus, because it can be demonstrated that all kinds of violent crime have higher concentrations among blacks than among whites, this does not mean that the same factors that produce the difference in one type of violent crime operate with the same intensity and effect for other violent crimes. If lumping together violent and nonviolent offenses to support theories of black crime is a demonstrable aggregation error, that should alert us to the likelihood that lumping together all kinds of violent offenses may also be a fundamental mistake.

To return to the data presented in Figure 5.1, arrests for rape in the Federal Bureau of Investigation statistics are about half as concentrated among black offenders as arrests for robbery. Just because robbery and rape are two subcategories of violent crime, that provides no basis for concluding that rape behavior by African-American offenders should be explained in the same way as robbery behavior by African-American offenders. While rape arrests are more concentrated among blacks than burglary arrests, the concentration noted for rape is closer to that found in burglary than to that found in robbery. So discovering one aggregation error is a poor excuse for spawning a somewhat narrower generalization that might still involve attempting to put very different kinds of eggs into the same basket.

The second caveat that is required for a balanced assessment of racial concentrations in arrest statistics is that race is being used as what scientists call a "marker" for the discussion of differences rather than as an explanation. Substantial differences between races in violence as well as significant differences in pattern by race may tell us a great deal about what sorts of phenomena should be studied. But such differences tell us nothing about what might explain the significant differences in pattern that we observe. We have at best a factor that predicts significant differences in violence but that can explain none of them.

Not a Black Problem

Whatever the data that we have just reviewed may mean, there is one thing that they do not mean: It is beyond foolishness to regard American violence as solely, or mainly, or even distinctively a black problem. Large segments of the black community in the United States are located in those areas of the social distribution where one would expect a generally higher American propensity to violence to be most concentrated. We will show that the tendencies toward lethal violence documented in the previous section are, in the words of H. Rap Brown's celebrated cliché, "as American as apple pie."

Some observers of crime statistics greet the data showing the extraordinary concentration of violent offenses among African-American males as a definitive exoneration of the general American culture, society, and government from responsibility for the higher overall rates of violent offenses in the United States (see Bonger 1943; Wolfgang and Cohen 1970). What those data are taken to prove is that violence is a black problem. And if violence in the United States can be characterized as a black problem, then perhaps it should not be regarded as a "white" problem. Furthermore, perhaps the general social environment of the country should be regarded as bearing little or even no responsibility for the death rate from violence. Professor DiIulio's refrain bears emphasis in this regard: "America does not have a crime problem; inner city America does." Prior to his 1994 article, these sentiments had never been explicitly stated as a theory in academic criminology or policy analysis. But they constitute a common if not omnipresent subtext in policy discussion and in the opinions held by some governing elites and by segments of the general public.

The only problem with this particular hypothesis is that it is false, contradicted both by the available statistics and by elementary analytic techniques. Statistical analysis should begin with the reported rates of criminal homicide, which can be used both because homicide is the most serious violent crime and because those rates are good indices of the total rate of life-threatening violence. The previous chapter compared World Health Organization rates of reported homicide in the United States with those in

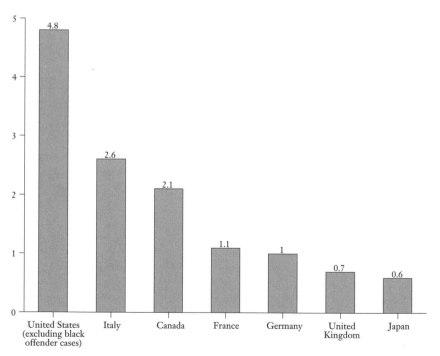

Figure 5.3. Homicide rates (per 100,000) for the United States (excluding black offender cases) and G7 countries, 1990. *Source:* World Health Organization 1990.

the other six members of the G7 industrial leadership nations. The U.S. homicide rate shown in Figure 4.1 was 9.4 per 100,000. Fifty-five percent of the 1992 homicide arrests in the United States were of blacks. Assuming that the 55 percent arrest figures means that black offenders were responsible for a similar percentage of homicide would imply a homicide offense rate for non-African-Americans of 4.8 per 100,000. This would be an extremely misleading statistic to use in international comparisons. The national experience of most other countries would benefit greatly if they could exclude their identifiable highest-risk subpopulations from any comparison.

But even with the cosmetic removal of all homicides attributable to black offenders, the U.S. homicide rate would still be a statistical "outlier," far beyond the experience of other industrial democracies. The "blacks excluded" estimated homicide rate of 4.8 for the United States is well over three times the average homicide rate of the other six nations and twice as high as the rate for the second highest nation, Italy.

The concentration of robbery in the United States would be much higher than other Western countries in 1992 if we assumed that black offenders were responsible for the same percentage of robbery offenses as they are of robbery arrests and then erased every robbery in the United States attributable to black offenders. Performing that operation on the data in Figure 1.1, blacks-excluded robbery in Los Angeles would still be three times the total robbery rates in Sydney, Australia. So the distinctive tendency of Los Angeles offenders to favor robbery over burglary when compared with offenders in other countries is pronounced for white offenders as well as for blacks.

So, the total exclusion of offenses attributed to blacks would not alter the distinctive position of the United States as an industrial democracy with extraordinarily high rates of high-lethality violence. But it must also be pointed out that "nonblack" rates of homicide and robbery are misleading and nonsensical. The truncation of one group in a national population in an international comparison produces a mythical part-country that cannot meaningfully be compared with real groups and nations. There is no more sense in removing an integrated group from a population in this way than one could amputate a person's leg and then compare that mutilated organism with another whole person.

In this connection, it is important to remember the distinction between factors that predict the distribution of violence in a social unit and the factors that explain levels of violence. As discussed in Appendix 1, race is like gender and age, a factor that tells us what groups in society will experience higher-than-average rates of violence. That does not imply that increasing the portion of African-Americans in the population would have any impact on rates of violence (see Appendix 1).

It will be helpful to contrast two contrasting assumptions that can be made about violent acts committed by blacks in the United States. One assumption is that of social independence, that is, that black violence is an outgrowth of generative processes that have nothing to do with the conditions of American life. This assumption hypothesizes a propensity on the part of blacks for violent attacks, which is both innate and immutable, and for that reason should not be expected to vary much over time or with changing social conditions.

There is no evidence that we know of to support this assumption. Moreover, there is much that contradicts it in the variable nature of both black and white violence in the United States since the midcentury. But this hypothesis of an innate and immutable black propensity for violence is worth mentioning because it describes the only set of circumstances in which a separate "nonblack" rate of American violence would make sense as an analytic tool.

The contrasting and, we believe, correct assumption is that rates of violence among racial and social subpopulations, black and white, are variable over time and with changed circumstances because they grow out of the social experience of American life. In these conditions, the rates of violence experienced by various subpopulations will, in large part, be determined by their location in the American social distribution.

On this assumption, the particular rates of violence of subgroups constitute a dependent variable. And the major social processes they depend on are generated by the social conditions of American urban life. Lethal violence must be regarded as an American problem in this essential respect.

Five-City Analysis

Part of the contrast between black and nonblack patterns in the national-level statistics on violence is an artifact of the fact that blacks and whites reside in different types of population areas, and there are substantial variations in standards of reporting and classifying crime in different parts of the country. Black population is concentrated in large urban areas in the United States. Because the nonblack category is so broad, it represents an aggregation of all community types in the United States. So differences between city populations and populations that reside in suburbs, small towns, and other areas may masquerade as differences between blacks and whites.

To find out how much of the race differences noted in the previous section might stem from different patterns of residence, we examined arrests by race in five U.S. cities: New York City, Los Angeles, Chicago, Houston, and Dallas. The analysis is reported in Appendix 4. When only city populations are analyzed, the contrast between African-American and white arrests changes in two respects.

First, the contrast between assault-to-homicide ratios that existed at the national level all but disappears. The fact that whites have nearly twice as many assault arrests for every homicide arrest as blacks is almost completely the result of policies of police departments outside of cities. In the five-city sample, the eighteen assault arrests per homicide arrest for blacks was 20 percent greater than the 15-to-1 ratio for whites. Eighty percent of the differences between the races in the national statistics disappear when the comparison involves only city populations.

The second substantial finding of the study was that the contrast between black and nonblack violence arrest rates shrinks when the comparison is restricted to city dwellers. While the robbery arrest rate for African-Americans is more than ten times that of whites at the national level, the difference is reduced to 6 to 1 in the five-city comparison. For homicide, the concentration among blacks is cut almost in half, from eight times the nonblack rate at the national level to four times the nonblack arrest rate at the city level. So a major element in the explanation of the larger concentration of violence among African-Americans is the fact that they more often reside in cities where violent crime rates are high generally. Here is a concrete demonstration of how the general social structure helps to account for what appears as differences between racial groups.

Black Violence, Black Victims

To focus on rates of victimization among African-Americans is again to confront the stark contrast between crime and violence discussed earlier, as well as the equally sharp discontinuity between victimization rates for broad categories of conventionally measured violent crime and victimization rates for lethal violence. What careful analysis shows for African-Americans is not two patterns of victimization, but three distinctly different concentrations of vulnerability. The more serious the loss, the larger the concentration of victimization among African-Americans.

Police statistics do not provide racial detail on patterns of victimization for most crimes. For this reason, victim survey data are the primary source available on racial concentration of criminal victimization apart from homicide, where health statistics provide reliable racial detail. Figure 5.4 (see p. 84) provides information from the U.S. National Crime Survey for two categories of nonviolent property offense, and the two most common violent offenses as well as official statistics on patterns of homicide victimization. To parallel our earlier analysis, the figure measures the extent of racial concentration by expressing African-American rates for each offense as a percentage of white rates. The rates of personal victimization provided in Figure 5.4 are for males, while rates of victimization for household crimes are for all persons in the household.

Data are gathered at the household rather than the individual level for household larceny, burglary, and automobile theft. The distribution of common property crime victimization rates by race varies. African-Americans report about the same rate of household larceny as others and 47 percent more burglary. Only rates of automobile theft are reported as more than twice white rates.

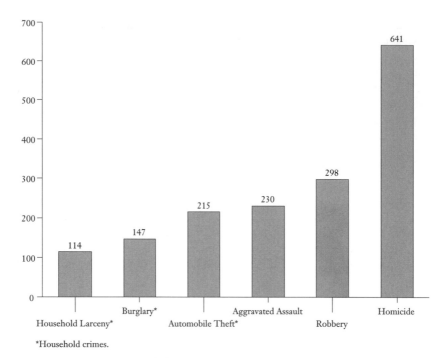

*Household crimes.

Figure 5.4. Comparison of black male and black household victimization rates as a percentage of white male and white household rates, 1992. *Source:* U.S. Department of Justice, Bureau of Justice Statistics, 1993 (household larceny, burglary, automobile theft, aggravated assault, robbery); U.S. Department of Justice, Federal Bureau of Investigation, 1993 (homicide).

The concentration by race for common offenses of violence is more pronounced, with black men reporting over twice as many aggravated assaults per capita and three times as many robbery victimizations. But even this concentration is small by comparison to the vulnerability to homicide among black males. The per capita rate of homicide among black males is over six times the white male rate, so that the concentration in homicide is over twice that found for any common offenses of violence in the victim survey.

We do not have reason to doubt that the National Crime Survey statistics accurately reflect the racial concentrations of assault and robbery as broadly measured. But the 6-to-1 concentration in homicide risk is a much more accurate reflection of the concentration of lethal violence in the African-American community. When the assault rate among African-Americans is estimated at twice the white rate but the homicide rate six times greater, the homicide concentration more accurately reflects the extent to which black males are more likely to be victimized by attacks that carry a substantial risk of death. If the only available data were those in

Figure 5.4 and we were asked to guess how much more likely a black man was to be shot or stabbed and survive his wounds than a white man, our estimate would be based on the 641 percent homicide risk differential rather than the 230 percent risk differential in aggravated assault. The less life-threatening assaults are those where white victimization rates are much closer to black victimization rates.

A limited amount of information is available regarding the distribution of lethal violence within African-American population groups: Death statistics constantly show concentrations within age groups fifteen to thirty-five for men and geo-coding the addresses of homicide victims shows large concentrations of homicide in high-density, low-income housing areas in Chicago (Block 1977). The residual of these concentrations would be rates of victimization much lower than age—and gender—averages for those African-Americans in more advantaged economic circumstances and locations. While the extent to which lethal violence is concentrated at the bottom of the economic scale cannot be precisely estimated, the geographical studies leave little doubt that in regard to the violence among African-Americans, the poor pay more.

But there is good reason to suppose that not only the poor pay more. Economic resources provide middle-class African-American households with some choices, but most American cities are divided geographically into racial zones where the black not-poor live in physical proximity to the black poor. The influence of social processes related to race may mean that economic resources are a less effective insurance policy against lethal violence for city-dwelling African-American families than for whites who live in suburbs.

The only national estimates available on African-American victimization by income group come from the National Crime Survey and detail the heterogeneous categories of assault and robbery. Table 5.1 shows robbery victimization by race and income. For whites, the rate of robbery victimization drops with increasing income. The rate in the income category above 50,000 is 70 percent less than rates reported by the two lowest income categories. For African-Americans, rates of victimization are higher at all levels and do not drop consistently as income increases. The robbery victimization of high-income blacks is six times that of high-income

Table 5.1

Robbery Victimization Rates per 1000 by Race and Income

	Under 7,500	7,500– 9,999	10,000– 14,999	15,000– 24,999	25,000– 29,999	30,000– 49,999	Over 50,000
White	8.2	8.8	6.6	4.5	4.00	4.2	2.8
Black	20.0	20.9	11.0	13.4	29.00	13.7	17.6

Source: U.S. Department of Justice, Bureau of Justice Statistics, 1993.

Table 5.2

Aggravated Assault Victimization Rates per 1000 by Race and Income

	Under 7,500	7,500– 9,999	10,000– 14,999	15,000– 24,999	25,000– 29,999	30,000– 49,999	Over 50,000
White	21.3	8.0	6.8	8.7	6.1	6.4	5.7
Black	28.9	17.3	23.1	16.4	10.3	8.8	6.9

Source: U.S. Department of Justice, Bureau of Justice Statistics, 1993.

whites, and also more than twice as large as for the lowest-income white group.

The pattern for aggravated assault, by contrast, shows significant decreases for reported victimization by income for both races, as shown in Table 5.2.

Aggravated assault rates for whites drop sharply when the lowest-income group is compared with all others, then decline a further 30 percent from the next lowest to the highest income level. The decline with ascending income is steadier among blacks, with assault rates lower at each step up in income level except $10,000 to $15,000. The highest black income group has a rate of aggravated assault only one-fifth higher than the highest white income group, and indistinguishable from middle-income white rates.

The extent to which higher-income African-Americans are at risk for lethal violence is not known, but should be. Detailed studies of socioeconomic status and risk of homicide by race and ethnicity are a priority need in the sociological study of lethal violence. This is one of many important issues that have yet to receive serious study.

There is one other respect in which African-Americans of all classes are placed at risk by high rates of lethal violence attributed to African-American offenders. The social reputation of blacks for violence is one element in white resistance to integration. So the same high violence rates that place blacks at risk of victimization also hinder mobility away from high violence areas. Black violence thus functions as a double burden on the black middle class, both a direct threat to personal security and a barrier to integration because a social reputation for violence is imputed to all men with dark skin.

As indicated in Chapter 1, the relationship between fear of violence and fear of black men is a two-way street. Anxiety about dark-skinned strangers can produce substantial levels of fear with no support in the crime statistics. But the reality of high levels of violence among African-American males reinforces white fear in ways that palpably contribute to the exclusion of blacks from the social mainstream. To the extent that a dark complexion provokes fear of violence, it will continue to be a visible stigma that exacerbates America's most serious social problem.

Conclusion

Life-threatening violence is more concentrated among African-Americans than among any other major population group in the United States. The likelihood that African-Americans will be involved in homicide either as victims or offenders is far greater than their proportionate share of crime, and also greater than the proportion of violent crime attributable to black offenders. So, the more life-threatening the offense, the greater the concentration of both victims and offenders among African-Americans. In this segment of the American community, as in the rest of American society, it is life-threatening violence, not a general propensity toward crime, that demands attention.

African-American violence is by no means the totality of the U.S. violence problem. Rates of life-threatening violence among other population groups are much higher than in other countries, and African-American patterns of violence are not dissimilar to those found in other groups. The concentration of violent crime arrests among African-Americans is substantially reduced when the comparison is restricted to populations living in the five major cities we examined, but the rates of life-threatening violence among African-Americans are also higher than among other urban populations. Violence is not just a black problem, but it is an American problem that has the largest proportional impact by far among African-Americans.

The extent and nature of the violence problem among different segments of the African-American population is not well documented. A plea for more research is always the first resort of academic commentary. But what we do not know about the incidence of lethal violence at different social and income levels among African-Americans is quite surprising.

Coming to know that lethal violence rather than crime is the significant American problem makes clear the undemocratic distribution of the most feared consequences from crime and violence in the United States. African-Americans are no more than twice as likely as whites to become victims of property crimes; they are more than five times as likely to be killed. Until life-threatening violence becomes the special concern, the largest crime burden of black America will continue to be ignored.

II

CORRELATES
AND CAUSES

THE INTELLECTUAL REPUTATION of discussions about the causes of violence is abysmal. Merely to announce causation as a topic of discussion will provoke the derisive groans of sophisticated scholars in the United States. Everybody agrees that the issue of causation is important. There is, however, also universal agreement that what is said about the causation of crime and of violence is simplistic and confused.

The next four chapters show how changing the subject from the causation of violence generally to searching for the proximate causes of lethal violence can clarify issues and provide a basis for both science and public policy. The first chapter in this part reviews the problems associated with discussion of the causes of violence and proposes narrowing the subject to determine what factors cause deaths and serious injuries.

The remaining chapters in this part illustrate how a shift to the specific issue of lethal violence can bring a series of important problems into sharper focus. Chapter 7 shows how guns assume huge importance when general concerns about crime rates are replaced with the search for the proximate causes of death from assault and robbery.

Chapter 8 deals with mass media impacts on lethal violence. Here the shift in focus from violence generally to lethal violence renders the mass media a much less important influence than contemporary discussion assumes. Careful comparative study disproves the notion that the intensity of media exposure is a generator of homicide in developed nations.

Chapter 9 addresses the relationship between illegal drugs and lethal violence. We question the assertion that the absence of a legal market is a sufficient condition for high rates of lethal violence, but acknowledge that drug markets in the United States do generate high death rates under current conditions. The significance of seeing that lethal violence is not an inevitable element of drug criminalization is the possibility that policies short of decriminalization may help to reduce the bloodshed now associated with drug wars in the United States.

The basic message of this section is that specific inquiry about the causes of lethal violence avoids much of the fuzziness that has made causal inquiry notorious. We know much more about what makes assault deadly than we do about the basic causes of criminal behavior or human aggression.

6

On Causes and Prevention

AMONG SERIOUS STUDENTS OF VIOLENCE there is an ambivalence about the discussion of causation that is of more than passing significance. On the one hand, nothing could be more logical and natural than to address questions about violence in causal terms. To seek to understand violence is inevitably to try to determine its causes; so that almost all discussions of violence quickly become discussions of causes.

On the other hand, so many discussions of the causes of violence have fallen victim to logical and empirical problems that many scholars avoid causal discourse as though the available literature had given the enterprise a bad name. In this chapter, we attempt to elucidate the prevailing ambivalence about causation by contrasting the approaches of two national commissions of inquiry into violence—the National Commission on the Causes and Prevention of Violence (1968–1969) (known as the Eisenhower Commission after its chairman, Milton S. Eisenhower) and the National Academy of Sciences Panel on the Understanding and Control of Violent Behavior—to questions of causation.

We then catalog some of the more common mistakes of causal attribution in the discussion of violence. A third section of this chapter discusses the appropriate link between understanding the causes of violence and seeking appropriate and effective ways of preventing violent outcomes.

The fourth section of this chapter attempts to bring issues of causation into sharper focus by arguing that the proximate causes of lethal violence should be the priority target for research. The singular character of U.S.

violence is its high death rate; this should be the aspect of U.S. violence we seek to explain.

Our motive in writing this chapter is not the desire to provide a text on causation. It is rather because we think that causal attribution is an important part of contemporary discussion of violence, and we believe that attention to the ways in which people think and talk about violent acts may be productive and illuminating. So the uses and abuses of causal theory concern us here as a way of organizing thought about the incidence and control of violent acts.

Two Views of Causation

The National Commission on the Causes and Prevention of Violence and the National Academy of Sciences Panel on Understanding and Controlling Violence were both designed as comprehensive efforts to survey knowledge about violent crime, with the object of facilitating its prevention. While similar in mission, these two bodies were quite dissimilar in their attitude to causal language and causal paradigms. The 1968–1969 Commission was established by President Lyndon Johnson by Executive Order No. 11412 as a commission on the *causes* of violence, and its progenitor's emphasis on causation was reflected and fulfilled in the Commission's analysis. The National Academy's Panel, by contrast, disavowed research into "the causes of violent behavior and of violent crime [and] accordingly, it focused more on issues and problems in understanding and control" (Reiss and Roth 1993:xv).

A Commission on Causes

The Commission was given a mandate "to investigate and make recommendations with respect to . . . the causes and prevention of lawless acts of violence in our society." The Commission was also instructed to investigate some other related matters such as "the causes of . . . disrespect for public officials." But our concern here is with the causation of acts of violence and what the Commission had to say on that topic.

The opening words of the Introduction to the Final Report of the National Commission on the Causes and Prevention of Violence published in December 1969 are explicit and unequivocal: "This Commission was created by the President in June 1968 to determine *the causes of violence* in the United States. . . ." Moreover, "In this report we analyze *basic causes* which underlie the chief varieties of contemporary violence. We make a number of recommendations directed to removing *these causes*." For the Commission believed that "we have identified *the causes* of much of the violence that plagues contemporary America" (U.S. National Commission 1969a:xxiii, xxv, xxviii; emphasis added).

The Report contains a chapter on violent crime that includes sections covering topics ranging from a "Profile of Violent Crime" to the "Prevention of Violent Crime." But one of those sections deals with the "Causes of Violent Crime" and is concerned specifically with what are referred to as "the root causes of a high percentage of violent crime." It is said there that because "violent crime . . . is heavily concentrated in large cities and especially among poor black young men in the ghettos," the focus of attention is on "the conditions of life for the youth of the inner-city" (U.S. National Commission 1969a:24).

"Violence," the Commission said, "is like a fear in the body politic: it is but the symptom of some more basic pathology." The nature of that more basic pathology is identified in the following passage:

> The way in which we can make the greatest progress toward reducing violence in America is by taking the actions necessary to improve the conditions of family and community life for all who live in our cities, and especially for the poor who are concentrated in the ghetto slums. It is the ghetto slum that is disproportionately responsible for violent crime, by far the most acute aspect of the problem of violence in the United States today. (U.S. National Commission 1969a:xxvi and xxx)

Following a brief review of conditions in ghetto slums, the report concludes that "an inter-related complex of powerful criminogenic forces" involving a combination of "poverty, dilapidated housing, high unemployment, poor education, over-population and broken homes" is produced by the ghetto environment. Moreover, these "social forces for crime are intensified by the inferiority-inducing attitudes of the larger American society." As a result, the slum ghetto generates "frustration that expresses itself in violent acquisitive crime."

The step to violence is explained briefly as follows:

> [I]n an effort to obtain material goods and services beyond those available by legitimate means, lower-class persons without work skills and education resort to crimes for which force or threat of force has a functional utility, especially robbery, the principal street crime.

But the ghetto also produces a "subculture" in which "aggressive violence tends to be accepted as normal in everyday life." For in the contemporary American city, "we find the necessary conditions not only for the birth, but also for the accelerated development of violent subcultures, and it is in these settings that most violent aggressive crimes in fact occur" (U.S. National Commission 1969a:30–31).

Throughout this section of the Commission's report, the analysis is conducted in etiological terms. "The root causes of a high percentage of violent crime" are to be found in "the conditions of life for the youth of the inner-city." There is a "causal link" between "slum conditions" and "crime and violence." Young men are subject to "a complex of powerful criminogenic forces" and

an enormous set of influences that pull [them] toward crime and delinquency . . . [T]he conditions of life for inner-city populations are responsible for
the . . . violent crime rates. (U.S. National Commission, 1969a:24, 31, 33)

The National Academy of Sciences Panel

If the Eisenhower Commission was enthusiastic in its search for causes,
the National Academy of Sciences Panel seemed to studiously avoid both
the use of the "C" word and any claims about causal linkages. A stunning
demonstration of this self-conscious avoidance may be found in Table 6.1,
with which, as we shall see, the Panel report illustrated what it called its
multifactorial approach to violent crime.

The 1993 Report of the National Academy of Sciences Panel on the
Understanding and Control of Violent Behavior both raises and answers
the question: "Is the United States more violent than other societies?" To
that question, according to the report summary:

> In general the answer is yes. Homicide rates in the United States far exceed
> those in any other industrialized nation. For other violent crimes, rates in
> the United States are among the world's highest. . . . Among sixteen indus-
> trialized countries surveyed in 1988, the United States had the highest
> prevalence rates for serious sexual assault and for all other assault including
> threats of physical harm. (Reiss and Roth 1993:3)

It is an obvious and inevitable corollary of that answer to ask the further
question: "Why do Americans so often resort to violent means?" Moreover, the desire for an answer to that further question was one of the principal reasons why the National Academy's panel was set up.

The Panel was established by the Commission on Behavioral and Social
Sciences and Education of the National Research Council in response to
the expressed interests of three federal agencies. Two of those agencies—
the National Institute of Justice and the Centers for Disease Control—
were primarily interested in an assessment of what was known about how
to prevent and control violent behavior. But the third—the National Science Foundation—specifically "sought a review of *current knowledge on the
basic causes of violent behavior*" (Reiss and Roth, 1993:xiii; emphasis added).

It might have been hoped that the Panel as a result of carrying out that
review would be able to offer some kind of general theory regarding the
causation of violent behavior; that it would make an attempt to carry out
what has been described by Albert Cohen as "the chief task of theory now"
in relation to crime causation, the integration of ideas "into a coherent
parsimonious and testable system of theoretical propositions" (Cohen
1983:352). But the Panel made no such attempt.

What the Panel actually did was to briefly review the existing knowledge regarding some aspects of violent events and behaviors. It declared
itself, however,

Table 6.1

Matrix for Organizing Risk Factors for Violent Behavior

Units of Observation and Explanation	Predisposing	Proximity to Violent Events and Their Consequences Situational	Activating
Social			
Macrosocial	Concentration of poverty Opportunity structures Decline of social capital Oppositional cultures Sex-role socialization	Physical structure Routine activities Access: weapons, emergency medical services	Catalytic social event
Microsocial	Community organizations Illegal markets Gangs Family disorganization Preexisting structures	Proximity of responsible monitors Participants' social relationships Bystander's activities Temporary communication impairment Weapons: carrying, displaying	Participants' communication exchanges
Individual			
Psychosocial	Temperament Learned social responses Perceptions of rewards/ penalties for violence Violent deviant sexual preferences Cognitive ability Social, communication skills Self-identification in social hierarchy	Accumulated emotion Alcohol/drug consumption Sexual arousal Premeditation	Impulse Opportunity recognition
Biological	Neurobiological[a] "traits" Genetically mediated traits Chronic use of psychoactive substances or exposure to neurotoxins	Transient neurobiological[a] "states" Acute effects of psychoactive substances	Sensory signal processing errors Interdictal events

[a]Includes neuroanatomical, neurophysiological, neurochemical, and neuroendocrine. "Traits" describes capacity as determined by status at birth, trauma, and aging processes such as puberty. "States" describes temporary conditions associated with emotions, external stressors, etc. *Source:* Reiss and Roth 1993:20.

frustrated to realize that it was still not possible to link these fields of knowledge together in a manner that would provide a strong theoretical base on
which to build prevention and intervention programs. (Reiss and Roth
1993:21)

Rather than provide a strong theoretical base, the Panel observed:

> Multiple factors . . . have been found to correlate with the probability of vio-
> lent events. The correlations are low by conventional standards, inconsis-
> tent across settings, and usually specific to particular types of violent events.

Moreover, it said, "The causal mechanisms that underlie the correlations
are not well understood" (Reiss and Roth 1993:19).

Some of the multiple factors said to have been found are summarized in
Table 6.1. Most notable for present purposes is the fact that the table
makes no reference to "causal mechanisms." It refers rather to "Risk Factors for Violent Behavior" and "Units of Observation and Explanation."
This seems odd when the primary interest of one of the federal agencies
involved in the establishment of the Panel — the National Science Foundation—was "*the basic causes* of violent behavior." Despite this, no causes as
such, basic or otherwise, appear in the table. Moreover, neither the word
"cause" nor such cognate expressions as "causal factors" appear in the
index to the Panel's report.

Yet reluctance to indulge in simplistic etiological speculation is under-
standable. One of the contributors to a 1985 "update of the National
Commission on the Causes and Prevention of Violence" (which had published its final report in 1969) makes the point that social and behavioral
scientists have too often

> employed an unfortunate focus in their thinking about crime and violence.
> They have tended to look for a root or primary cause. . . . To understand
> crime and violence, a perspective is needed that takes into account the
> complex way in which multiple factors interact . . . the web of causation, or
> the notion of multiple interacting factors, rather than a root or primary
> cause is particularly useful in thinking about crime and violence. (Comer
> 1985:65–67)

What is obvious in the 1993 Panel report is an attempt to avoid references to causation at almost any cost. What is not obvious is whether this
linguistic strategy produced any substantive benefits. The "notion of multiple interacting factors" has, of course, a long history. But neither its utili-
ty as an analytical tool (except perhaps as a warning against simplistic
explanation) nor its implications have ever been entirely clear. And it may
be significant that Table 6.1 with its "Matrix for Organizing Risk Factors
for Violent Behavior" (factors that, it is said, "have been found to correlate
with the probability of violent events") presents a curious pattern of heterogeneous elements including such diverse items as "decline of social

capital," "violent deviant sexual preferences," and "cognitive ability" with no obvious heuristic significance at all.

For example, it is implied in Table 6.1 that certain neurobiologic (which "includes neuroanatomical, neurophysiological, neurochemical, and neuroendocrine") traits (which "describes capacity as determined by status at birth, trauma, and aging processes such as puberty") may be "predisposing" to violent behavior. And in the text accompanying the table, it is said that "awareness of these [risk] factors [for violent behavior] does suggest opportunities for understanding and preventing particular types of violent events." Moreover, "neurobiologic processes" are included in "the array of potential intervention sites for violent interpersonal events" (Reiss and Roth 1993:19–20). But no indication is given of the kind of opportunities for preventing violent events that might occur or of the type of intervention that might be possible.

Indeed, it is said explicitly that "to date no known neurobiological patterns are precise and specific enough to be considered reliable markers for violent behavior." Although it is suggested that "specific neurobiologic markers for an elevated violence potential *may eventually be discovered*" and "promising sites for discovering such markers" are mentioned, the principal conclusion is that "knowledge of the neurobiological underpinnings of violent behavior is limited." And the principal practical suggestion for preventing violence is, in this context, that "neurobiologic research on violent behavior should be expanded" (Reiss and Roth 1993:12; emphasis added).

According to the Panel, an essential prerequisite for the design of effective "violence prevention strategies" was the answer to one "basic question." That question was, "How do psychosocial, biomedical, and social processes operate and interact to explain violence patterns in the United States today?" Accordingly, the Panel "with a twelve- to fifteen-year perspective in mind" called for "a multi-community longitudinal research program to investigate the psychosocial, biochemical, and social processes" that would explain patterns of aggressive behavior (Reiss and Roth 1993:156–157). In fact, the principal message of the report was the need for more research.

So, the Panel's report was ingenious in its avoidance of causal language, speaking instead of "markers," "correlates," "predisposing traits," "explanations," and "risk factors." But only the language of causation was exorcised from the Panel report; the enterprise of searching for causal theory and causal tests remained central to understanding and controlling violence. And causation issues are difficult no matter what names we give them.

Causation and Control: Five Common Fallacies

One reason for the low social reputation of causal rhetoric in criminology is that analysis of causation in relation to violence has often led to errors of the most straightforward and fundamental kind. Far from testing the limits of causal analysis, much that has been said about the causes of violence can be shown to be both fallacious and misleading. It is those elementary errors that we examine in this section.

The Categorical Confusion of Crime and Violence

One common characteristic of contemporary discussions of violence that has given causal theory a bad name is the assumption that searching for the cause of violence is the same as searching for the causes of crime. In fact, as soon as crime and violence are used interchangeably in any discussion of causation, the enterprise is doomed.

There are two important reasons why using the categories of crime and violence interchangeably is fatal to any search for the roots of violence. First, crime itself, rather than being a single category of behavior, is a complex amalgam of all those behaviors classified as criminal by political units. It would indeed be astonishing if incest, embezzlement, armed robbery, and seditious libel could be explained by a single causal scheme.

The extraordinary heterogeneity of crime as a behavioral category is not necessarily paralleled in the case of serious forms of interpersonal violence. While there are many forms of violence that differ from one another, violence as a category of behavior is both narrower and contains more common elements than the all-inclusive category of crime. So that not all of those who despair of any productive discussion of the unitary causes of crime would necessarily be forced to reach a similar conclusion in regard to the causes of violent crime.

The second major problem associated with confusing crime and violence is that the phenomena have very different distributions and therefore very different causal histories. The reader will recall that levels of crime are not efficient predictors of levels of violence cross-nationally. Under these circumstances, it is ludicrous to suppose that causal explanations could work interchangeably for crime and violence.

Yet assumptions about the interchangeability of crime and violence are pandemic in the literature, and categorical confusion of crime and violence is not confined to the inexperienced and the unscholarly. Treatises on the nature and distribution of crime commonly lump violent and nonviolent behaviors together despite the substantial differences in the distribution of the two types of behavior (see, e.g., Wilson and Herrnstein 1985: 213–244). Analyses that principally focus on violence mix in data on the incidence and prevalence of nonviolent offenses without any major qualification (see Silberman 1978:86–116).

One cost of this kind of confusion is a form of guilt by association that assimilates causal explanations relating to violence to the explanation of the causes of crime and all the problems attendant on that broader enterprise. There is also a tendency to avoid positing theories that might not explain the broad spectrum of criminality even though they might plausibly illuminate the major categories of interpersonal violence. As difficult as it might be to analyze the causes of violence, researching for the common root of crime *and* violence is a fool's mission of a distinctively different order.

Singular Causation

The assumption of a single cause, that is, the assumption that violent acts should have one and only one cause, is probably the most frequently found error in the rhetoric of violence. The rhetorical use of single-cause statements is commonly to dismiss as insignificant any factor other than that which the speaker is nominating. The use of this device is a feature of two of the most familiar American examples of the single-cause fallacy. The first of these is associated with opposition to gun control and it is the slogan, "Guns don't kill people; people kill people." This is a single-cause phrasemaking at its catchiest.

In that case, the nominated single cause for homicide is human agency —people kill people. Since that is the single cause of homicide, having established that, it therefore must follow that no other agency or factor can have any significant causal relationship to homicide, ergo, guns do not kill people. While the phrasing of the slogan is not explicitly causal, the logic of the relationship between the fact that people kill people and the conclusion that guns do not is of the single-cause variety.

Another example of this fallacy that is more explicit in its causal phrasing can be found in the assertion that all crime is caused by criminals. On the one hand, there are lawbreakers, and on the other, honest citizens. Or as James Q. Wilson puts it, there are "the wicked" and "the innocent," and the solution to the problem of crime is to apprehend the "wicked people" and "set them apart from innocent people" (Wilson 1975:209).

This view of crime causation is also often expressed by saying that crime is the work of "naturally bad men" (van den Haag 1975:264) or that it is due to "selfishness" or "self-interest uncontrolled" (Hoover 1938: 310–311). The suggestion that crime is the product of social conditions is ridiculed. As Richard Nixon stated during his presidency, so far from it being true that society was responsible for crime, "Society is guilty only when we fail to bring the criminal to justice" (Nixon 1973:246).

Liberal analysis of violence is by no means immune from the dangers of single-cause assumptions. In the nineteenth century, Peter Kropotkin maintained that the "anti-social passions" which inspired crimes of violence were "the result of bodily diseases" (Kropotkin 1887:368). But currently the single causes nominated tend to be social and structural rather than matters of individual psychology or morals. The emphasis of the National Violence Commission on the slum ghetto is typical of liberal explanations of the roots of violence. Pet theories like human wickedness and the urban ghetto become a single-cause error when the dominant role of the favored theory is used to refute the possibility that other factors contribute to the incidence and cost of violence.

Confounding Causes and Prevention

One cardinal mistake associated with the discussion of violence is the assumption that the only way to prevent violence or reduce the harm from its incidence is to deal with its causes. This is a logical error that leads to profound problems in the analysis of violence control policy. One example of this phenomenon was discussed earlier in relation to single-cause theories of violence: the assumption that the prevention of violence should be confined to the removal of factors that are properly classified as causes, which is both popular and nonsensical.

The parable of the cashless bus might serve as a useful introduction to the confounding of causation and prevention. The most effective and most general response to the problem of the armed robbery of municipal buses in the 1960s was the design of cash boxes beyond the immediate access of the bus driver. These were commonly called cashless buses, which is in fact a misnomer. This mechanism merely deprived would-be robbers of *access* to the cash proceeds by locking the money in nonportable strongboxes for which the driver did not have a key.

Perhaps the definition of causation is sufficiently amorphous so that the relatively easy availability of cash from bus drivers can be regarded as one of the causes of municipal bus robberies in the 1960s, along with such other factors as structural inequality in society, easy access to handguns, and the anonymity of big city living. But whether or not cash is a cause of robbery, as long as the removal of access to cash takes away the incentive for bus robbery, the installation of inaccessible locked cash boxes will be an efficient preventive mechanism.

The logical point is that many things can serve as effective means of reducing either the incidence or cost of violence quite independently of whether they deal with those factors that play a causally significant role in generating violence. Bulletproof vests save the lives of police officers who wear them quite independently of whatever causes people to shoot at police (Butterfield 1997). If the use of a gun increases the likelihood that death will result from a violent assault, then reducing access to guns can reduce the death toll from violence even if the number of violent assaults experienced is unaffected. And the fact that "crime is caused by criminals" is irrelevant to the lower death rates experienced when guns are removed from the scene. What causes violence and what may prevent it are two different topics. When they are confused, only mischief results.

What makes the confusion of the causation and the prevention of violence particularly problematic is that many of the elements that play causal roles in bringing about violence can be extremely difficult to alter.

One problem with "root causes" is that they may be deeply rooted in attitudes and social circumstances that are strongly resistant to change. Effective prevention and cost reduction strategies are more likely to be found following the path of least resistance. So that an exclusive focus on causal mechanisms is likely to lead to the neglect of more promising strategies of loss reduction or prevention from the range of options that might be considered.

Confusion of Levels and Types of Causation

One reason for the low estate of causal frameworks that address violence is the confusion of what we would call different levels and types of causation. Earlier in this chapter we reproduced "Matrix for Organizing Risk Factors for Violent Behavior" from the report of the National Academy of Sciences Panel on Understanding and Controlling Violence (Table 6.1). That report subdivided what it called "Risk Factors" into Predisposing, Situational, and Activating "Proximity to Violent Events," as well as into Social and Individual "Units of Observation and Explanation" (Reiss and Roth 1993:20).

As a matter of logic, there is no reason why it is necessary to avoid the language of causation when referring to the different types of factors or levels of proximity to violent events. There can be any number of different necessary causes of particular types of violence that operate at different levels of proximity to acts through different social, psychosocial, and biological mechanisms. But those who speak of root causes often seem to associate causal language with zero-sum competitions and singular approaches to the causes of violence, in effect confusing necessary with sufficient conditions. This confusion may simply be an example of a logical category mistake. On the other hand, the association of causal claims with simplistic schema for the explanation of violence may be a matter of misleading connotation.

In fact, there is no reason why diverse factors ranging from television programming to loaded guns cannot play different types of causal roles in violence. But scholars often tend to associate causal language with the exclusive claims and problematic assumptions that were the subject of this section. And this kind of confusion has been the cause of many of the excesses associated with causal claims in contemporary discussions about violence.

Differing Thresholds of Violence

One further element that confuses discussion about the causes of violence is the lack of agreement about the extent of harm that is necessary to constitute problematic violence. Even relatively modest differences in the threshold used as a standard for violence can lead to substantial differences in the type of events and their frequency. Even relatively rigorous definitions of problematic violence can use importantly different thresholds and thus describe significantly different phenomena.

Two elements contribute to the definition of a particular category of violence: the type of harm inflicted and the extent of that harm. Specifying the type of harm that characterizes violence should not be confusing because physical injury is both a common and correct defining element of violent harm. Sometimes the term "violent" is extended metaphorically to cover categories of harm that are nonphysical, as when expresses like "verbal violence" are employed. This oxymoronic construction is usually justified on the grounds that the amount of harm that can be done by the use of words may in fact be as great as the quantum of harm persons suffer if beaten or hit. This metaphorical extension seems an easily avoidable silliness.

But within the category of physical harm, where should the line be drawn that separates violence from less serious physical damage? Is a parent spanking a child committing a problematic violent act if the spanking leads to no palpable or longstanding injury? Is a fistfight between eleven-year-olds in a schoolyard problematic violence? If not, what about a fistfight between their fathers in a pub?

In pointing out the confusion produced when different speakers use different thresholds of violence, we need not take a position on whether violent acts can properly be arranged on a single continuum, on whether spankings and shootings have different or common origins. Instead, it seems sufficient to suggest that two persons engaged in a dialogue about the causes of violence are likely to disagree and to misunderstand each other if one speaker is referring to schoolyard fistfights and the other is confining his definition of problematic violence to events as serious as "drive-by" shootings. There is no method available to measure precisely the amount of confusion produced by different thresholds, but we think it is considerable.

Policy Perspectives on Cause

Searching for the causes of violence is not merely defensible as an activity, it is inevitable. But more circumspect claims about the identification of the causes of violence will be necessary to rehabilitate the reputation of the enterprise. It is mildly ironic, however, that much of the enthusiasm for the etiological enterprise will probably be dispelled once the proper limits of causal claims are understood.

Identifying causal elements in the production of violent acts is an important part of understanding the nature and distribution of interpersonal violence, and may also be important in the development of promising strategies of prevention. That statement may appear so obvious that it might be questioned whether it needs to be defended in a book with some pretension to scholarly value. But the negative connotations associated with extravagant claims have to be taken into account in any contemporary analysis of violence research and policy. We discussed some of the major errors associated with causal claims in the literature on violence in the previous section. And avoiding the repetition of those mistakes is an important element in securing a proper place for causal inquiry.

There are two further steps that should be an integral part of an affirmative action plan for determining the proper role for notions of causation in the scientific study of violence. First, it is necessary to distinguish claims of predominance that may be made for various theories of violence from basic questions of causation. Second, it is necessary to avoid assigning a preferred position for the etiology of violence in the hierarchy of violence prevention.

Causation and Policy Priority

There is in contemporary discussion of the subject a competition between theories of violence that emphasize social, individual, and public health approaches to the explanation and prevention of violent acts. We would like to call these *claims to predominance* in that the proponents of each approach are arguing that their particular perspective should receive more attention and resources than other ways of viewing violence. But these are not competing schools of violence causation in any real sense.

Debates about which are the most important causes of particular types of violent acts are not really disputes about causation at all, nor are findings about causation necessarily of direct relevance in determining the correct predominant theoretical emphasis in relation to violence policy. Whether or not variations in serotonin levels may influence the propensity of individuals to act in violent ways (see Reiss and Roth 1993:120–121) is only marginally relevant to whether biochemical or biological approaches to violent behavior and its prevention should receive greater emphasis than other approaches.

Once we reject the paradigm of singular and exclusive causation, a large number of necessary causes can be viewed as coexistent, at different levels of explanation and in no logical sense can they be regarded as competitive with one another. Yet one of the reasons why causal claims and causal language in theories of human violence have been viewed with skepticism and distrust is the assumption that they represent attempts to displace competitive paradigms that emphasize other aspects.

Causation and Prevention

Just as statements about causation do not necessarily imply that particular influences deserve greater priority than other influences, finding that a particular factor is a cause of violence does not imply that it should have a preferential position when choices are made between alternative measures for the prevention of violence. In the previous section, we discussed the confusion between causation and prevention that is frequently encountered in current discussion. It is a problem that is sufficiently serious to warrant corrective advertising. For classification as a cause of violence should not guarantee high priority when resources are being allocated for the prevention of violence.

The relationship between conclusions about causation and priorities for preventive programs is probably an asymmetrical one. Evidence that a particular factor is not a cause of violence may be used properly to downgrade the priority of particular preventive program if the original reason for design of the preventive measure was the belief that that factor was a cause of violence. If antigang initiatives have been urged because the level of gang organization was thought to increase homicide rates, evidence that undermined the causal hypothesis would diminish the attractiveness of gangs as a target for preventive measures.

But if work with groups of young people is thought to prevent violence because of the propensity for group organization to moderate and control individual tendencies to violence, the argument for group-based prevention is irrelevant to data on gang causation of violent acts. As a general rule, attempts to control factors that are thought to be causes of violence should compete on an equal footing with other plausible methods of reducing violent behavior.

Sometimes the determination of a causal link between risk factors and outcomes can lead directly to best-case preventive programs. In the annals of public health, the outstanding twentieth-century example of this is the conversion of findings on cigarette smoking and lung cancer into smoking cessation programs of epic proportions.

In other cases, precautions outside any obvious chain of causation can pay handsome and immediate dividends. Half an aspirin tablet a day as a regime for persons at risk of heart attacks is an excellent example of a preventive measure only loosely tied to findings about causation. Indeed, aspirin tablets were relieving headache pain for decades before physical medicine had a clue about the causes of headaches. The great diversity of linkages between cause and prevention suggests that a formal policy of equal footing that allows potential remedies to compete with each other regardless of causal linkage to violence should be encouraged.

Why the necessity for corrective advertisement on the subject of causation and violence policy? At the heart of the confusion about the implications of causation for policy purposes is a gap between popular and scientific understanding of causation. To the ordinary citizen and to the legislator, the concept of causation connotes a more simple and mechanical linkage than that implied by the use of causal language in the physical sciences. When the term "cause" is used in this context, the layman is tempted to conclude that the causes of violence are few, direct and intimately linked to preventive efficacy, so that the determination of causes will almost inevitably lead to the discovery of effective countermeasures.

Many people get excited about violence on television as a cause of violence in the street because they believe that a causal link means that changes in television programs will have an immediate and significant influence on street violence. It is this misperception we believe that leads reports like that of the National Academy of Sciences Panel to avoid speaking of causation. So a proper understanding of the limited role of causal analysis in research and policy making toward violence will almost certainly diminish the enthusiasm of citizens and governments for emphasis on causal analysis. This diminished enthusiasm is an unfortunate necessity.

On the Proximate Causes of Lethal Violence

The relatively thin layer of violent acts that frequently produce the death of their victims is the distinguishing feature of violence in the United States. This lethal violence is not the only type of physical insult that is properly called violent. Lethal attacks are also not the only type of violence that troubles citizens and properly concerns the criminal law.

But violence that generates a high risk of death does seem to be the most important problem confronting the criminal process when it occurs with relative frequency. It is also the particular type of violence that most distinguishes the United States from other developed nations. A focus on lethal events is in large part a consequence of the empirical findings set forth in Part I of this book. The types of attack that frequently lead to victim death are not the only violence problem in the United States, but they are the most important problem.

This emphasis in the analysis that follows should permit greater clarity in argument and meaning. The multiplicity of kinds of violence present in American society and the multiple layers of violence discovered in the empirical assessments discussed in Part I of this book frequently produce confusion. Consistent emphasis on a single priority is our antidote of choice to the confusions that are a constant hazard in studies of the causes of violence.

The consistent focus on lethal violence provides a pragmatic guide through many of the conceptual confusions of violence causation discussed in this chapter. The three remaining chapters in this section will be looking for the proximate causes for lethal violence, the conditions and intersections that best predict variations in rates of death associated with intentional injury. Our primary attention is not on the causes of anger or of conflict, but on the potentially lethal forms of human attack.

7

Firearms and
Lethal Violence

WHEN DISCUSSING AMERICAN LETHAL VIOLENCE with any foreign criminologist, guns are always the first factor to be mentioned as an explanation of the distinctively high rates of death in the United States. What sets the foreign criminologists' comments apart from our American colleagues is not the unanimity with which they focus on guns, however, because this topic is inevitably mentioned by American criminologists as well. But our foreign colleagues are frequently unwilling to discuss any other feature of American society or government *except* gun ownership and use. In Europe or Japan, any mention of social, demographic, or economic factors as a cause of homicide is commonly regarded as an evasion of the most obvious reason why American violence is specially dangerous. This singular preoccupation with guns and gun use overstates the degree to which U.S. lethal violence can be explained by a single cause, but not by much. Firearms use is so prominently associated with the high death rate from violence that starting with any other topic would rightly be characterized as an intentional evasion.

This chapter discusses the role of firearms use in explaining the high rate of lethal interpersonal violence in the United States. This is but one element of a complex set of issues that concerns that relationship between guns and violence in the United States. Self-inflicted and accidental gunshot cases are excluded from this analysis. We will not discuss general patterns of gun ownership and use in this chapter or survey the many different types of control strategy that might reduce gun violence. The central concern here is whether and to what extent our distinctive patterns of gun use explain the high death rates from American violence.

The first section of the analysis discusses the way in which the topic and method of this study push firearms to a position of central importance. The second part of the chapter examines what we call global approaches to firearms as a contributing cause to lethal violence. The third section of the chapter sets out a variety of different explanations for why firearms use increases the death rate from violence and surveys what is known about each of those mechanisms. A concluding section talks about issues of causation, in discussions of the relationship between gun use and lethal violence.

Why Guns?

There are two features of the approach of this volume that put special emphasis on gun use: the emphasis on lethal violence and the frequent use of cross-national comparisons. Figure 7.1 shows the special connection between gun use and deadly violence in the United States by comparing the proportion of police-reported gun use in total index felonies, violent

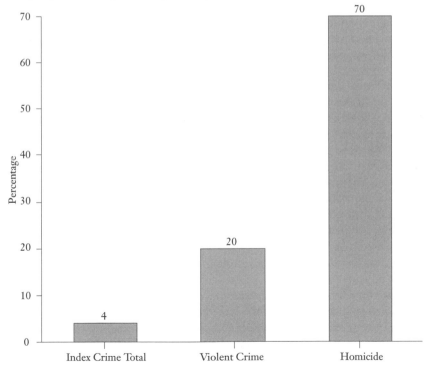

Figure 7.1. The prevalence of firearms use in three crime categories, United States, 1993. *Source:* U.S. Department of Justice, Federal Bureau of Investigation, 1993.

felonies in the crime index, and killings resulting from intentional injury.

The estimates presented in the figure probably understate gun use in index and violent felonies recorded because gun use is not reported for forcible rape and cannot be assessed for noncontact property crime. But the conclusions to be drawn from Figure 6.1 are far too robust to be seriously affected by this problem. The 4 percent estimate for the proportion of total index offenses involving guns confirms what the National Rifle Association has been insisting upon for some time: only a very small proportion of all criminal offenses in the United States are known to involve guns. If all crimes are of equally serious concern to citizens and policy makers, the low prevalence of firearms in serious crime would be a significant reason to look for other instrumentalities and approaches when attempting to reduce crime.

What the middle bar shows is that when the crimes analyzed are restricted to those that threaten or inflict bodily injury—homicide, rape, robbery, and aggravated assault—the proportion of gun involvement increases fivefold, from 4 to 20 percent. When the subject of the inquiry shifts again to criminal injuries that take life, the prevalence of guns jumps again, this time rising to 70 percent. A shorthand way of communicating the importance of the shift to lethal violence as the focus of inquiry is this: If crime is nominated as the problem, guns are involved in one of every twenty-five cases; if lethal violence is nominated as the problem, then guns are implicated in seven of every ten cases.

The contrast between the one-in-five share of violent felonies committed with guns and the 70 percent gun share for American homicide makes guns appear very much more important when the focus shifts from all violence to lethal violence; this contrast also provides a preliminary basis for concluding that attacks with guns are more dangerous than attacks with other weapons. The 20 percent share of violent crime committed with guns in the United States is significant, but very far from cornering the market. The majority of robberies, rapes, and criminal assaults are committed with personal force, knives, or blunt objects. Even the elimination of all firearms incidents would leave a very high volume of violent offenses. But the 70 percent of all lethal attacks committed with firearms represents a statistical dominance that is difficult to ignore or to minimize. Guns alone account for more than twice as much homicide in the United States as all other means combined.

And the contrasting percentage of gun use for lethal and nonlethal violence also provides circumstantial evidence that guns are far more dangerous than any other instruments when used in violent assaults. If 25 percent of all aggravated assaults produce 70 percent of the lethal outcomes, then that 25 percent of gun attacks are seven times more likely to produce death on the average than the 80 percent of all serious assault that does not involve guns and that cumulatively accounts for only 30 percent of all killings. These are only preliminary indications, because gun attacks may be the product of different motives and situations from attacks employing other means. But the dominance of gun cases in the whole of the lethal violence category makes firearms use a necessary first step in the explanation of American lethal violence.

While solely domestic statistics implicate firearms as a dominant cause of American lethal violence, the sort of international statistical comparison that we have used as a primary tool in earlier analysis also calls attention to firearms. No large industrial democracy other than the United States reports firearms as the cause of a majority of its homicides. Thus, scholars engaging in international comparison are confronted with two extraordinary distinctions between homicide in the United States and in the rest of the developed Western world: very much higher rates of homicide in the United States, and a uniquely high percentage of gun use in U.S. violence. Concluding that the elevated gun use is a cause of the distinctively high homicide experience seems natural.

One example of this reasoning from a statistical comparison may be found in an essay by Ronald V. Clarke and Pat Mayhew, "The British Gas Suicide Story and Its Criminological Implications." Clarke and Mayhew compare homicide rates per one million population for England and Wales and the United States for firearms, handguns (also counted in the firearms category), and all means other than firearms. Their results are set out in a table, which is reproduced here as Table 7.1.

All forms of homicide are more frequent in the United States than in England and Wales. Killings by all means other than guns occur in the United States at a rate per million population that is 3.7 times the nongun

Table 7.1

Gun and Nongun Homicides, England and Wales and the United States, 1980–1984

Type of murder	Homicides		Average annual rate per one million population[a]		England and Wales to United States ratio
	England and Wales	United States	England and Wales	United States	
All gun[b]	213	63,218	.86	54.52	1 to 63.4
Handgun[b]	57	46,553	.23	40.15	1 to 174.6
Nongun[b]	2,416	41,354	9.75	35.67	1 to 3.7
Total[c]	2,629	104,572	10.61	90.19	1 to 8.5

[a]Annual average population for 1980–1984: United States, 231.9 million; England and Wales, 49.55 million.

[b]Figures for the United States involved some extrapolation from homicides for which weapon was known.

[c]Figures for England and Wales relate to offenses currently recorded as homicide.

Source: Clarke and Mayhew 1988, Table 2, p. 107.

homicide rate reported in England and Wales. But homicides by handguns occur in the United States at a rate per million population that is 175 times as great. This comparison leads the authors to conclude that "there is little doubt that limiting the availability of firearms in the United States would have a substantial effect on homicide and probably also on other violent crime" (Clarke and Mayhew 1988:106).

Even though this conclusion cannot be established solely from population statistics of the sort presented in Table 7.1, the tendency to reach it is inevitable when both the magnitude of gun use and the aggregate death toll differences are that high. The fact that homicide rates with handguns in the United States are 175 times as high as in Great Britain may be only coincidental to the large difference in total homicide rates between the two countries. But few who have studied these international differences are willing to accept the coincidence hypothesis. Instead, those who analyze American violence by first making international comparisons tend to be adamant in their belief that gun use is a major explanation of the elevated death toll from violence. As we have said, it is hard to get them to consider anything else.

And the obvious conclusion about the relationship between firearms and lethal violence in the United States is also the correct one. High levels of gun use in assault and robbery are a very important contributory cause to elevated U.S. death rates from violence. While the magnitude of the difference that can be attributed solely to gun use cannot be determined with precision, as much as half of the difference between American and European homicide rates may be explained by differential resort in the United States to the most lethal of the commonly used instruments of violence.

On Global Comparisons

The type of data featured in Figure 7.1 and in Table 7.1 are global statistical comparisons that show the extent of the overlap between firearms and violence in the United States. We use the phrase "global comparison" to denote efforts to estimate the impact of gun use on the death rate from violence by obtaining a correlation between variations in gun use and variations in homicide rates. Such comparisons do not directly address issues of causation. A further limitation of most global comparative analyses is that they do not directly distinguish what features of firearms use might contribute to elevating death rates from those associated with other types of violent attack. So the global comparative approach should never be the endpoint of any analysis of firearms and violence. Nevertheless, the cautious use of basic comparison can tell us a great deal about the extent to which gun use increases death rates from violence.

One early test of global relationship was reported by Stephen Seitz in 1972 (Seitz 1972). Seitz observed a 0.98 correlation between the firearms homicide rate in a U.S. state in 1967 and the total rate of homicide experienced in that state, so that a higher-than-average death rate from firearms injury would almost predict a higher-than-average death rate from injury by all means. The interpretation of this relationship was: "[I]t is almost impossible to conclude that the relation between firearms and criminal homicide is merely coincidental" (Seitz 1972:597).

The problem with inferring a causal connection between gun homicide and total homicide from this sort of correlation is that this type of relationship studied by Seitz has been categorized as a "part–whole correlation." Gun homicides constitute the majority of all homicides in the United States. Thus, if a state has a higher-than-average gun homicide rate, the total homicide rate would automatically tend to vary in the same direction as the gun homicide statistics.

The problem can be illustrated by imagining a study of the effect of weight loss strategies that found that those men and women who lost the largest amount of weight from their thighs, legs, and feet during a diet period also tended to lose the largest total amount of body weight. Does this tell us that a priority strategy of a diet regime should be weight reduction in the thighs, legs, and feet? The alternative to concluding that thighs are of special significance in weight reduction is understanding that the bottom half of the body is an important part of the body's weight and for that reason alone persons who lost considerable weight from their legs would have lost more total weight on a diet than those who lost a smaller percentage of their southern extremity poundage. Losing a substantial amount of weight in the legs, far from being an independent variable causing success in a dietary regime, is one of the major effects of having been on a diet.

Is there a way of eliminating the impact that death rates from firearms would have on total homicide rates only because they are such a substantial part of the homicide total? One promising approach would be to measure the influence, not of the number of people killed by guns in any given state, but of the proportionate use of guns rather than other methods of inflicting death. Suppose we compare, for each state, the proportion of fatal attacks using firearms with the total homicide rate for the particular state instead of comparing the rate of gun deaths with the total rate of all deaths, the notorious part–whole correlation. We are now predicting that a high proportionate use of guns will yield a higher-than-average homicide rate while states with lower relative gun use in deadly attacks will also have smaller-than-average total homicide rates. The correlation when we use a percentage homicide variable rather than the gun homicide rate for the fifty states in 1967 is 0.55, suggesting that gun use explains about 30 percent of cross-state variations in homicide in the year that the Seitz analysis was run.

There are a variety of different global comparisons of gun use and death rates that point to gun use as a positive influence on homicide rates.

One stategy is to study the relationship between gun use and homicide rates over time in the United States. The correlation between total gun share of homicide and total homicide rates in the United States for the years 1964–1990 is 0.77, indicating that years in which the proportion of all killings committed by guns is high are associated with high total homicide rates by all means, and vice versa.

To the same effect, a recent research note by one of us finds the correlation over time between percentage gun use and total homicide rate for offenders under eighteen was 0.9 over the years 1977–1992, and that changes in gun use were also efficient predictors of which age groups would exhibit the largest increase in homicide (Zimring 1996).

Even this variety of correlational study results cannot establish a definitive causal sequence. Perhaps both the rate of gun use and the death rate from attacks increase because more people who intend to kill their victims select guns to achieve that goal. Because the proportion of all assaults committed with guns may signal changes in the nature of violent attackers as well as in violent attacks, it is not possible to isolate firearms as a cause of increases in death rate through the use of this kind of comparison.

In the second place, even if we believe that global comparisons make it probable that gun use causes an increased death rate, this kind of global statistical analysis cannot reveal what characteristics of guns or their use in attacks is the operative cause of increased lethality. What is there about guns that produces more homicides than other weapons when they are used in assaults? Simply knowing that those periods of maximum gun use in the recent history of the United States are associated with much higher death rates from intentional injury cannot produce any insight into why gun assaults acquire their extra measure of dangerousness. In this sense, then, global statistical comparison is important as an estimate of the strength of the general relationship between gun use and death from homicide and as a precursor to more specific investigation of the mechanism of guns and the effect of these on violent assault.

The basic problem that limits the policy significance of the global comparison is that changes in gun use may signal changed intentions by attackers as well as increasing the chances that an attack will result in death because the gun is a more lethal instrument. When Clarke and Mayhew assert that reducing gun availability will reduce deaths, they either assume that more deadly intentions are not the cause of a high rate of death from gun assault or believe that the absence of available guns will modify or frustrate an attacker's lethal intentions.

The prudent conclusion from global comparison is that when gun use increases, both the larger capacity of firearms to cause death and the greater manifest desire of the attacker to risk a victim's death will increase the death rate. The global comparison can estimate the joint impact of altered instruments and intentions, but cannot apportion any effects on death rate between these two elements.

As to the magnitude of the relationship between gun use and homicide rates, studies over time in the United States are associated with substantial estimates of gun use effects. More than half of the variations of homicide rates in the United States are linked systematically to variations in the proportion of shooting fatalities in the 0.77 correlated reported previously. And parallel statistics for selected cities and subgroups produce even larger correlations (see Zimring 1996).

No matter how large the noted association between guns and homicide, however, the global comparison is a self-limiting methodology. The more likely it is that such comparisons implicate gun use as a cause of homicide, the more important it becomes to supplement such statistics with different empirical strategies that promise to provide information about why guns are particularly lethal.

The Causes of Differential Lethality

Guns may cause increases in the death rate from assault in a variety of different ways. The use of guns as opposed to other weapons in assault may be associated with both mechanical and social changes in violent assault that can increase death rates. Among the mechanical or instrumentality aspects of gun use that can increase death rates are: the greater injurious impact of bullets, the longer range of firearms; and the greater capacity of firearms for executing multiple attacks. Among the features in social setting related to gun use are: the need to use more lethal instruments of assault in situations where an attacker fears that his adversary may have a gun, the need to sustain or intensify a deadly assault because an opponent possesses or is using firearms, and the increased willingness to use guns and other lethal weapons in personal conflict because such weapons are used generally. All of these aspects may increase the lethality of assaults committed with guns, but by no means to the same degree. There are also two social impacts of gun possession and use that can lower death rates: the deterrence of assaults because of fear of gun-owning victims and the prevention of attempted assaults by an armed victim.

Instrumentality Effects

Of all the possible ways that gun use increases the deadliness of attacks, the theory that gunshot wounds inflict more damage than other methods of personal attacks is considered the most important and has been the subject of the most research.

The early debate about the influence of guns on deaths from assault involved different theories of the types of intention that produced assaults that lead to death. Marvin Wolfgang in his landmark study of homicide doubted that the weapon used in an attack made much difference in the chance that a death would result since so many different weapons could produce death if an attacker tried hard enough (Wolfgang 1958). Zimring responded to this assertion with a study of knife and gun assaults and killings in Chicago (Zimring 1968).

Zimring's data suggested that many homicides were the result of attacks apparently conducted with less than a single-minded intent to kill. Unlike the Wolfgang study where only fatal attacks were examined, the first Zimring study compared fatal and nonfatal gun and knife assaults in Chicago over four police periods. The study found that 70 percent of all gun killings in Chicago were the result of attacks that resulted in only one wound to the victim, and most attacks with guns or knives that killed a victim looked quite similar to the knife and gun attacks that did not kill (Zimring 1968). From this data, Zimring argued that most homicides were the result of ambiguously motivated assaults, so that the offender would risk his victim's death, but usually did not press on until death was assured.

Under such circumstances, the capacity of a weapon to inflict life-threatening injury would have an important influence on the death rate from assault. The 1968 Chicago study found that gun attacks were about five times as likely to kill as knife attacks, and this ratio held when the comparison was controlled for the number of wounds inflicted and the specific location of the most serious wound (Zimring 1968). Since knives were the next most deadly frequently used method of inflicting injury in attacks, the large difference in death rate suggested that substituting knives or other less dangerous instruments for guns would reduce the death rate from assault.

This weapon dangerousness comparison was first reported for Chicago in 1968 and has been replicated in other sites (Vinson 1974; Sarvesvaran and Jayewardene 1985). Follow-up studies have shown that a difference in weapon as subtle as firearm caliber can double the death rate from gun assaults (Zimring 1972). The summary conclusion from this line of research can be simply stated: the objective dangerousness of a weapon used in violent assaults appears to be a major influence on the number of victims who will die from attacks. This "instrumentality effect" is the major documented influence of guns on death rate (see Cook 1991).

The use of guns in robbery is different from their use in wounding since the weapon is not necessarily used to inflict harm. Because robberies with guns frighten their victims into complying with the robbers' demands more than other robberies, a smaller number of gun robberies result in woundings than personal force robberies and robberies with knives. Still, the greater dangerousness of guns when fired more than compensates for the lower number of wounds. For street robberies and those that take place in commercial establishments, the death rate for every 1000 gun robberies is about three times that generated by robberies at knife point and about ten times the death rate from robberies involving personal force (see Zimring and Zuehl 1986; Cook 1991:17).

Another way of estimating the impact of gun use on the dangerousness

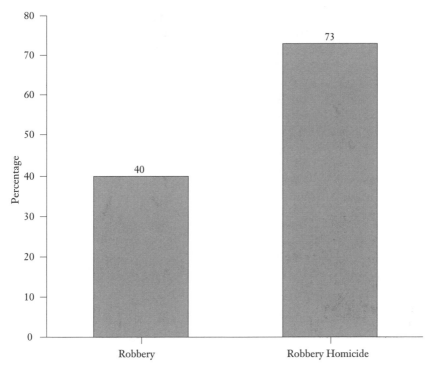

Figure 7.2. Firearms use in U.S. robbery and robbery homicide, 1992. *Source:* U.S. Department of Justice, Federal Bureau of Investigation, 1992.

of robbery is to focus on the prevalence of gun use in fatal and nonfatal robbery incidents. Figure 7.2 contrasts the firearms share of robberies and robbery killings in the United States for 1992.

The contrast in Figure 7.2 is about half that noted between violent crime and homicide in Figure 7.1. Firearms are responsible for 40 percent of robberies and 73 percent of all robbery killings in the United States, so that the apparent death rate from gun robbery nationwide is four times that of nongun robberies in the aggregate. The data presented in New York City robbery in Chapter 3 estimate a 10-to-1 difference in death rate.

The death rate comparison in Figure 7.2 is subject to at least two qualifications. In the first place, the difference in death rate noted in the figure already takes into account whatever savings of life results from the lower rate of resistance to gun-using robbers. So the difference in death rate from gun robbery as a result of the greater injury potential of bullet wounds may be larger than the 4-to-1 ratio derived from the data in Figure 7.2.

The second qualification cuts in the opposite direction. Many of the robberies committed with guns involve commercial entities and other relatively well-defended robbery targets. These robberies might involve a greater risk of injury or death that is to some degree independent of the weapon used by the robber. The switch to knives or blunt instruments in such cases might lead to a higher rate of victim injury or death than is generated by other types of knife and blunt instrument robbery. Of course, some of these difficult target robberies might not be committed if firearms were not available. So the calculus of comparison between gun robberies and other types of robbery is both multidimensional and complex.

There is one sense in which what we call global gun-versus-nongun comparisons in robbery are less problematic than global comparisons involving assault. Because persons committing assault intend to injure, the weapons they select may be probative of their intention to risk a lethal outcome. Since robbery involves only the threat of force, the choice of weapon may not directly reflect an intention to do harm and the choice of more dangerous weapons may not as closely reflect a more serious intention to injure. The robber may not intend any harm at the point of choosing weapons, and differences in total death rate may thus reflect only instrumentality effects.

RANGE

One obvious way in which firearms differ from other frequently used instruments of personal attack is the long distance across which bullets remain potent messengers of lethal force. Sticks, stones, knives, and blunt objects can be used to deadly effect, but not at great range. Killing with a knife or a blunt instrument is both hard work and close work. The only practical limit to the range of a firearm as an instrument of deadly attack is the marksmanship of the shooter. Hunting rifles are designed to inflict life-threatening force at great distances. The bullets fired from handguns can travel considerable distances before losing their capacity for injury, although most handguns are more difficult to employ with accuracy at long range.

How important the greater range of firearms might be in elevating the death rate from assault depends on the types of situation and the distance between victim and assailant that occur in life-threatening assaults. The majority of life-threatening assaults in the United States are carried out at close range even when a firearm is the instrument of attack. For this reason, the long range of guns should not be a major influence on the death rate from attacks in most cases. Indeed, handguns are nine times as likely to be involved in a homicidal assault in the United States as long guns even though the longer barreled weapons are much more efficient in respect of aim and accuracy over great distances. Lethal violence in the United States is for the most part hand-to-hand combat where the handgun's maneuverability is more important than the long gun's superior long-range accuracy.

In those circumstances where attacks are initiated or completed at long range, a firearm is a necessary weapon. Included in such attacks are sniper incidents, many assassination attempts, other assaults from a distance at a defined and frequently guarded target, as well as more common "drive-by" shootings where a target may or may not have been preselected, but where the defining characteristic of the attack is shooting at long range. The official records on such killings are not complete. The Federal Bureau of Investigation reported a total of ninety-seven sniper killing cases between 1990 and 1992, but did not have a code for drive-by shootings. The Los Angeles police estimated about thirty drive-by fatalities in 1991 out of about 1000 cases (no national-level estimates are available).

CAPACITY FOR MULTIPLE ATTACK

Most firearms have the capacity to shoot many separate bullets in a relatively short period of time and with a minimum of physical effort on the part of the shooter. A revolver typically has a six-shot capacity and is easy to reload. Pistols typically carry six to nine rounds and can carry many more. Rifles vary from single-shot weapons to some with very large capacity clips and magazines.

There are two ways in which the capacity for multiple-wound infliction can produce a higher death rate from assault than would occur if more time and effort were required to repeat or intensify an attack. In the first place, several shots can be fired at the same victim producing wounds where the first attempt missed or resulting in multiple wounds that involve a much higher probability of death. In the second place, the multiple-shot capacity of many firearms can mean that more than one victim can be wounded—and put at risk of death—during the same assault.

Very little research has addressed explicitly the impact of a firearm's capacity for multiple attack on the outcome of gun assault. There are a number of different questions to be studied. First, single-victim attacks could be studied to assess whether attacks with guns result in a greater number of woundings than attacks with knives. Second, firearms assaults could be studied to determine whether attacks made with weapons that carry a single load of many bullets produce a higher number of multiple wounds and a higher rate of fatality.

The assault studies conducted in the late 1960s and early 1970s did not show a high proportion of multiple-wound attacks. Indeed, the failure of most shooters to exhaust the capacity of their firearms is cited as strong evidence against the proposition that most gun fatalities were not the result of kill-at-any-cost intentions (Zimring 1972). The more specific study of whether firearms with multiple capacity are more often used to produce multiple wounds has not yet been attempted.

Crude empirical soundings regarding whether guns are more often used in multiple-victim killings are not difficult to conduct in the age of the computer, but an all-fatality sample may be biased. Using data from the Federal Bureau of Investigation's Supplementary Homicide Reports for the years 1976–1992, we tested the hypothesis that guns would more often be the instrument of attack in assaults that resulted in more than one

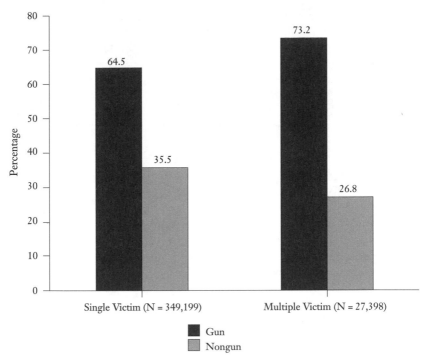

Figure 7.3. Firearms by single or multiple victim (excluding child cases), United States, 1976–1992. *Source:* U.S. Department of Justice, Federal Bureau of Investigation, 1994.

fatality than in assaults in which only one victim died. We found a modest but consistent confirmation of the hypothesis. In all seventeen years covered by the data set, the proportion of gun use in multiple-victim killings was higher than in single-victim killings. When cases involving young children are deleted from the analysis, weapons other than guns are used in about one out of every four multiple-victim incidents, as compared with one out of three single-victim killings, as shown by Figure 7.3.

The larger proportion of multiple killings committed with guns probably represents an increase in death rate on top of the differential deadliness effects discussed earlier, but these two effects overlap in a study that considers only multiple killings. A larger proportion of attacks on multiple victims with knives or clubs may result in only one death because other victims survive a knife attack but are killed in a gun attack. The research question is whether gun attacks on multiple victims produces even higher differential deadliness over knife attacks than is found in single-victim assaults. A study of nonfatal as well as fatal attacks might decide this issue, but has not yet been undertaken.

Social Factors

The mechanical factors just discussed are characteristics of guns that may influence the death rate from attacks committed with firearms. What we call social factors are the many ways in which a social environment where many people possess and use firearms in interpersonal assault may have an influence on the extent to which assaults lead to fatal conclusions. There are at least three different theories as to how a social environment of high gun use can increase killings and at least two theories about how a social environment of extensive gun ownership and use might reduce violent deaths. But precise and specific empirical evaluation of theories about social and environmental effects is not easy.

One way in which a social environment of frequent gun assaults can increase the death rate from assault is by making those engaged in physical combat resort to more lethal instruments of assault and also to continue and intensify an assault because an opponent is armed. A social environment of frequent gun use multiplies the number of cases where both sides in a conflict possess lethal weapons. This should increase the death rate from both gun and knife attacks by motivating more sustained application of lethal force because of the counterforces risked if the attacker desists too soon.

One common feature of a two-way gun fight is that each combatant is unwilling to stop shooting until it seems clear that his opponent is incapable of shooting back. For this reason, it seems likely that the death rate from bilateral gun fights will be much higher than in situations where one party is armed with a gun and the other party has no deadly weapon. An attack where only one participant uses lethal force should be less likely to produce death because the combatant who controls the lethal force can stop pressing his attack without risking being shot or stabbed.

A second environmental influence closely related to the problem of bilateral lethal force is the way in which fear that others may have guns may motivate people to arm themselves with deadlier weapons than they might otherwise feel would be necessary for either self-defense or attack. When approaching a conflict in which guns are believed to be present, a potential combatant is more likely to feel it necessary to arm himself with a knife or a gun. The irony here is that one element that may increase the use of firearms in combat is a fear of guns in the hands of others. In this way increases in gun use can, in many social settings, become self-fulfilling prophecies.

A third effect of an environment where gun use is frequent that might increase mortality rates from assault is that a high frequency of gun use might lead citizens to expect that firearms are used in interpersonal conflict. On this theory, an increase in gun use would occur, not only out of fear, but out of social habit as the widespread practice of carrying and using guns generates a belief that gun use is a normal part of interpersonal conflicts. The use of a gun in many serious conflicts may no longer be regarded as deviant behavior. This could increase gun use over time substantially. We know of no way to directly measure the extent of this type of legitimation of the use of deadly force, but it is an influence that could be of considerable significance.

There are two current theories about how a social environment of frequent gun use might reduce the death toll from criminal violence: self-defense and deterrence. The self-defense theory argues that a larger number of firearms produces a larger proportion of gun ownership and self-defense gun use. Potential crime victims will use guns to prevent or thwart attack and thus reduce the death toll—at least among nonoffenders—from assault. The extent of this direct self-defense dividend from high gun ownership is the subject of a lively debate (cf. Kleck 1991 with McDowall and Wiersema 1994).

One major methodological problem with measuring self-defense is that asking persons in a survey whether they have used a gun to prevent a criminal act produces self-serving statements that cannot be verified. *Each* party to an argument that turned violent is likely to regard the other party as a criminal aggressor, and to think that his own use of force was permissible self-defense. When talking to only one of two combatants, the story one is likely to hear is that a crime was prevented by a gun even though the respondent's opponent would swear that in fact a crime was committed by the person representing himself as the victim. Official police statistics on assault involve an umpire's decision made by police about the culpability of the parties. But survey research cannot generate a valid test of the allegations of a self-serving respondent.

A final theory of social influence argues that widespread gun ownership and use deters criminal assault because would-be offenders recognize the high probability that a criminal attack will be met with lethal force. The probability of substantial across-the-board crime reduction from this kind of armed citizen deterrence is emphasized frequently by opponents of gun control legislation in the United States. And it has been associated with legislative proposals to loosen restrictions on carrying concealed guns. Indeed one small city in Georgia passed an ordinance requiring citizen possession of firearms for which the stated rationale was deterrence (see Benson 1984).

The measurement of the types of social impact that have been outlined in this section is difficult and some of the most important social influences are the most difficult to assess empirically . The degree to which widespread ownership and use of guns leads to the expectation that they will be used in personal assaults could have a substantial impact on the amount of lethal violence experienced in a society incrementally over a long period of time. But the rigorous empirical assessment of this would be practically impossible to execute because it would be a process taking place gradually over decades without any specific landmarks to be the focus of evaluation.

Yet the potential importance of this factor in determining a society's rate of lethal interpersonal violence is not smaller merely because it is not susceptible to rigorous measurement.

Some of the theories of social influence outlined above can be tested in relatively straightforward ways. The quantity and quality of self-defense uses of firearms can be assessed using police statistics and, to a lesser extent, surveys. Police statistics can provide a minimum estimate of incidents of citizen self-defense where a neutral factfinder affirms that the person using the force was not to blame for the event. Survey reports of self-defense can be useful in defining issues even if the factual accounts in the survey cannot be verified. When surveys show that 70 percent of all claimed incidents of crime prevention concern the offense of aggravated assault, the criminologist can pay specific attention to assault and homicide statistics in studying the influence of gun ownership and use on crime.

Another opportunity for straightforward evaluation is the comparison of multiple-wounding and case-fatality rates in one- and two-way gun battles. That sort of specific assessment would be a logical next step in the epidemiological research into intentional injury that is in progress in the United States (see Kellerman and Reay 1986; Wintemute 1995).

There are a number of hypotheses that cannot be isolated and separately measured. If high gun ownership environments are associated with higher-than-average proportionate use of guns in assault, is this because would-be attackers are afraid their opponents may be armed or is it another manifestation of a general social expectation that it is permissible to use guns in certain types of social conflict? If the widespread availability of handguns prevents some lethal attacks but also increases the death rate from attacks, how can these two countervailing tendencies be isolated and measured?

To some extent, the difficulties of isolating each element of gun influence for individual assessment are intractable, but the precise measure of individual influences on death rates may also be relatively unimportant. From a social policy standpoint, the sort of global assessment that was discussed earlier may tell us all that we have to know because it provides an estimate of the magnitude of the net effect of variations in gun use over time and cross-nationally.

The major problem with many such global estimates by themselves, however, is the issue of causal ordering. But once the mechanical ways in which gun use increases the death rate from assault have been identified and measured, it may be possible to approach the sort of global estimates discussed earlier with more confidence that variations in gun use are, for the most part, independent variables in the equation and that variations in homicide rates are, again for the most part, the dependent variables. If so, a large positive correlation between percentage firearms use in homicide and rates of homicide over time tells us that mechanical and social elements that accompany increases in gun use have a much greater elevating

influence on death rates than any restraining influence that may be con-
current. If lethal violence is the focus of social concern, such an aggregate
conclusion may be more important than the precise assessment of the
impact of specific aspects of firearms use.

Firearms Use as Contributing Cause

The use of firearms in assault and robbery is the single environmental feature of American society that is most clearly linked to the extraordinary
death rate from interpersonal violence in the United States. But the
strength of this relationship does not mean that firearms ownership and
use has a simple, invariable, or independent influence on homicide rates.
In this section, we consider the question of the causal connection between
gun use and lethality. We do this not only because it is an important issue
in relation to firearms and lethal violence, but also because reflecting on
the questions of causation that arise in connection with firearms teaches us
an important lesson about the role of many other environmental influences on the incidence of lethal violence.

The American debate about guns has produced one of the few causal
critiques ever to appear on a bumper sticker: the famous "Guns don't kill
people, people kill people." Behind the strong sentiment that inspired this
and a multitude of related appeals lies an important logical point. Firearms
ownership and use is neither a necessary nor a sufficient cause of violent
death in the United States. Firearms are not a necessary cause of killings
because of the wide array of alternative methods of killing that are available ranging from the strangler's hands to car bombs. Even in the United
States in 1996, nearly 30 percent of all killings did not involve guns. Moreover, the widespread availability of firearms is not a sufficient condition for
intentional homicide by a wide margin. One-half of all American households own guns and it is estimated that one-quarter of all households own
a handgun—the weapon used in three-quarters of all gun homicides. Yet
only a small fraction of all gun owners become gun attackers. The logical
point here is that guns do not become dangerous instruments of attack if
they are not used in an attack.

If gun use is neither a necessary nor a sufficient cause of violent death,
what is the proper descriptive label for the role gun use plays in deaths due
to intentional injury? The most accurate label for the role of firearms in
those cases of death and injury from intentional attacks in which they are
used is *contributing cause*. Even where the availability of a gun plays no
important role in the decision to commit an assault, the use of a gun can be
an important contributing cause in the death and injury that results for
gun attacks. When guns are used in a high proportion of such attacks, the
death rate from violent attack will be high. Current evidence suggests that
a combination of the ready availability of guns and the willingness to use
maximum force in interpersonal conflict is the most important single con-

tribution to the high U.S. death rate from violence. Our rate of assault is not exceptional; our death rate from assault is exceptional.

The role of gun use as a contributing cause means that the net effect of firearms on violence will depend on the interaction of gun availability with other factors that influence the rate of violent assaults in a society and the willingness of people to use guns in such assaults. So the precise contribution of firearms to the death toll from violence is contingent on many other factors that may influence the number and character of violent attacks.

Some implications of this contingency deserve emphasis. Introducing 10,000 loaded handguns into a social environment where violent assault is a rare occurrence will not produce a large number of additional homicide deaths unless it also increases the rate of assault. The percentage increase in homicide might be considerable if guns become substitutes for less lethal weapons. But the additional number of killings would be small because of the low rate of attack. Introducing 10,000 handguns into an environment where rates of attack and willingness to use handguns in attack are both high is a change that would produce many more additional deaths. The net effect of guns depends on how they are likely to be used.

One corollary of viewing guns as an interactive and contributing cause to intentional homicide is that societies with low rates of violent assault will pay a lower price if they allow guns to be widely available than will societies with higher rates of violence. The sanguine sound bite encountered in American debates about guns is: "An armed society is a polite society" (Handgun Control Inc. 1995). This does not seem particularly plausible to us, but it seems likely that only a very polite society can be heavily armed without paying a high price.

The United States of the 1990s is far from that polite society. Our considerable propensity for violent conflict would be a serious societal problem even if gun availability and use were low. But the very fact that the United States is a high-violence environment makes the contribution of gun use to the death toll from violence very much greater. When viewed in the light of the concept of contributing causation, the United States has both a violence problem and a gun problem, and each makes the other more deadly.

8

On Mass Media Effects

THE RATE OF HOMICIDE is much higher on the television screens of the United States than in even her meanest streets. Media portrayals of violence and messages about violence are a pervasive part of modern life in every industrialized nation. And media portrayals of violence are more common than first-hand experience of violence for most citizens. Only a minority of citizens are directly touched by serious violence in any given year; but most citizens will be repeatedly exposed to mass communication versions of murder and mayhem every night of their lives. Television news and entertainment programs, motion pictures, music in the age of its mechanical ubiquity, magazines and books, computer games—all these media of mass communication are saturated with violence.

Mass communications are full of violence because they reflect the interests, values, and concerns of their audience. But do these communications increase the level of real-world violence in the United States as well as reflect it? There is widespread belief that they do. Eight out of ten American adults believe that media renditions of violence are themselves a problem, and the topic is considered important enough to have attracted the attention of Senator Robert Dole of Kansas in the early stages of campaigning for the presidency of the United States (Broder 1995). The issue of mass media effects on violence was one of the small number of topics that generated a full-blown task force investigation by the National Commission appointed by Lyndon Johnson in the late 1960s (U.S. National Commission 1969b:xi). And it has been the subject of recurrent research by behavioral scientists for decades.

This chapter considers the link between mass communications and rates of lethal violence as a case study in attenuated causation. Of all the important social phenomena that might plausibly be linked to rates of lethal violence, the mass media present the sharpest contrast to firearms use. The first section of this chapter spells out the contrast between gun use and the mass media. The second section of the chapter illustrates the multiplicity of different issues it is necessary to distinguish in any rigorous inquiry about mass communications as an influence on rates of lethal violence. What is often posed in debate as a single question in reality involves a variety of different media, messages, audiences, social contexts, and hypothesized effects.

The third section of this chapter discusses studies that claim to have established a direct link between television viewing and lethal violence. The final section in this chapter suggests some additional research that would be of value to students of mass communications with particular concern about lethal violence.

The Attenuated Link to Lethal Violence

One reason why we selected the link between the media and violence for extended discussion is the contrast that pertains between firearms and mass communications when using international comparisons to discover the proximate causes of life-threatening violence. A concern with life-threatening violence rather than violence generally makes firearms seem more salient because guns are three and a half times more prevalent in deadly violence than in crimes of personal force where the victim survives. By contrast, a specific focus on life-threatening violence makes the particular role of mass media communications seem much less important, at least on first impression.

Why would a special concern with deadly violence diminish the apparent significance of media effects? In the first place, while the death toll on television is quite high there is no hypothesized link between mass communication messages and deadly violence specifically to parallel the increased importance of firearms in lethal attacks. In the second place, a focus on *lethal* violence creates a larger gap between available laboratory evidence on media effects and the behavior of concern than would exist if the focus were all varieties of physical force. As we will see later in this chapter, it is not clear how much of a link exists between the aggressive acts that psychologists measure in media studies and serious incidents of real-world violence. But however great this gap might be for violence generally, it widens considerably when the focus shifts from fistfights to stabbings and shootings. Human aggression as measured in media studies and lethal violence on the streets may or may not be located at two different points on a single behavioral continuum. But even if they are, they are located at a very great distance apart.

There is still another respect in which a focus on lethal violence makes mass communications seem less important. While there are some differences between industrial countries in the specific contents of their motion pictures and television, the similarities in media content among modern industrial states seem much more significant than any differences one encounters when moving from one G7 nation to another. If the issue under discussion is the relation between media and general rates of violence and aggression, a major media role might be plausible if societies exposed to similar kinds and amounts of mass communications have similar rates of violence.

There are some forms of violent behavior that may be spread relatively evenly throughout Europe and the Americas, but Part I showed that lethal violence is not one of them. For this reason, a special concern with lethal violence tends to diminish the apparent importance of any social or environmental influence that is not present in the United States in much larger quantities than in other developed countries. Since the dependent variable is so heavily concentrated on American soil, the search for proximate causes of lethal violence favors proposed causes that exhibit a similar skewed distribution. The relatively even spread of modern mass media is not an example of such a skewed distribution.

And the even spread of media throughout developed countries is only the first reason to downgrade media as a cause of lethal violence. The relationship between changes over time in media exposure and rates of lethal violence is also problematic. For most of the developed nations, exposure to the media of mass communication has increased on a linear basis since 1950, while Chapter 2 showed rates of lethal violence have usually fluctuated in relatively brief cyclical patterns. There is no obvious fit over time between mass communications as a presumed independent variable and lethal violence as a dependent variable.

Failure to discern a close fit between variations in mass communications and the body count from lethal violence does not, of course, exhaust the possible linkages between murder and the media. Television and motion pictures may be having a worldwide impact on the toleration of violence, the kind of effect that would not show up in cross-national comparisons or short term trends. And what the media do may also have a direct effect on small subpopulations at particular risk. But the basic framework of this inquiry stacks the deck against such media influences appearing to be a significant proximate cause of high rates of homicide in the United States.

A Multiplicity of Issues

Anyone who expresses an interest in studying what is described as the effect of mass media on violent behavior misunderstands either the English usage of the plural form, or the nature of mass communications in modern society, or both. There is, in fact, a wide variety of different effects that have been hypothesized as the results of communications as well as many different methods of communication, types of message content, and audiences. Figure 8.1 is our deliberatingly intimidating attempt to illustrate the variety of different questions that can be generated about communication effects on the propensity toward violence. This figure itemizes different possible media effects and lists some of the other variables that may be of crucial significance in predicting the nature and extent of those effects. The most important introductory point we can make about the figure is that it is *illustrative* of a number of discrete issues concerning mass communications, but is far from *exhaustive*.

The right-hand box of the figure distinguishes between short-term and long-term communication effects and gives examples of each. We assume that most short-term effects take the functional form of the typical stimulus–response model in psychology in which the communication is the stimulus and it is hypothesized that behavior is produced in a relatively short period of time as the organism responds. There are three different forms of short-term response that have concerned media observers, and a fourth significant effect that has not been mentioned. In the first place, communications can alter the emotional state of audience members and produce excitement, anger, or some other affective state that makes physical aggression more likely in the short term. In this aspect, it is the emotional level that is important. Changes in affect that increase the probability of violence are called an "excitation effect" in Figure 8.1.

A second form of short-term affective impact has been called the catharsis effect, "the idea that the probability of aggressive behavior is reduced by observing the kind of violence seen in the mass media" (U.S. National Commission 1969b:453). The notion is that aggressive impulses might either be vicariously satisfied or inhibited by the observation of

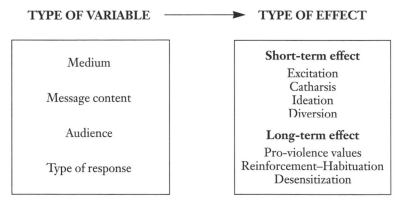

TYPE OF VARIABLE ⟶ **TYPE OF EFFECT**

Medium	**Short-term effect**
	Excitation
	Catharsis
Message content	Ideation
	Diversion
Audience	**Long-term effect**
	Pro-violence values
Type of response	Reinforcement–Habituation
	Desensitization

Figure 8.1 Some potential effects of mass communications on violence and significant variables in predicting media influence.

some forms of violence. This is, of course, the precise opposite predicted by excitation. The two impacts might not be mutually exclusive, but rather occur with different types of communication or different audiences.

A third form of short-term communication effect that may be relevant to the incidence of violence is ideational or informational. This type of effect has also been called observational learning (De Fleur and Ball-Rokeach 1975:226). The clearest model of this to be found in public discussion of communication effects is the so-called "copycat" reaction in which members of an audience reenact particular forms of violent behavior that they have seen portrayed in movies, television, or other media. The key ingredient of an ideational effect is that it provides information about a course of conduct that some members of an audience might wish to follow. Studies have looked for copycat effects in homicide and suicide as well as more specific behaviors described in mass media. While ideational and excitational effects can be distinguished, the same communication can produce both.

The fourth short-term effect of mass communications on rates of lethal violence—which we will call diversion—is not discussed in the behavioral science literature. The media of mass communication prevent thousands of violent acts each year by diverting the attention of their audience from alternative forms of occupation or recreation. In the United States of the 1990s, a television set is switched on for more than seven hours of every day in the average American household. The average male adolescent reports watching television 3.1 hours per day, about one-fifth of his waking hours and a much larger share of his potential leisure time (Information Please Almanac 1995).

Time spent watching television, reading, playing video games, and watching motion pictures is time that is not spent in other social settings or pursuits. Reading and watching television removes participants from physical environments where interpersonal violence is an immediate possibility if pursued as solitary occupations. Time spent reading a mystery novel is as far removed from the social circumstances that produce violent conflict as it is possible to get. The hundreds of billions of hours that Americans spend watching car chases, shootouts, and newscasts represent a significant amount of time not spent in activities that would generate a higher risk of immediate social conflict and violent outcomes.

The diversionary or "babysitting" function of mass communications should be taken into account when calculating the net effect of those communications on the incidence of violence. The presence of violence as the subject matter of the mass media probably contributes to the size of the audience willing to watch the media and to the amount of time audience members are willing to devote to that pursuit. In this way, the depiction of violence on the mass media has a preventive effect in relation to rates of violent behavior that is largely independent of the psychology of audience response.

Long-Term Effects

The short-term effects of exposure to the media are a matter of stimulus and immediate response—the usual subject of behavioral psychology. Changing the focus to extensive and repetitive exposure to mass communications dealing with violence places more emphasis on personal habits and social values, as well as the cumulative psychological response that is obliquely referred to as desensitization. The principal concern of most media critics is that the positive portrayal of violence increases the social acceptability and status of violent persons and responses and that this leads to a social framework in which force is considered an acceptable means of responding to a variety of problems. We think that concern about something like this motivated Senator Robert Dole's 1995 critique that

> A line has been crossed—not just of taste, but of human dignity and decency. It is crossed every time sexual violence is given a catchy tune. When teen suicide is set to an appealing beat. (Broder 1995)

An additional concern that is expressed about the cumulative impact of a large number of favorable portrayals of violence is that they tend to create a habitual association so that a frustration or a personal problem suggests a violent response to a person who has been programmed by years of media exposure (see Freedman 1984). If persons are already committing violent acts in these circumstances, the media portrayals are seem as reinforcements (De Fleur and Ball-Rokeach 1975:229). This sort of habitual association might link to individual and collective responses that range from committing homicide to supporting the dispatch of troops to foreign trouble spots.

A final long-range effect frequently mentioned is that repeated exposure to violence in the media of mass communication leads to the desensitization of the audience. What sorts of exposure produce that effect and how that effect should be defined and differentiated from other long-term processes is by no means clear in published discussions of desensitization. Thus, for example, De Fleur and Ball-Rokeach speak of "a numbing or *desensitization* effect" where prolonged exposure may promote "insensitivity or the lack of a desire to help others when violent encounters are witnessed in real life" (De Fleur and Ball-Rokeach 1975:271).

Significant Variables

Each of the categories of variable presented in Figure 8.1 signifies a large number of factors that can have substantial impact on the effect of mass communications on the incidence of violence. There is, first of all, the matter of the different kinds of media. Books, motion picture, television, magazines, e-mail, radio, compact discs, and computer games are all different means of communication. This affects the way in which messages

can be communicated, portrayed, and perceived. But the list of importantly different forms of media is very short when compared with the number
of significant differences in message content that may have a significant
impact on the effect of the communication.

The nightly news is television violence. So was *Ben Hur* with Charlton
Heston when it was televised. So is the live presentation of a prize fight
from Las Vegas. Messages differ in the type of violent acts depicted, in
how and whether violence is rewarded, in the views on violence expressed
by persons on the media, and in many other ways. We would not be at all
surprised if modern psychology could produce a list of twenty different
kinds of violence that should not be aggregated or confused when predicting the effects of the mass communication of violent scenes. Different
kinds of messages might have different effects on audiences. But what
might be the significant differences in the kinds of portrayal of violence is
the subject of unresolved debate.

There is also the question of the many different kinds of audiences that
are at the receiving end of modern mass communications. Here, to mention only a few, are some of the dimensions of an audience that can make
a difference to audience responses to violence in the media: gender, intel-
ligence, current mood, maturity, age, educational background, value orientation, and a variety of other social and demographic characteristics.
Because serious violence is statistically a rare event, media effects that
occur only among small and atypical audience segments may produce
very large variations in rates of serious violence. But searching for those
effects in a general population sample would be very much like hunting
for a needle in a haystack.

The final variable mentioned in Figure 8.1, the type of response being
measured, is by no means the least important. The elements measured as
behavioral responses to mass media violence vary from reports of emotional states such as anger or frustration, to the punching of large stuffed
effigies called Bobo dolls, to willingness to administer what the subject
believes to be electric shocks to persons who are experimental confeder-
ates, to incidents of homicide and suicide after public events such as box-
ing matches and executions (Phillips 1980 and 1983; Bollen and Phillips
1982).

But most of the experimental work involves attempts to measure what
the researchers call the aggressive responses of persons who have been
subjected to different types of media communication. Some nonexperi-
mental longitudinal research counts self-reports of violence such as fistfights as the dependent variable and some statistical comparisons over
time take aggregate counts of homicide or suicide incidents in the general
population. The time during which behaviors used as dependent variables
are collected also varies from short-term responses to periods of years.

Perhaps there are important linkages between measures of aggression
such as hitting a Bobo doll and propensities toward starting fistfights or

inflicting gunshot wounds. Perhaps also the same sorts of communication produce both short-term and long-term impacts. But the nature and extent of such linkages are not known. And because the intrinsic nature of these behaviors may vary from innocuous to quite harmful, it is not safe to assume that communications that produce one sort of response—e.g., hitting a Bobo doll—would also have a potential influence on the willingness of an experimental subject to hit or stab a human being. From that perspective, the dependent variables employed in mass communications research should not be lumped into conclusory aggregate categories like aggression or violence, but considered separately.

Indeed, some of the different behaviors designed to measure aggression measure different types of response, and this may explain different patterns of response that confuse some analysts. For example, catharsis and excitation are listed in Figure 8.1 as directly opposed hypotheses, in the sense that one predicts a greater tendency to aggression while the other predicts the restraint of a tendency to aggressive action. But if excitation is a matter of physical tension and the need to discharge energy, an energizing communication might lead to a number of Bobo doll punches that might have no important link to the propensity to commit a serious assault on another human being. At the same time, a so-called catharsis effect may influence attitudes and not energy states. If one measures verbal hostility after a communication, one might find catharsis. If one measures the punching of Bobo dolls, one might find excitation.

One or both effects may be produced by a given set of stimuli. And the same stimuli may have different effects on different audience groups. Assume that watching a fistfight generates physical energy and tension in an audience no matter which fighter is winning. Assume further that watching such a fight to its conclusion generates satisfaction for those whose favorite fighter wins and frustration for those who were rooting for the loser. A Bobo doll test might find the two groups responding in the same fashion, while a test of willingness to inflict pain on another might find differences between the two groups. These, then, may not just be two different measures of aggression, but also two different kinds of aggression being measured.

Under these circumstances, the different types of behavior that are used as dependent measures in research may very well be measuring different kinds of subject response, not merely different levels of the same emotional or cognitive response. These important potential differences in effect limit our capacity to generalize across studies that have used different measures of aggression or violence. The only response pattern in most communication research that would downplay the importance of the type of outcome measure used would be a consistency of the type and magnitude of response produced by different media violence cues. That kind of consistency cannot be found in the psychological literature dealing with media communication of aggression.

From our perspective, then, the effect of mass communications on violence is not a single question, but a categorical label for a myriad of quite different questions about communication and response. Very few of these questions have been answered definitively. Some of the specific questions that have been asked are more closely connected to issues about variations in lethal violence than others. Because the principal focus of this book is lethal violence, the empirical research exploring the linkage between mass media effects and lethal violence is of special interest.

Mass Media and Lethal Violence

We found only two lines of published research suggesting a causal relationship between mass media and increases in lethal violence. One line of studies compared trends over time in television ownership and in homicide rates in four nations (see Centerwall 1989a,b, and 1992). The research concluded that homicide rates increase substantially about fifteen years after increases in television ownership. The second sequence of studies tests the effect of widely publicized prize fights on homicide rates in the days following the fight (Phillips 1983). These studies reported increased levels of homicide three days after widely publicized prize fights.

Appendix 5 presents our detailed analysis of these two lines of research. We demonstrate that a causal link between increases in television ownership and subsequent increases in homicide is disproved by the homicide record in the G7 nations over the past generation. For that research, it is not that insufficient data is available to test the theorized relationship; rather, the trends over time rather clearly show no major influence of television ownership and viewing on homicide.

The studies that examine the short-term impact of media events suffer from methodological flaws that prevent us from concluding that good evidence for short-term homicide impact exists. But the data now available also do not rule out the existence of such effects, and further research seems warranted. Since the work of Gabriel Tarde, the possibility of media-induced imitations of violent crime have been discussed (Tarde 1912).

With the substantial modern emphasis on media research, the lack of studies examining the relationship between media cues and lethal violence is surprising. We would not assign a high priority to media studies as part of a research program on the proximate causes of lethal violence. But we would consider any plausible hypothesis about media influence on lethal violence to be a high priority for those interested in assessing the social impact of mass media.

Some Next Steps

There are literally thousands of studies that have attempted to assess the impact of messages conveyed by the mass media on the behavior of their audience. One large subsegment of these studies, about 500 in number by 1984, has addressed the effect of portrayals of violence and aggression (Freedman 1984:229). The short-run effect of many different kinds of message has been to increase the probability of behaviors that are associated with low levels of aggression (Freedman 1984).

Longitudinal studies of television viewing have also associated extensive exposure for boys during particular childhood periods with a higher probability of aggressive behavior later in life (Eron 1972, Milavsky et al. 1982). The evidence on short-term effects comes from research methodologies that include controlled experimentation. The longitudinal comparisons are not the product of random assignment experimentation, so that those who were exposed to extensive early television viewing were self-selected and might well have differed from the less exposed subjects in the cohorts in other ways that could trigger higher rates of problematic behavior later in life (see Freedman 1984:241–242).

From the standpoint of research into the proximate causes of lethal violence, further studies of the impact of aggregate television exposure should probably be assigned low levels of priority in the competition for scarce resources. The reason for this was stated at the outset of this review: Exposure to common elements of the mass media is extensive throughout the Western world. And there is no clear pattern that links aggregate media exposure to increases or decreases in lethal violence.

In coming to this conclusion, we find ourselves in disagreement with a recent communication to the *Journal of the American Medical Association* by Dr. Brandon Centerwall in which empirical evidence on television and violence is given a more dramatic interpretation:

> The epidemiologic evidence indicates that if, hypothetically, television technology had never been developed, there would today be 10,000 fewer homicides each year in the United States, 70,000 fewer rapes and 700,000 fewer injurious assaults. (Centerwall 1992:3061)

There are two problems with this assertion as a basis for future research. First, the evidence does not support the conclusion that television exposure produces anything close to these claimed effects. The "epidemiological evidence" referred to is Dr. Centerwall's own study of television ownership in English-speaking countries. We have already shown his conclusion is contradicted by following the countries he studied further in time and adding trends in television ownership and homicide for several other Western nations. These further data falsify the hypothesized link between increasing television ownership and increases in homicide.

The second problem with this kind of analysis is that it operates at a level of aggregation that is inappropriate for both scientific and policy analysis. The only way to study the total effect of a phenomenon as socially pervasive as television is crude before-and-after comparisons that cannot take into account all the other changes that time brings to a modern social system. Such a level of aggregation is also inappropriate because it assumes the literal truth of the Marshall McLuhan cliche: "The medium is the message" (McLuhan 1964:7). Do television game shows increase the homicide rate? How about *I Love Lucy* reruns or the rebroadcast of *The Sound of Music*? If message content is important in the production of audience response, phrasing hypotheses about the aggregate effects of a particular medium of communication is bad science. As Jonathan Freedman concluded, "the effect of viewing violence (or anything else) on television must depend on the specific content of the program" (Freedman 1984:244). In other words, the medium is not the message.

There are many different kinds of communication carried on television screens, available in movie theaters, transmitted by radio and mechanisms for the reproduction of sound. There are also many different kinds of people in the audience of mass communications. To the extent that scientific progress tends to be in the direction of producing and testing more specific hypotheses, scientific values would be well served by studies of particular types of media content and their effects on different types of audience. For those whose interest in media studies is motivated by a special concern about the role of mass communications in respect to lethal violence, the need for specificity and subdivision in media research is particularly acute. We need to identify those specific content elements most plausibly linked to serious violent behavior; and we need to test the effects of such communications on groups at particularly high risk of violent behavior.

With regard to media effects on violence, it would seem most important to test the impact of portrayals of violence, of appeals that seek to encourage a violent response, and also of communications that might alter or reinforce audience values regarding when violence is justified. Within these broad categories, there are many different kinds of violence and a myriad different ways in which violence may be presented and portrayed. The way in which violent incidents are depicted, the value context, the presence or absence of aesthetic appeal, the degree of realism—all these may make night-and-day differences in the responses of audiences to the portrayal of violent activity. In this connection, it is pertinent to recall the advice of the psychologists Seymour Feshbach and Robert Singer at the conclusion of their discussion of television and aggression a quarter of a century ago:

> We suspect that if television fare equivalent to such violent epics as *Macbeth*, *Medea*, or *Treasure Island* were substituted for *The Untouchables*, *Combat*, and similar programs, there would be much less concern about the depiction of violence on television. (Feshbach and Singer, 1971:159–160)

The division of messages and portrayals related to violence into behaviorally significant subcategories is not an easy task. There is no general agreement about what the significantly different kinds of violence are for the purpose of predicting audience response to the portrayal of violence. But this lack of consensus makes the subdivision of cues all the more necessary even as it renders the process more difficult to achieve.

A special concern about life-threatening violence suggests a special interest in the audience reaction of population groups at higher-than-average risk of becoming engaged in serious violence. Homicide and serious assault are low-frequency behaviors that are also far from evenly distributed across the population. Mass media communications might have effects on very few people and yet still dramatically escalate rates of violent predation. Some of the subgroups of particular importance stand out because of a presumed vulnerability to media messages: young children and the emotionally disturbed are two such groups. Other groups are of particular interest because of a higher-than-average likelihood of involvement in particular kinds of violence. Examples of such high-risk groups would include depressives (for studies of suicide) and the inmates of juvenile and adult correctional facilities (for studies of criminal violence).

The use of controlled experimentation to test the differential impact of particular forms of violent communication on some high-risk groups might be objected to because of inadequate protection of human subjects from research-generated risks. Exposing young children or emotionally disturbed subjects to larger doses of mass media violence than they would otherwise encounter could be objected to on protection of human rights grounds. But withholding violent communication from children or disturbed persons as an experimental condition while allowing control subjects ordinary access to media messages seems unobjectionable.

Moreover, there are substantial opportunities, in prisons and institutions for older juvenile offenders, to conduct controlled experiments on the short- and long-term impact of different media communications. If freedom of speech and message reception questions can be resolved by securing the consent of research subjects, well-controlled media experiments can be conducted on older subjects who are at elevated risk of the commission of serious violence. There is some precedent for conducting media research in a correctional environment (see Goldstein and Kent 1974). But particular interest in life-threatening violence would suggest a much higher concentration on individualized populations in future studies.

Before producing our own short list of candidates for media research, it is necessary to note the sharp differences in priority concerns that one is likely to find when contrasting the research priorities of those with a special interest in life-threatening violence and researchers with a more general interest in the impact of the mass media on human behavior. Students of lethal violence are interested in statistically abnormal behavior; their focus is on what can or might happen to the behavior of a small number of persons monitoring messages rather than on the typical responses of most audience members. Those more broadly interested in mass media effects will want to document the entire range of those effects and will be more interested in modal responses to media communications.

The compilation of our short list of topics has been influenced by the priority concern with lethal violence. From this perspective, our highest priority among media research topics would be for qualitative assessment of the impact of particular types of media on patterns of suicide and homicide. Do various types of youth suicide portrayed in movies or on television result in higher rates of youth suicide after broadcasts? If measurements were confined to aggregate rates of suicide in conducting such research, many of the same difficulties encountered by the heavyweight fight research (discussed in Appendix 5) would bedevil attempts to model expected suicide rates. But data can also measure the quality of suicides, particularly on patterns by age, to produce specific hypotheses that generate far lower risks of false inference. Similar kinds of studies can be carried out on the impact of television broadcasting or the theatrical release of films that feature teenage gang violence. Time-series researches can determine whether the particular type of homicide emphasized in the medium increases after mass communication.

Imitation is a widely confirmed mechanism in the literature of social psychology. The kind of qualitative study we recommend holds the best prospect of isolating discrete media events that might be the proximate cause of fluctuations in rates of lethal violence. In this sense, the style of research engaged in by David Phillips can serve as an inspiration for more qualitatively oriented studies of the impact of the mass media on violent death.

We would place a high value on such studies even though we believe that the null hypothesis should be regarded as a strong favorite in any study of the short-term consequences of media exposure. Homicides and suicides are infrequent occurrences and particular subclasses of these events—for example, youth suicides—are even more infrequent. Existing statistical methods may be too weak to detect all but the most extraordinary of short-term media effects. Indeed, one of the things that made us suspicious of the modeling strategies recorded in the Phillips research was the wide variety of different significant results that were produced by his methodology. (see Phillips 1978 and 1979).

A second type of research that merits the special concern of those interested in the impact of mass media on lethal violence is controlled experimentation on the responsiveness of high-risk populations to media cues about violence. Are imprisoned adults far more likely to respond to particular media cues than normal subjects? Are those with a prior history of violence more prone to special responses than nonviolent offenders? The currently crowded prisons of the United States represent a research opportunity that should command more attention than it has received to date.

Conclusion

There is a large gap between folk wisdom and the best available data from behavioral science on the impact of the mass media on rates of lethal violence. There are at least two explanations that may help to account for the gap between popular sentiment and scientific assessment. In the first place, violence in the mass media is a source of discomfort and concern to many of those who observe it. That is the case whether the cornucopia of gore that spills from modern television sets generates or merely reflects social tendencies. And when such media communications provoke discomfort and anxiety, it is natural for citizens to regard them as a cause of violence. Blaming the messenger who brings bad tidings is a recurrent phenomenon. As Shakespeare put it: "The bringer of unwelcome news hath but a losing office."

The second reason why public sentiment condemns media violence more than social science data is that the public may be right. Media portrayals of, and emphasis on, violence may produce long-term citizen desensitization and value changes; a tolerance for violence that might interact with other American social conditions to elevate rates of lethal violence. Such long-term, subtle, and contingent influences are very difficult to measure statistically, but may be important nonetheless. What little we know about the specific effects of mass media communications suggests that it is not a major cause of variations in the amount of life-threatening violence. But we may lack the capacity to measure significant dimensions of the pervasive influence of mass media communications.

9

Only in America?
Illicit Drugs and the Death Rate
from Violence

CONVENTIONAL WISDOM is firm in the belief that the use and marketing of illicit drugs in the United States is a major cause of homicide. Indeed, the belief that illegal drugs generate violence is one of the very few propositions that commands the agreement of both those who support the intensified prohibition of presently illicit drugs and those who urge complete decriminalization. Confirmed "drug warriors" argue that the violence associated with illegal drug markets proves the necessity for strict punishment of the drug criminal: "tough and coherently punitive anti-drug measures . . . should be employed" (Office of National Drug Control Policy 1989:7). The partisan of decriminalization believes that homicide is the product of the illegalization of drug trafficking and that homicide would diminish dramatically if the criminal prohibition were removed, "saving in excess of 10,000 lives a year" (Friedman 1991:57). The belief that illicit drugs are a major cause of urban homicide is common ground in the drug control debate of the 1990s.

This chapter exposes that common ground to the same kind of statistical scrutiny that was used in the earlier analysis of firearms and mass communication. The first section of theis chapter will summarize and critique the statistical evidence used in support of a causal connection between illicit drugs and lethal violence. The second section will contrast U.S. data with some information about homicide and trends in illicit drug taking that casts doubt on the belief in the inevitability of lethal violence as an outcome of expanding rates of illicit drug use. The third section of the chapter will outline our own argument that the expansion of the illicit drug market in the mid-1980s interacted with other conditions to produce an increase in the death rate from intentional injury.

We present this chapter as a case study in contingent causation illustrating the important role of the interaction of social conditions in predicting variations in rates of lethal violence. In one sense, then, a capsule summary of our treatment of guns, the mass media, and drugs as significant causes of lethal violence is: "Yes, no, and sometimes." In a deeper sense, however, all of the social conditions that contribute to lethal violence are contingent causes. Even loaded guns do not produce homicide unless they are fired. What transnational comparisons regarding illicit drugs can show is the enormous practical effect of the different social contexts in which illicit drug use occurs, and the special vulnerability of the United States to lethal violence from a wide variety of conflicts.

The American Scene

The relationship between illegal drugs and crime in the United States, and in particular the linkage between drugs and lethal violence, has been documented extensively in the aftermath of a high-intensity "war on drugs." The overlap between illegal drug use and involvement in other forms of criminal activity is extensive. The so-called "drug use forecasting" studies in the United States found that the majority of persons arrested for other than drug offenses in most American cities had recent evidence of drug use in their urine (U.S. Department of Justice, National Institute of Justice, 1990). This chemical evidence is supported by extensive survey research in prisons and jails. More than three-quarters of all jail inmates surveyed in 1989 reported some lifetime illicit drug use, and 40 percent of the inmates reported using drugs in the month prior to their most recent arrest. About two-thirds of all prison inmates reported using drugs once a week and more than one-third claimed to be under the influence of drugs at the time of committing the offense for which they had been imprisoned (U.S. Department of Justice, Bureau of Justice Statistics, 1992:196).

There are no data parallel to those available for arrested populations to establish the proportion of all drug users who also commit other criminal offenses. That sort of calculation could be made if a representative sample of illicit drug takers were available and could be asked about the extent of and reasons for other forms of criminal activity. Studies of active drug takers have reported high rates of nondrug crime but low rates of robbery and no details of lethal violence (Johnson et al. 1985:77). But even if estimates existed of the prevalence of lethal criminal activity not related to drug use, finding an extensive overlap between criminal drug use and other forms of criminal activity would not establish any cause and effect relationship for reasons which we have discussed (see Appendix 1).

The published research on the relationship between illicit narcotics and lethal violence goes beyond documenting the overlap between drug use and serious violence to analyze the causal role that drugs and drug transactions might have played in homicidal events. Paul Goldstein studied police accounts of New York City homicide to determine how many such killings could be directly linked to illegal drugs. Three types of drug-related cases were postulated: those in which illegal drugs had a pharmacological influence on a homicide because the assailant was under the influence of a drug at the time of the act; those in which obtaining illicit drugs were an instrumental motive for the attack, in that the events that produced the killing were part of the assailant's effort to obtain either drugs or the money to buy them; and systemic drug-related killings in which the robbery or conflict that produced the homicide was the consequence of some aspect of the commerce in illegal drugs (Goldstein 1985; Goldstein et al. 1990).

Little is known about the mechanisms of various illegal drugs that might produce aggressiveness and there is no good methodology currently available for assessing the causal impact of illicit drug intoxication on homicide (see Fagan 1990). In any event, the effect of illegal intoxicants on inhibition and aggressiveness would have with be compared to the pharmacological impact of potential substitutes such as alcohol before any net difference in homicide could be attributed to the illegal agent. So the impact of illicit drug intoxication on homicide rates is not known and not believed to be large.

It is also difficult to estimate the amount of homicide produced by persons trying to obtain drugs or the money to buy drugs. The amount of published evidence available on this topic greatly exceeds its probative value. Anecdotal lore about the homicidal activities of the desperate drug addict is considerable. The amount of crime reported by heavy drug users is quite substantial. But these kinds of data are far from rigorous tests of the hypothesis that drug hunger causes homicide.

A potentially more rewarding data set concerns the variations in the self-reported crime commission rate of drug users. Persons narrating life histories report much more criminal activity during periods when they were also frequently using illicit drugs, and it has been suggested that the increase in drug use is a plausible cause for this pattern. There are, however, two rival hypotheses that would explain covariation in crime rates and drug use. The first is that increased drug use is a consequence of increased income from criminal activity but not necessarily a cause of the other crime. The theory here is that drug use is an important form of recreation that would be expected to expand with increasing levels of discretionary income, whether or not obtaining the drug was a specific motive for the increase in criminal activity. The second possibility is that other factors such as increased agitation or freedom from outside monitoring might be a cause of both higher levels of drug use and of nondrug criminality.

An additional problem that confronts the "man with a golden arm" scenario as an explanation of homicide is that lethal violence has never been the specific focus of this kind of research. Given the causal attribution problems associated with such studies and the low incidence of lethal violence among drug-using populations, a major research undertaking on this topic might not be a wise investment.

Systemic Homicide

It is the systemically related drug killings that prompt the conclusion by most observers that expansions in the use and purchase of illegal narcotics cause additional homicides. The theory of how illegal drug markets produce systemic homicide was described by Hope Corman, et al. as follows:

> Many believe that violence associated with drugs is primarily due to the illegality of the market. Drug producers and sellers have no other recourse to settling disputes and force is a typical method in obtaining market power. Some claim that individuals involved in crack production and distribution are a younger, tougher breed of drug marketeers, more violent and more indifferent to human life than in prior generations. (Corman et al. 1991:113)

How many homicides occur as a consequence of these illegal markets? The prize for the most grandiose claim would probably go to Milton Friedman for suggesting that only the decriminalization of drugs stands between the United States of the 1990s and the lowest homicide rates experienced in the twentieth century:

> I believe one can have great confidence that if drugs were decriminalized the homicide rate would fall sharply, most likely back to the level that it maintained throughout the fifties. That is no small matter. A reduction in the homicide rate from its average during the eighties to its average during the fifties would, with our current population, mean a saving in excess of 10,000 lives a year! (Friedman 1991:57)

Professor Friedman's estimate of the impact of drug markets on homicide is high, but how high? The evidence available on the number of systemic homicides produced by illegal drug markets comes from two separate types of statistical analysis. The first analyzes the circumstances of homicides in a particular jurisdiction and then makes assumptions about the impact of changes in policy on the likely homicide rate. Examples of this kind of work have been produced for New York City and Washington, D.C. In Goldstein's study of New York City, it was estimated that 24 percent of homicides in 1984 were drug-related and that the majority of these were systemic (Goldstein 1985). By 1988 the same team of investigators estimated that 53 percent of all New York City homicides were drug-related and more than 40 percent of all killings fit the systemic drug pattern (Goldstein et al. 1990). A study of homicide in Washington, D.C. estimated that fifty-three percent of all District of Columbia homicides in 1989 were drug- or alcohol-related and that a substantial majority of these were systemic (Office of Criminal Justice Plans and Analysis 1991). These are city-level estimates derived from cities with notoriously high levels of illicit drug commerce, so that they cannot be extrapolated to other cities or to nonurban areas.

There is also a problem with inferring that all these systemic homicides would disappear if the illicit market in drugs that generated them were abolished. There is more hope, surely, that killings arising out of drug commerce would diminish if the legal status of narcotics were changed than there is hope that homicides associated with drug intoxication or the need to obtain narcotics would fall in an atmosphere of decriminalization. But just as a wide variety of legal and illegal intoxicants are associated with violence, the well-armed and violence-prone young men who shoot each other now in disputes about drug markets could not be expected to have homicide rates near zero after they leave the drug business.

Perhaps the majority of systemic homicide incidents would disappear if major illegal drug markets ceased to exist. But a study that merely classifies drug killings as systemic cannot generate estimates of the killings that will remain if the high-conflict entrepreneurs who are now responsible for drug killings do not have drugs to fight about. Studies that provide censuses of homicides in major cities thus provide preliminary information on the range of killings that might be preventable under different drug policies without any more precise estimates.

A second method of estimating the number of additional killings produced by changes in drug markets is to compare homicide rates before and after significant changes in the nature and extent of drug marketing. Corman and her associates performed that kind of trend analysis on New York City, focusing especially on the presumed introduction of crack cocaine markets in New York City in 1985 and its impact on homicide volume. The study was an interrupted time series of all killings and did not separate out offenses that had been separately identified as related to drug traffic. Instead, it assumed that any increases in killings that occurred in 1985 were attributable to the crack phenomenon. The study found an increase in the total volume of homicide of less than 7 percent attributable to the new crack activity in 1985 (Corman et al. 1991:134). But this new volume may have been in addition to the almost one-quarter of New York City killings that Goldstein estimated to be drug-related in 1984. So an aggregate drug involvement estimate for New York City in the late 1980s might exceed 30 percent.

The District of Columbia homicide experience since the 1980s is not as well documented with reference to drug involvement, but shows much wider fluctuation in drug-related homicide and homicide generally.

An analysis of the District of Columbia, reported in Appendix 6, suggests that increases in drug-related homicides over the 1980s increased the total level of homicide in Washington, D.C., substantially. But virtually all of the additional homicides involved young minority males, so the risks associated with drug conflicts, were even more concentrated than homicides generally. And there is some evidence that expanding drug markets reduced the robbery and robbery homicide totals in Washington, D.C., during the mid-1980s by providing more lucrative alternatives to robbery as a means of income. So drug commerce not only increases risks of homicide, but may also redistribute risks of homicide, and some groups of potential victims may benefit from the increase in drug focus of urban violence.

National Trends

Figure 9.1 extends the analysis by showing trends in the proportion of all homicides the police believed were drug involved by year from 1980 to 1992. The data come from the Federal Bureau of Investigation's Supplementary Homicide Reports.

Trends in the aggregate of all reporting jurisdictions follow the general pattern noted in New York City and Washington, D.C. But the proportion of cases involving illicit drugs is much lower in the national aggregate and the extent of the increase over the 1980s is much more modest than in highly drug-impacted New York City and Washington, D.C. Between 1980 and 1989 the proportion of homicide cases in which the police thought drugs were a motive increased from 2.5 to 9.2 percent. By 1989

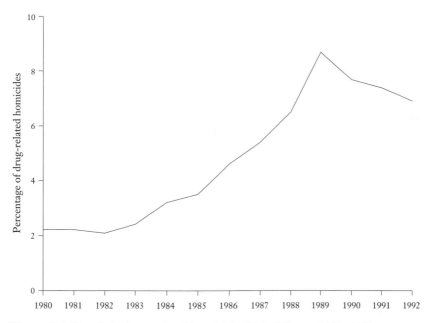

Figure 9.1. Trends in drug-related homicide, United States, 1980–1992. *Source:* U.S. Department of Justice, Federal Bureau of Investigation, 1994.

drug homicides accounted for three times as many killings as in the earlier time period. But the proportion fell back to 7.8 percent by 1992.

Conclusion

Extensive data are available on the overlap in the United States of illegal drugs and lethal violence. By far the most significant connection between illicit drugs and homicide is the large number of killings that the police believe are related to the markets for illegal drugs, what analysts have called "systemic" drug violence. Conservative police estimates put drug-related killings at just under 10 percent of total homicide. Studies of individual cities push this estimate up to about one-half of all killings at peak periods in Washington, D.C., and New York City and also suggest that there may be a large gap between official police estimates and actual drug involvement.

It appears also that expanding rates of drug-related violence are associated with higher rates of overall homicide in many cities, although the magnitude of the relationship between drug violence and overall homicide rates may be more modest than some observers have thought. No fewer than 10 percent of American homicides and perhaps as many as 25 percent have important linkages with some illicit drug. In recent years, cocaine has been the illicit drug most prominently associated with lethal violence in the drug trade. The evidence in relation to heroin and other illicit drugs is less substantial.

Given the substantial attention devoted to the impact of illicit drugs in the United States since the mid-1980s, the amount of research devoted to illegal drugs and lethal violence is really quite small. The reason for the neglect is the general tendency, as noted earlier, for the specific issue of lethal violence to be downplayed, while the amorphous and general topic of "drugs and crime" has occupied centerstage. The typical textbook or policy analysis discusses a wide variety of criminal behaviors ranging from petty theft to contract killing as if all those were of equal importance and emerged from the same systemic roots (see U.S. Department of Justice, Bureau of Justice Statistics, 1992:2).

The standard critique of the criminalization of hard narcotics often seems to rely on the same confusion between crime and lethal violence that was considered in Chapter 1 of this book. In the debate about the legalization of drugs, that confusion is reflected in the assumption that making drug transactions criminal is the equivalent of making such transactions inherently likely to generate life-threatening violence. On some occasions, the assumption that criminal markets inevitably produce violence is simply implicit. In other analyses, the argument is that the unsuitability of mechanisms like law courts for the enforcement of the promissory aspects of illegal drug transactions inevitably will lead to the kind of systemic violence that escalates rates of homicide (vide Corman et al. 1991:113).

In fact, the threat of lethal violence is one way of maintaining commercial expectations in illegal markets but by no means the only way. Unless lethal violence with all its attendant risks has inherent advantages over other strategies of risk management in illicit drug markets, high and constant rates of lethal violence will not be the inevitable outcome of the criminal prohibition of drugs. We will return to this issue in the third section of this chapter.

For present purposes, however, it is sufficient to note that equating crime and violence is one way of ensuring that fundamental questions about the linkage between criminal prohibitions and criminal homicide never get asked and never get tested. In this regard, it is worth noting that commercial transactions in illicit drugs are not the only arrangements that are unenforceable in the American courts because they are illegal. Price-fixing agreements between firms, bookmaking accounts, other gambling debts, and a wide variety of other bargains struck in the shadow of the criminal law cannot come to court.

Do they produce large numbers of criminal homicides? Is whatever link exists between unenforceability and violence not susceptible to any legal policy controls? Does the specific social environment of the illegal activity make a difference? These are the sorts of questions that never get asked when the equivalence of crime and violence is assumed because it is implicitly assumed that all criminals are equally violent.

A Transnational Perspective

Data from foreign countries might assist us in understanding the relationship between illegal drug markets and lethal violence in the United States. The strategy to be used in examining this data is parallel to the comparison that was used in our analyses of firearms and the mass media. Unfortunately, the data on both illicit drugs and on drug-related homicide are not comparable in quality to the information available on television and firearms ownership.

Legal policy toward drugs such as cocaine, heroin, and marijuana in the other developed Western nations is formally similar to the drug laws in the United States. Since the possession and use of these drugs is prohibited by law in all G7 nations, whatever markets exist for narcotics in those nations are illicit. One problem with illicit markets is that the commerce goes unreported to the government and is rendered unmeasurable by conventional methods (see Morris and Hawkins 1977:21). So estimates of the prevalence and incidence of illegal drug taking is more difficult to verify than is the case with goods and services that are not the subject of prohibition. Estimates of illicit drug taking in foreign countries are less than reliable and the same problems are found in the American statistics. Under these circumstances, transnational comparison of the incidence of illicit drugs may generate problems of compounded uncertainty.

The available evidence suggests that the United States has a higher rate of illicit drug consumption than any other industrialized nation. Yet all of industrialized Europe reports the existence of illicit markets in heroin, cocaine, and cannabis (Hartnoll 1994). Without denying the unique scale of illicit drug marketing and consumption in the United States, it still seems possible to learn from the overlap between illicit narcotics and lethal violence in other-than-American settings.

A Statistical Thought Experiment

Figure 9.2 reanalyzes the homicide data for Sydney and Los Angeles discussed in Chapter 1 to separately report the number of 1992 homicide cases that the police believed were related to illicit narcotics.

The data on drug involvement in Los Angeles come from the Supplementary Homicide Reports discussed in the previous section. There, the Supplementary Homicide Reports were considered to provide conservative estimates of drug involvement and were more likely to err on the side of understatement than overstatement. Data on the Sydney killings comes

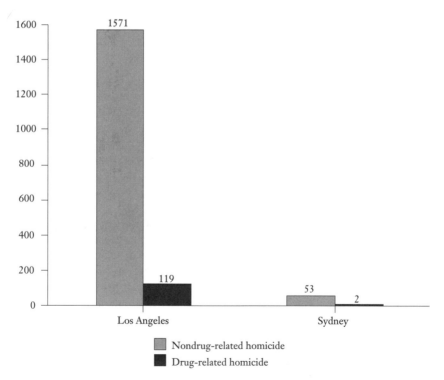

Figure 9.2. Homicide and drug-related homicide, Los Angeles and Sydney, 1992.
Source: U.S. Department of Justice, Federal Bureau of Investigation, 1994 (Los Angeles); data provided by New South Wales Bureau of Criminal Statistics (Sydney).

from the reanalysis of the homicide case records by Roseanne Bonney of the New South Wales Bureau of Criminal Statistics and Research.

Figure 9.2 reports total homicides as well as drug-related homicides for each city and these four data elements permit three different kinds of two-way comparisons that are of potential value. In the first place, each city's drug-related homicides can be compared with that city's total homicides. In the case of Los Angeles, the comparison yields estimates that about 11 percent of all Los Angeles killings are drug-related. For Sydney, the parallel figure is 4 percent. A second comparison that might be useful is between drug homicides in Los Angeles and total homicide volume in Sydney—a city of the same population (3.6 million). What this comparison shows is that more than twice as many drug-related homicides occurred in Los Angeles in 1992 as the total homicides in Sydney during that year. A third comparison that can be made is between the volume of Los Angeles and Sydney drug-related homicides, and the ratio there is: sixty Los Angeles drug killings for every one Sydney drug killing.

Why are drug-related killings so much more numerous in Los Angeles that in Sydney? No precise estimates are available of the incidence or prevalence of the various different illicit drugs in Sydney. Both heroin and marijuana are widely available in illicit markets in Sydney, as is cocaine although to a lesser degree. It seems highly unlikely that the difference in the incidence of drug-related killings between Sydney and Los Angeles is wholly attributable to a difference in the scale of drug taking. Indeed, one implication of the data in Figure 9.2 is that even the belief that illicit drug markets mechanically increase lethal violence would yield two very different predictions about the impact of expanding illicit drug markets in Sydney and that city's homicide.

If we believe that the same kind and amount of illegal drugs would produce an impact on lethal violence in Sydney similar to its impact in Los Angeles, there are two very different definitions of equivalent reactions that seem plausible. On one hand, such a theory might predict that the expansion of the relative importance of drug markets in Sydney would make the relative impact of illicit drugs on Sydney homicide approximately equivalent to the impact of illicit drugs on homicide in Los Angeles. On this account, one would expect that an expansion of Sydney drug markets to Los Angeles levels would generate enough killings to constitute 11 percent of Sydney's homicide: that would be five deaths at 1992 levels. On the other hand, the prediction might be that an expansion of illicit drug markets in Sydney to Los Angeles levels would produce the same number of homicides that illicit drugs generate in Los Angeles, i.e., 119 killings at 1992 levels.

The first thing to notice about these two predictions is how different they are. The second projected homicide total is twenty-four times the size of the first. Another noteworthy characteristic of these two divergent estimates is that each produces an apparent anomaly. If increasing the volume of illicit drug marketing in Sydney to Los Angeles levels produces only five killings a year in Sydney, why would the same level of illicit enterprise generate twenty-two times as many deaths in Los Angeles? Something other than the size of the drug market would have to be responsible for more than 90 percent of the variation in killings generated by the same level of traffic in the same drugs.

On the other hand, if the same level of drug transactions is expected to produce the same number of killings in Sydney as it does in Los Angeles, drugs would have a dominant position in Sydney violence, starkly different from their role in Los Angeles. The same number of drug transactions would be accounting for 11 percent of all Los Angeles homicides and two-thirds of all the homicides in Sydney. Why should the relative share of drugs in homicidal violence be six times as great in Sydney as in Los Angeles?

If drug transactions in Sydney are just as likely to lead to death as in Los Angeles, then the drug market would dominate the homicide statistics because all other social interactions in Sydney generate much lower rates of lethality than do social interactions in Los Angeles.

So our view is that the lower estimate of homicide volume is the more accurate of the two. The reason for this we believe is that the social context that determines the rates of lethal violence generally also has a major influence on the death rate from illicit drug transitions. This is a simple insight, but it might be a very important one.

Cross-National Data

Available data on narcotics and lethal violence in industrialized countries suggests that substantial domestic markets in illicit drugs frequently are found in countries where extensive drug-related lethal violence is not in evidence. One indication that drug-related lethal violence is not a major problem in Europe is the absence of scholarly attention to what Americans call systemic drug violence. One can read, for example, an extensive analysis of illicit drug markets in a variety of Italian cities without encountering a single reference to homicide (see Ruggiero and Vass 1992). A lengthy analysis of Dutch drug policies and their efforts in the drug field is similarly bereft of any mention of drug-related violence (see Leuw 1991). The scholarly literature on drugs in Europe shows no indication of a major violence problem.

There is also an extensive quasigovernmental literature on illicit drug use that includes the efforts of multinational, regional, and United Nations organizations. With regard to the industrialized nations, which are primarily consumers, not producers, of hard narcotics, two generalizations seem secure even given the manifold problems of data reliability in these reports. First, illicit drugs and illicit drug markets are present and problematic in every industrial nation; and second, lethal violence generated by illicit drug traffic is not a problem that appears worthy of special attention in most industrial democracies.

On the extent of illicit drugs and drug markets, Table 9.1 is reproduced from a 1989 Canadian report because of the uncharacteristic economy with which it rates the relative prevalence of six different drugs in eleven different countries.

The estimates in the table cover the period 1975–1980 and cannot be considered up-to-date on any scale. The prevalence of illicit drug use in the United States, however, was at its all-time highest modern elevation during this period (Zimring and Hawkins 1992b). Table 9.1 uses four different rankings based on estimated drug abuse rates in the population. The rating of "1" indicates extensive abuse; "2" signifies moderate abuse; "3" indicates minimal abuse; and "4" denotes either no abuse or no reporting of it. Alone among the eleven listed countries, the United States earns the highest abuse score on all six of the drugs rated. With these consistently high ratings, it is to be expected that the size of illicit markets in the United States and the scale of the problem that they cause would be higher than in other countries.

But the World Health Organization ranking also estimates that nine out of the eleven nations surveyed experienced "extensive abuse" (number one rating) for at least one illegal drug and therefore had at least one substantial illegal drug distribution network. Australia and Italy appear to have extensive numbers of known heroin abusers. Seven out of the eleven surveyed nations have extensive concentrations of cannabis use.

Table 9.1

Comparative Drug Abuse by Country, 1975–1980[a]

Country	Heroin	Cocaine	Cannabis	Hallu-cinogens	Amphetamines	Barbituates/tranquilizers
Canada	2	2	1	2	1	1
United States	1	1	1	1	1	1
Brazil	4	2	1	3	2	2
Argentina	4	1	2	3	3	2
Mexico	3	1	1	2	1	1
Sweden	2	3	1	4	2	3
France	3	3	3	3	3	3
Great Britain	3	3	2	3	3	3
Australia	1	3	1	2	3	3
Italy	1	3	1	3	3	3
Japan	3	3	2	3	1	3

[a]Key: abusers per population;
(1) extensive abuse (less than 1:1,000)
(2) moderate abuse (more than 1:1,000 - 1:10,000)
(3) minimal abuse (more than 1:10,000 or verbal estimate)
(4) no abuse or no report

Source: Eliany 1989: 14.

And Canada experiences extensive or moderate abuse levels for every drug on the list (World Health Organization 1993). If illicit markets inevitably generate deadly force, then the homicidal byproduct of criminal drug traffic should be an extensive and visible problem in a number of countries.

One quantified index of drug use is the rate of drug overdose deaths reported in various locales. The mean rate of eleven different cities reporting drug use deaths for 1989 in the Council of Europe report was 6.9 per 100,000 (Hartnoll 1994:122). Combined heroin and cocaine overdose death rates for Cook County (which includes Chicago) were 12.2 per 100,000 that year and 13.1 for Los Angeles. The death categories for Cook County and Los Angeles are not fully comparable with the European cities and the mix of drugs in the United States contains much more cocaine. But if the rate of reported overdose deaths is a measure of abuse, the prevalence ratio for drugs with lethal overdose potential appears on the order of 2 to 1.

But there is little evidence in the literature of concern about illegal drug markets and lethal violence. The subject of drug-related violence is almost completely absent from the discussion of contemporary drug abuse problems and their effects in most developed nations. The Council of Europe, for example, published in 1994 an extensive statistical and observational study of illegal drug markets and their effects in thirteen major European cities. This report, overflowing with statistical graphs, did not mention, let alone document, systemic drug violence as a problem in any of the cities under review.

What is particularly striking about the invisibility of drug market violence in Europe is the much higher visibility one would expect for drug-related homicide in countries with much lower general homicide rates. The low-end estimate of drug-related killings in New York City in 1990 was about 200 or a total that by itself exceeds the total homicide volume in London. An extra 200 homicides should certainly draw the attention of the law enforcement authorities in London where it would double the homicide rate. And yet the risk of intentional homicide arising from the manifold problems associated with illegal drugs has not been a visible problem to the law enforcement authorities there.

One further cautionary tale concerning the functional independence of the traffic in illicit drugs from lethal violence concerns the impact of expanding rates of heroin use and addiction on homicide in England. As Professor Geoffrey Pearson told the story in 1990:

> Britain was plunged into a heroin epidemic in the early 1980s from which it has yet to recover. In 1983, the number of heroin seizures doubled over the previous year, with a sixfold increase compared to the annual average for 1973–1978. There was a forty-two percent increase in the number of addicts notified to the Home Office, with a fifty percent increase in the number of new addicts notified in 1983 as against 1982 (Home Office, 1984). The trend, which had already been established a year or two earlier although at a much less accelerated pace, was almost entirely confined to heroin misuse. And it

was set to continue, so that by 1985 the number of newly notified heroin addicts had reached 5,930—a fivefold increase in the figure recorded in 1980, with a fourfold increase in persons found guilty of drug offenses in connection with heroin (Home Office, 1987). In 1986 and 1987, this trend appeared to level off, and there was even a recorded decrease in the number of newly notified heroin addicts to 4,082 by 1987. One would expect a heroin epidemic to "peak out" in this way . . . although it is not clear to what extent these declines might also have reflected alterations in the notification procedures that followed the introduction of a new computer system. Indeed, the numbers of drug addicts recorded as receiving notifiable drugs in treatment continued to increase, with the numbers receiving methadone almost doubling between 1984 and 1987 from 5,160 to 9,763, having more than doubled between 1980 and 1984 (Home Office, 1988). (Pearson 1991:181)

What was the impact of this heroin epidemic on the rate of homicide in Britain? By all available accounts, the additional homicide generated by the expansion in drug users and drug markets was nil. Figure 9.3 shows trends in heroin abuse and homicide from 1973 to 1988.

The upward surge in heroin indicators began just as homicide rates fell in England and continued to increase while the homicide rates stabilized at a rate substantially below the level of the mid-1970s. We sought to supplement this data with information from the Home Office on homicide in

Figure 9.3. Trends in homicide, heroin arrests, and known heroin addicts, England, 1973–1988. *Source:* Pearson 1991 (heroin); World Health Organization 1993 (homicide).

London with known or suspected drug involvement. The Home Office reports, however, that this data was not reported during the years before 1995 (Home Office 1995). Apparently, there was no strong feeling in Great Britain during this period that the traffic in heroin was a major source of lethal urban violence.

It is not our ambition to provide a comprehensive portrait of illegal drug markets in England or in Europe. Instead, the information on lethal violence and the drug markets abroad is intended to put the data about drugs and lethal violence in the United States in a broader perspective. The people who sell heroin in England are no less criminal than the people who sell heroin in New York City, but evidently they are not as violent. Illicit drug sales in Paris and London produce tens of thousands of debts that cannot be collected through the law courts. And all of the other transactional contingencies that are associated with high levels of violence in the United States are also found in the drug markets of Europe. But the rates of violent death associated with European drug markets are evidently much smaller. Why? What can that tell us about the levels of violence generated by the illicit markets for drugs in the United States? What does this tell us about the general relationship between crime and lethal violence?

Should the absence of a prominent connection between illicit drug markets and criminal homicide in Europe be used to challenge the theory that the expansion of crack cocaine markets was the proximate cause of an expansion of homicide rates in the United States? Just as the stable homicide rates in Europe could be used to disprove a causal relationship between television and lethal violence in the United States, why not argue that the absence of the striking connection between drug markets and homicide in Italy, England, and France provides evidence that drug markets do not generate large amounts of lethal violence in the United States, either?

We prefer an alternative hypothesis that can harmonize the available data. It might be that the creation or expansion of illegal markets poses problems of territory, credibility, and quality control wherever such markets exist. Where potential drug sellers have the habits and skills of violent predators, the overlap between hard narcotics and violence can be expected to be substantial because problems of credibility and nonenforceability would seem to call for violent measures. On the other hand, where lethal violence is not part of the background and predilection of those who organize and engage in illegal drug transactions, the rate of violence generated by the drug trade will be smaller.

On this theory, the expansion of drug markets should be regarded as a potential or contingent cause of expanding rates of lethal violence. And the presence or absence of factors that influence the contingencies will be the primary explanation of the resultant level of lethal violence. Under these circumstances, the lack of a strong link between the narcotics trade and high mortality rates in Europe should be regarded more as a qualification of some of the findings on violence and drug markets in the United States than as a refutation of the drug-violence connection.

Toward a Theory of Contingent Causation

The overlap between illegal drug markets and lethal violence in settings like New York City is sufficiently substantial to convince all but the most dedicated of agnostics. When more than one-third of all killings might plausibly be linked to drug taking, drug selling, or the organization of the traffic in narcotics, the permissible boundaries of coincidence probably have been exceeded. Yet drug taking and drug selling do not produce high rates of lethal violence wherever drugs are illegal. Illegal drug markets are a contingent cause of lethal violence and the important work is determining the significant contingencies.

In predicting the impact of illegal markets on rates of homicide, the contingencies about the type of product involved, the people who buy and sell it, and the larger social environment in which this commerce takes place are more important than the bare facts of illegal commerce. Little is presently known about the specific conditions that promote or retard the escalation of lethal violence in drug markets. One reason that little is known about the specific conditions that promote violence is that unjustified generalizations about the inevitable connection between violence and illegality have been the conventional wisdom about drugs in the United States.

There are three broad hypotheses that we believe best describe the relationship between drug markets and lethal violence. None of these has been tested in the social science literature on drugs and crime. First, the creation and expansion of illegal markets will produce extra homicides when social circumstances conducive to lethal violence already exist. If the people involved in making and selling illegal goods or services are violence-prone to begin with, then rates of life-threatening violence will increase with the creation or expansion of illegal markets.

Second, the creation or expansion of illegal markets might also increase homicides in some environments where a high rate of lethal violence has not existed previously. When violent persons enter nonviolent illegal markets, they may make the whole of the illegal market a more violent environment. In this way, the opportunities of an illegal market may also introduce lethal violence in some environments where it was not prevalent previously.

But there are illegal markets in the United States and retail drug markets in many nations that do not experience epidemic rates of lethal violence. The notion that illegal markets are a sufficient condition for lethal violence does not survive even cursory exposure to the many forms of non-drug criminality in the United States or to the national experience of most of Europe with most illicit drugs. There is no iron law that illicit markets will generate a high body count.

If these broad propositions are true, it is necessary to determine what aspects of the illegal markets in drugs and other commodities are most likely to promote or retard rates of lethal violence. Such data would also be useful for law enforcement policy. To date, the debate about decriminalization has proceeded as if only changes in the legal status of a commodity could be expected to influence the death rate from intentional killing. If other less basic policy shifts can either suppress violence or prevent its expansion, government policy should pay attention to some tactical changes in policy that might save lives without resolving the ultimate strategic issues.

If the hypotheses set forth are verified by investigation, the change in orientation that we would recommend for those concerned about drug-related violence reflects the same logic that we suggested for violence policy generally. The first step is to move away from the unquestioning assumption that all that is criminal is violent, and violent to the same degree. Instead, prudent policy will search for the specific elements of illegal markets that increase or decrease the death toll that is associated with these activities.

If the death rate from drug traffic is responsive to tactical shifts in the enforcement of drug prohibition, it will be necessary to determine how high a priority should be assigned to the reduction of the lethal violence associated with illegal drugs, as opposed to other illicit drug problems such as the incidence and prevalence of drug use, HIV transmission, drug overdose deaths, police corruption, and collateral property crimes committed by drug users. Those who approach illicit drug markets as a public health problem tend to assign high priority to the reduction of death and serious injury produced by drugs. From that perspective, systemic drug homicide would receive a priority rank close to that of HIV and drug overdoses as a threat to life, with the number of deaths and serious injuries and the ease with which they can be prevented helping to determine the priorities within life-threatening conditions.

There is, however, a prominent approach to drug control that might assign considerably less priority to reducing the death toll from illicit drug markets. What we have elsewhere called the "legalist" approach to drug law enforcement puts great stress on reduction in the incidence and prevalence of illegal drug use, and regards the health and violence consequences of illegal drug taking as less important than those other kinds of drug costs, and also less important than most other kinds of intentional homicide victimization (see Zimring and Hawkins 1992b:8–9, 10–15). The reason for downgrading the priority of those killed in systemic drug conflicts is that they are rarely innocent bystanders of the illicit drug trade. When one drug dealer shoots another it could be argued that the morbidity or mortality that results represents far less of a social cost than when the victims of violence are themselves innocent of any crime.

This kind of "assumption of risk" argument is distinguishable from downgrading the death toll from domestic violence because the victim chose to live with the perpetrator. Participating in the illegal drug markets is not only a voluntary choice like that involved in cohabitation or marriage, it is also illegal conduct. And while it would be unjustified to approve the death toll of noninnocent participants in the drug trade, there might not be a priori reason to suppose that such deaths should be given equal weight in making decisions about the allocation of scarce law enforcement and penal resources. The deaths of drug dealers may be regarded as social harms, but they need not, on this view, be regarded as social harms equivalent to the deaths of bystanders or of battered wives.

Yet assuming that the social loss from lethal violence can be properly measured by reference to the social standing and risk-generating activity of its immediate victims represents a dangerous oversimplification. When drug sellers shoot other drug sellers the communities in which these incidents occur experience citizen alarm and social disorganization that cause innocent people to suffer. The impact of lethal violence is always much more widely diffused than the actual harm inflicted on the immediate victims. Indeed, a substantial part of the fear and revulsion associated with the perceived crisis of illegal drugs in the late 1980s involved lethal violence associated with the growth of crack cocaine use. What if we can reduce lethal drug violence without making major inroads on drug sales and use?

Ironically, the ability to ameliorate systemic drug violence might reduce public resistance to drug decriminalization and at the same time make the case for the decriminalization of drugs less persuasive in an important respect. A significant part of the fear of drugs in the 1980s and 1990s has been fear of lethal violence. The existence of illegal markets without extensive lethal violence such as those of London and Amsterdam could reduce both citizen fear and also citizen support for stringent antidrug law enforcement. Fewer conspicuous casualties might lessen support for an unqualified war on drugs.

Yet the death toll from drug-related violence is also the rhetorical trump card frequently played by those critics who seek the repeal of the criminal sanctions on drugs. When Professor Milton Friedman suggests that all that stands between the United States and the revival of all-time low homicide rates is the repeal of criminal drug sanctions, he is implicitly arguing that only drastic action can reduce drug violence (Friedman, 1991:57). Tactical remedies for lethal drug violence would undercut the arguments for more radical strategic reform.

The analysis of lethal drug violence thus exemplifies many of the themes encountered in the analysis of lethal violence generally. The confusion of the specific problem of lethal violence with the general relationship between illegal drugs and crime has discouraged policy analysts from considering specific policy responses to death and serious injury. And consideration of the specific priority that should be accorded to the reduction of lethal violence has quickly illustrated the complexities and ironies that are inevitably encountered in that process.

III

PREVENTION

THE TWO CHAPTERS in this section concern the policy implications of identifying lethal violence as the central problem that diminishes the quality of American urban life. Chapter 10 examines how a clear priority on reducing lethal violence should change the substantive criminal law. The adjustments required to make the criminal law an effective instrument of violence prevention are many. The uncertainties encountered when making specific judgments about the effects of various rules are substantial.

Chapter 11 concerns the larger question of how a democratic government should organize and execute a program to reduce lethal violence. How should priorities be determined? How should problems be defined? What mistakes from comparable government programs should be avoided? What issues must be examined in a program to reduce the cost of lethal violence? How many resources need be and should be committed to reducing the deaths and injuries from interpersonal violence?

Making policy for the prevention of lethal violence involves a mixture of simple and complex issues. The complexity is encountered when seeking appropriate means to reduce violence and the fear of violence. The tactical issues in violence prevention are multifaceted and refractory. Specific policies will be established and evaluated on a trial and error basis. But the strategic choice is simple. The strategic core of government policy must be personal safety. And unvarying commitment to that priority has huge implications for the policy process.

10

Lethal Violence and the Criminal Law

How MIGHT THE CRIMINAL LAW better serve to reduce lethal violence? How much more prevention can be expected from a system that is almost the exclusive antiviolence agency of government now? This chapter addresses these questions by exploring the implications of making the prevention of life-threatening violence the priority concern of American criminal law.

We start our analysis of the means of violence prevention with the criminal law because it is the narrowest of the concerns to be addressed in this section. The penal law is only one mechanism that is required for a balanced program of lethal violence prevention, a necessary but not sufficient condition of public safety. But prevention of lethal violence should be the very highest priority of the criminal law. The only challenging questions about the use of criminal law as a means of reducing lethal criminal violence are questions of tactical choice rather than strategic priority. The primacy of life, of feelings of bodily security, and of being able to negotiate well-known environments without fear are the central concerns of the criminal law of every modern state. The high rate of life-threatening violence in the United States simply underscores the larger significance of this problem in the United States.

The task of this chapter is to imagine a criminal law in which safety from life-threatening violence is a dominant but not exclusive value. We would not argue that saving a single life justifies a billion-dollar investment in the criminal justice system or that policies that would produce 50,000 extra burglaries are worthwhile if one life fewer is lost. But making this concession is far from retreating to the amorphous language of general cost and benefit in crime control. The real-world trade-offs between preserving life and other values are close enough so that a preference for personal safety can serve as a practical guide to specific policies.

This analysis is divided into five sections. The first analyzes the substantive criminal law as both a cause and effect of violent behavior. The second outlines some of the major mechanisms available in the criminal law to achieve the partial prevention or diminution of life-threatening violence. The third discusses the appropriate criteria for making the choice between criminal law strategies. The fourth examines the criteria for choosing between the criminal law and other mechanisms designed to prevent or diminish lethal violence. And the final section reviews the reasons why across-the-board increases in penal severity might not result in reducing life-threatening violence.

Cause and Effect

Before discussing the ways in which the criminal law may influence violent behavior, we believe it is necessary to illustrate some of the ways in which the kind of violence experienced in a society may influence the provisions of substantive law and the way in which that law is applied in particular circumstances. A recurrent pattern that causes foreign observers to despair about American society and values is the case where a foreign visitor or student approaches or enters the dwelling of a stranger at night in the United States and is shot to death by the householder, who mistakes him for a burglar.

The violence itself generates negative publicity in countries like Scotland and Japan, the domiciles of two recent victims. But the subsequent failure to find the gun-toting householder guilty of any crime for his lethal mistake provokes even more pointed criticism of American criminal law and societal values. Some foreign commentators appear to believe that laxity in the enforcement of American criminal law is one of the main reasons why rates of violent crime in the United States are so high. In fact, what such cases best illustrate is the extraordinary pressure that high rates of violence exert on the standards of the criminal law. The greater the risk of violence that a citizen confronts, the more likely it is that judges and juries will find that citizens have acted reasonably when they have used violence to deal with a threatening stranger.

It is not fair to make judgments about criminal law and law enforcement in the United States without recognizing that the path between the criminal law and the social reality of lethal violence is a two-way street. The level of violence in a society can and should influence the nature of police work, criminal law standards for the justifiable use of deadly force, and many other ways in which a society responds to the risks of lethal violence.

One product of the way in which the threat of violence influences criminal law is the paradox of the justified use of force as an index of social well-being. If Smith is the only person in a crowded bar room with a loaded gun and he shoots someone, the chances that a prosector or a jury will conclude that his action was a justified use of deadly force would appear remote. In such circumstances, Smith's possession of an instrument of deadly force argues against the conclusion that the hostile action of another person in that bar created a reasonable belief that shooting the attacker was necessary to preserve his own life.

But what if two-thirds of the people drinking in that bar are carrying loaded guns? The greater manifest danger of Smith's physical environment now makes it much more likely that he is acting on a reasonable belief that his life is in danger when he shoots. One product of the proliferation of deadly weapons might well be a greater tendency for those who administer the criminal law to believe claims of self-defense.

The paradox of justification is this: the greater the proportion of violent events that result from bipolar lethal violence, the larger the proportion of violent acts that the law will accept as justified. The number and percentage of justified violent acts then becomes an index of social pathology. The more willing the law is to accept explanations for lethal violence, the more dysfunctional the societal circumstances that spawned this justifiable violent behavior. So what is not culpable behavior at the individual or "retail" level constitutes in the aggregate a picture of societal regression toward violence. The acquittal of the armed householder in Louisiana is discouraging not so much because of the legal standard that absolves him from liability, but because of the social forces that transform what the citizens of other countries might regard as paranoia into a belief that a Louisiana jury might regard as reasonable.

The paradox of justification is only one of the number of legal and behavioral responses to violence that are an important part of fin de siècle American life. Our police must be armed and must wear bulletproof vests because so many citizens carry guns—well over 90 percent of all killings of American police are committed with firearms. The pressure on both police and private citizens to carry and use guns is generated principally by the fear of guns in the hands of others. This phenomenon has many of the characteristics of a vicious circle. Widespread handgun possession and use is a major contributing cause of high rates of American homicide. But the principal reason why Americans buy guns and keep them loaded is the fear of crime generally and of lethal violence in particular.

Foreign observers who disapprove of America's social and legal tolerance of deadly force identify an important symptom of social pathology. But it is an error to place the blame on those who create and administer legal standards. Not the least of the corruptions produced by chronic fear of lethal violence is the creation of widespread tolerance of deadly force inspired by fear of bodily harm. But the problem is not those legal standards of necessity so much as it is the social conditions that force hard choices.

Third Cause

There is also the possibility that a patterned relationship between the provisions of the criminal law and rates of violence in a society might exist, because some of the same social forces that influence rates of violence also determine criminal law priorities. For example, assume that a particular culture abhors violent behavior and stigmatizes persons who engage in violence. That strong social value would tend to produce both relatively heavy penalties for unjustified acts of violence and relatively low rates of violent conduct among those persons who subscribed to the dominant social values. Under those circumstances, the severe criminal penalties in the law are neither the cause of the low rates of violence nor an effect of them. Instead, the cultural stigma associated with violence is a feature of social life that influences both the provisions of the criminal law and also the behavior of citizens, whether or not those legal provisions and rates of behavior have any influence on each other.

A similar third cause possibility exists in situations where tolerance of life-threatening violence is more pronounced. A culture that places high positive value on violent self-defense is unlikely to severely punish episodes involving violent defense of honor or property that may exceed the boundaries of the permissible use of force. A society that approves of the extensive use of personal force will be more apt to extenuate, if not entirely overlook, acts of violent self-help that do not measure up to the standards for excuse in the criminal law. That sort of social system might generate high rates of violence even if its punishment policy had little or no independent influence on its crime rate. The same social values that restrict the use of the criminal prohibition will also encourage violent self-help.

The existence and power of social values as a potential influence on both the criminal law and the rate of lethal violence makes the comparative assessment of the influence of penal codes on behavior a subtle and complicated process. The same attitudes and values that may influence rates of violence and the provisions of the criminal law may also be influenced by the way the law is enforced. No statistical formula can unravel the interconnections of criminal behavior, cultural values, and legal standards. Thus, the value of discussing the difficulties of causal attribution lies in the caution that such reservations might inspire, rather than in the provision of a curative algorithm. The fact that this is an unavoidable problem renders ignoring it more, rather than less, perilous in conducting sociolegal research.

Mechanisms of Prevention in Criminal Law

At least three different mechanisms of prevention are mentioned as ways in which the prohibitions and punishments of a criminal code might prevent criminal conduct or ameliorate the harm caused by crime: the educative and moralizing effect of punishment; the deterrent effect of the threat of punishment; and the incapacitative effect of those criminal punishments that deprive persons of the capacity to violate prohibitions, usually by means of secure confinement. Each of these mechanisms has potential for the prevention of life-threatening violence in a variety of different ways. This survey of the major mechanisms of the criminal law seeks to identify ways in which new programs might prevent life-threatening violence.

Educative and Moralizing Effect of Punishment

The educative and moralizing influence of criminal prohibitions and punishments is the least tangible of the commonly mentioned methods of crime prevention. The notion involved here is of the criminal law as a teacher of societal values. The publicized fact of the criminal prohibition demonstrates to a population that society views the prohibited behavior as wrong and also reinforces the population's already existing negative feelings about that conduct. Moreover, the punishment of offenders for particular violations becomes a separate moralizing and educative enterprise. It reinforces the negative social attributes of both the offense and those who commit it.

The separate consideration of these educative and moralizing influences of criminal punishment is most prominently associated with the writings of Johannes Andenaes in the 1960s and 1970s (Andenaes 1974). Students of punishment generally have acknowledged the probable existence of distinct educative and moralizing effects. But there has been little detailed analysis of how such effects are generated, modified, or neutralized in the administration of the penal law.

The severe punishments meted out to those convicted of murder, attempted murder, and life-threatening assault no doubt contribute to the shared social belief that those behaviors are morally wrong. But how might the educative and moralizing influence of criminal punishment be better used to prevent lethal violence? Where there is substantial social and legal consensus that a behavior is wrong, there is correspondingly little leeway for the educative and moralizing influence of the criminal law to improve its performance and prevent a larger number of offenses. It is where the social and legal messages about violence are mixed that the potential may exist for substantial additional prevention. The dynamic role of the criminal law and criminal punishment is much more important where social feelings are not well defined or are ambivalent.

The three specific areas where the further educational potential of the criminal law for violence prevention might best be tested are: the punishment of behavior that, while formally prohibited is traditionally not prosecuted, such as nonfatal domestic assault; the punishment of risk-generating behavior where the population traditionally has not regarded the behavior as serious, such as gun control infractions; and the redefinition of criminal law offenses so as to punish previously justified use of life-threatening force, such as the use of lethal countermeasures to protect property interests.

Removing the de facto exemptions from the criminal law of violence is one way to enhance prevention. The most important shift in morality for the criminal law in recent years has concerned the treatment of domestic violence cases by the police and the criminal courts. The changes being advocated and achieved in this branch of domestic violence policy have little to do with the formal legal definition of criminal conduct—"the law on the books"—and much more to do with the discretion exercised by legal officials—"the law on the streets." Shooting, stabbing, or beating a domestic partner has been criminal conduct throughout the twentieth century and for a long time before that. But this formal criminality was undermined by a tradition of nonprosecution of those who committed acts of violence against intimates, unless the injuries sustained in an attack were grievous. The tradition of nonarrest, nondetection, nonprosecution, and nonconviction in domestic violence cases was interpreted by many potential offenders as an implicit license.

For this reason, one major justification for more rigorous prosection of domestic violence cases was to revoke the implicit license to beat that previous policies conveyed. Did the reorientation of the justice system result in a reorienting of social values? There can be little doubt that hitting and other acts of physical force directed at a domestic partner are more negatively viewed by citizens of every age, gender, and class in the United States of 1997 than they were a generation before.

What is harder to determine is the extent to which the changes in criminal justice policy were a result of changes in attitude that preceded them rather than a cause of increasing social disrepute (Zimring and Hawkins 1970). In the intangible realm of attitude and value, it is hard to distinguish occasions when the criminal law is teaching a lesson to society from occasions when policemen and judges are changing their behavior in response to social pressures. The shifting perceptions of domestic violence in the United States after 1965 appear to be a case in which a change in social attitude and political pressure occurred before shifts in police and judicial behavior. But the changes in law enforcement reinforced and underscored the criminality and wrongfulness of domestic abuse, particularly after 1985.

The number of instances in which the criminal law can operate by itself in fashioning changes in citizen morality will be quite limited under a democratic system of government where citizen attitudes can nullify legal initiatives in a variety of ways. It is far more likely that the success stories regarding the use of criminal law enforcement as an instrument of social change will more closely resemble the interactive dance of legal and social changes that occurred in the case of domestic violence.

In such circumstances, it is difficult to isolate and measure the independent impact of the legal changes on behavior. The moralizing influence of the law is one of two intangible social forces operating at the same time on a large and diffuse audience. But saying that the role of the law is difficult to measure should not be equated with saying that the criminal law is unimportant. The effective criminalization of domestic violence in the United States was one of the most important legal reforms of the late twentieth century. Clearly the changes in attitude that have occurred already would have been much harder to sustain without the moralizing example of police and judicial sanctions.

One further issue concerns the type of domestic abuse most likely to decline as a result of attitude changes. The moral reorientation of domestic violence probably has had a more dramatic primary effect on the rates of less than life-threatening aggression than on deadly domestic attack. The reason for this is that the less serious forms of abuse had been more widely tolerated in the past. Shooting and stabbing a domestic partner were never regarded as benign. So a tightening of standards will probably bring down the rate of nonlethal abuse more than that of lethal abuse. Of course, if a common cause of lethal outcome in domestic violence is a predictable progression from the chronic to the life-threatening, either as a continuation of force by the initial aggressor or as a reaction to that force by the initial victim, then lethal violence rates might decline almost at the same rate of nonlethal abuse.

CRIMINALIZING RISK

A second category of behavior where the educative and moralizing example of the criminal law might not have exhausted its potential is the risk-generating infractions that are not intended to produce harm or cause injury, but all too frequently do so. The leading example of changing views of risk-generating behavior is drunk driving (Laurence et al. 1988). Very few of the millions of Americans who drive on highways with positive blood alcohol readings intend any harm to themselves or to others. But injury and death are the recurrent result of drunken driving. Because both drinking and driving are widely distributed behaviors, there was a long-standing tendency in the United States and in many other developed countries to regard driving under the influence of alcohol as a technical infraction of the traffic law, but not as truly criminal in the sense of an immoral act.

A combination of public education and legal change has engineered a thorough revolution in public attitudes toward drunk driving in most Western nations over the past generation (Zimring 1988). In the mid-1960s, drinking and driving was widely regarded as a serious matter only in Scandinavia. By the 1990s, drunk driving was the object of stern disapproval all over Europe, throughout North America, and in many other areas. The association of high blood alcohol with fatal collisions in the public mind became the basis for the moral reevaluation of driving under the influence of alcohol.

The role of criminal law enforcement in changing public attitudes toward drinking and driving was not unimportant. Again, however, distinguishing between changes in law enforcement that caused changes in public attitudes and changes in law enforcement that were caused by changing public attitudes is a far from easy task. In most countries, drunk driving became a much higher priority for the police and the criminal courts during the 1970s and the 1980s. Random stops, portable blood alcohol testing equipment, and increased police concern with detection widely increased the arrest rate for driving while intoxicated. And the number of persons punished or subjected to compulsory treatment as a result of drunk driving offenses increased substantially wherever drunk driving law enforcement became a high police priority.

The behavioral results of campaigns against drunk driving have been dramatic. By most estimates of alcohol-related fatal crashes, reductions in the amount and degree of driving while intoxicated save thousands of lives each year in the United States. From the standpoint of the impact on public health, the reevaluation of drunk driving has been the greatest success story of the criminal law in the modern era. One reason that the impact of this reevaluation has been so dramatic is because of the extraordinary public tolerance of driving while intoxicated that preceded the change.

Are there analogous risk-generating behaviors associated with lethal violence where the criminal law might lead to a reevaluation of behavior? One obvious candidate in the United States is the large number of attempts to regulate the transfer and use of deadly weapons. Many laws restricting the carrying of concealed firearms, forbidding all but prescribed methods of selling and buying guns, and forbidding particular population groups such as convicted felons and minors from acquiring or owning guns are currently regarded as involving only technical infractions rather than real crimes by many citizens. The key question is whether a combination of public education and strict law enforcement will lead citizens to regard transgressions as morally wrong because they increase the risk of lethal attacks.

The analogy with driving while intoxicated is a limited one. One important difference between driving while intoxicated and violating gun control laws is that the firearms injury is intended by someone in most violent assaults with guns. The nonaccidental quality of the infliction of injury with guns makes the relationship between a gun law violation and the subsequent injury or death seem more attenuated. Why regard the man who transfers the gun to the offender as a cause of the deadly attack when the intentions of the attacker played such an obvious causal role? If the evil that men intend is the major cause of death from violence, then those who provide only the instruments of violence can be regarded as playing a relatively minor role.

The most attractive candidates for moral opprobrium among gun control law violations are those cases where the intention of the person who shoots plays a less than overwhelming role in the moral evaluation of the lethal act. When a small child discharges a gun, we are much more interested in where the gun was obtained than in assessing the child's blameworthiness. That is because we do not expect small children to possess the capacity to safely handle loaded weaponry. For this reason, the most attractive target of current opportunity for taking gun control violations seriously is the enforcement of laws that forbid the transfer of handguns to minors. The more innocent and immature the perpetrator, the greater the culpability of those who provided that agent with access to instruments of deadly force.

The violation of gun control laws is not considered a serious matter in the folkways of the United States if the person who violates those laws intends no injury to result. This laxness of attitude is both an opportunity to change behavior (if a reorientation campaign succeeds) and also a warning that changing attitudes about gun transfers will be difficult. A shift in focus from concern about crime generally to priority concern with lethal outcomes might make the enforcement of firearms control more attractive to the general public. But creating a moral equivalence between unauthorized gun transfers and drunk driving will not be an easy sell.

THE LAW OF DEADLY FORCE

Most of the criminal laws relating to murder, manslaughter, and aggravated battery are the legacy of a long and uncontroversial tradition; so that the educative potential of legal change in this area appears quite small. Furthermore, criminal punishments for murder and life-threatening assault are close to the top of the scale for criminal punishment generally so that the exemplary potential of criminal punishment already has been fully realized.

There is one possible change in the legal standard for what constitutes the justifiable use of deadly force that would have a major influence on the educative and moralizing force of criminal law, if accepted by the population. Current law and practice in the United States allows the use of deadly force to the extent that it is necessary to prevent burglary. A restriction of the privilege to use deadly force to circumstances where death or bodily injury are at risk would quickly test the criminal law's capacity to alter citizen behavior. Such a change is unlikely, but not impossible.

As the discussion of the paradox of justification in the first section of this chapter implied, the justifiable use of deadly force by police and private citizens is a large-scale enterprise in the United States. The most reliable indicatior of the level of life-threatening force is the statistics collected by police authorities on deaths resulting from such force. In 1992 the Uniform Crime Reporting Program of the Federal Bureau of Investigation counted 415 killings by police officers that were classified as justifiable (U.S. Department of Justice, Federal Bureau of Investigation, 1992:22, Table 2.15). An additional 348 justifiable killings were reported to have been committed by private citizens that year (ibid., Table 2.16). The 763 cases reported in 1992 were about 3 percent of the criminal homicide total. On an international basis, however, the number of justifiable killings seems larger. The 348 killings by U.S. civilians that were classified as justifiable in 1992 constitute a larger volume than the total number of homicides that year in England and Wales. And the number of justified killings for that year in the United States by police and private citizens exceeds the total volume of homicide in France.

There are no national statistics available to provide separate estimates of justifiable deaths and injuries inflicted without imminent threat of injury or death. There are indications that the number of cases involving burglars is substantial and the number of shootings of "fleeing felons" by both police and private citizens is not trivial. There is a tendency for citizens to regard any shooting in the self-defense category not prohibited by the criminal law to have received the positive sanction of the authorities. For that reason, citizens are frequently eager to use lethal force in crime prevention whenever they think it is allowed.

When a shopkeeper kills a burglar, community sentiments usually side with the merchant. So that even if a concerted effort was made to restrict the use of justification in killing cases, it is not known how far shifting standards in the statute book would be reflected in changed enforcement activities on the streets. But if any substantial restriction were to occur, it would be a major experiment in the extent to which stateways can change folkways.

The prospects for a rapid shift in response to changing legal standards would be much greater among police than among private citizens. The existence of a command structure, an abundance of before-the-fact training and instruction opportunities and a detailed reward and punishment structure within the police department make changes in police behavior somewhat easier to engineer than citizen response. The average police officer is also much more likely to be involved in a potential use of deadly force. Private citizens are usually not at high risk of becoming victims of crime and they do not pledge obedience in a command structure. Extensive publicity of criminal prosecution and punishment would have the potential for making any change in the legal standards for lethal violence against nonviolent or fleeing felons widely known. But the police are much easier to retrain.

One striking confirmation of the impact of changing legal standards for police use of deadly force comes from a U.S. Supreme Court judgment in 1984 that invalidated state laws that gave police the authority to use deadly force to arrest burglars and others who had not committed violent crimes or otherwise threatened violence. In those states where the decision had the effect of cutting back on police authority to use deadly force, the number of killings by police dropped 24 percent after the judgment, or twice the decline noted in jurisdictions where the law of arrest was not changed by the Supreme Court. A number of other patterns that are consistent with the conclusion that the change in law produced the change in killings are also reported (Tennenbaum 1994).

One reason why further restrictions on the use of deadly force are not likely is a long tradition of public approval for violent citizen self-defense against property felons. The very attitudes that make the public educational role of criminal law of substantial significance also greatly diminish the likelihood that further restriction on the use of deadly force would command a legislative majority. When acts defined as criminal are not widely regarded as wrong, credible and effective law enforcement is difficult to maintain and irregular enforcement undermines the educational and moralizing influence of the criminal sanction. So the use of that sanction as what Professor Andenaes called "a moral eye opener" (Andenaes 1974:116) is most difficult to achieve in those settings where its contribution to crime prevention would be most productive.

Deterrence

The deterrent objective of the criminal law is to dissuade potential offenders from committing crime by threatening punishment. Pure deterrence can be distinguished from the educative and moralizing influence of punishment because changing attitudes about the wrongfulness of the conduct is not supposed to be an influence on the felicific calculus of the potential offender. The currency of deterrence is the fear of pain, disgrace, and the deprivation of liberty rather than the moral commitment of the threatened audience to the values that the criminal law serves. The same threat can teach and frighten simultaneously.

How might the deterrent strategies of the criminal law in the United States be modified to better serve the goal of reducing deaths and serious injuries? We address this question in three stages. First, we outline the different ways in which deterrent threats might serve to preserve life and prevent bodily injury from intended harm. Second, we identify some of the tensions between the different tasks of deterrent threats that compete for priority in the calibration of a particular punishment attached to a specific crime. Third, we address the extent to which a priority for the preservation of life helps us to choose between the conflicting objectives of deterrence in the control of violence.

There are three goals that deterrent threats should pursue in an attempt to minimize deaths and serious injuries. The first of these is to manipulate the punitive consequences threatened for conviction of crime so as to minimize the aggregate number of offenses committed. Even if the volume of total crime is not a major factor in the death rate from violence, the other social benefits of a low crime rate justify deterring crimes generally.

The second objective of the criminal law threat as an instrument of public health is to discourage those particular types of criminal behavior that produce especially high risks of death and serious injury to victims. This objective goes beyond the attempt to discourage crime generally and singles out for special attention those offenses that produce the highest rates of death and serious injury. The difference in priority between this and deterrent systems that seek to minimize all crime is the special attention reserved for life-threatening varieties of criminal activity. A deterrence policy that seeks to reduce crime generally will attempt to use the threat of punishment to discourage both robbery and burglary. A deterrence policy that concentrates on the prevention of those crimes that generate particularly high rates of serious injury and death will be more concerned with the prevention of robbery than with the prevention of burglary.

The final task of deterrent threats is to discourage the killing and serious injury that may occur in the course of potentially violent crimes. The distinction between this final task of leaving incentives in the penal threat to deter intentional killing and discouraging the more dangerous general patterns of crime is that the particular concern of this third objective is the reduction of the death rate from those robberies, kidnappings, and burglaries that were not in fact deterred by extensive threats. A large difference between the punishment threatened for robbery and the punishment threatened for robbery murder is an expression of this third objective.

These multiple tasks of deterrent threats are all well worth pursuing, but the range of punishments available to be threatened is finite; thus, the different types of crime prevention through deterrence must compete with each other for the wide distinctions in threatened punishment that might attract the attention of potential offenders. The best way to deter the general range of unaggravated property felonies that occur in the United States might well be with a large base penalty to be imposed on conviction for any felony property crime.

But the problem with a heavy penalty for the least serious of all property felonies from the standpoint of deterrence is that this will limit the law's capacity to discourage the more dangerous offenses by differential threats of punishment for life-threatening crimes. If most people who steal are sent to prison this would certainly serve the law's broad obligation to deter crime generally. But a smaller expected punishment for the unaggravated theft of property would produce a large difference in the punishment threatened for theft as opposed to armed robbery.

It seems inevitable that a choice has to be made between the sheer quantity of crime deterred and policies that might deter fewer crimes yet produce a mix of offenses of less inherent risk to victim's lives. Should we prefer a policy that minimizes the total number of property crimes yet generates 10 percent more robberies, or a policy that results in fewer robberies but more larcenies and burglaries? Only our ignorance of the marginal deterrent impact of different penalties has prevented us from directly confronting this kind of policy trade-off.

The situation is further complicated by the need for a deterrence strategy that keeps some punishment in reserve so that those who do commit life-threatening offenses such as armed robbery, kidnapping, and carjacking still have incentives not to injure or kill their victims. However much the criminal justice system wishes to deter crime generally, and life-threatening crimes like armed robbery and kidnapping more specifically, any rational system of deterrent threats will reserve an ample difference in punishment to separate the kidnapper who releases his victim from the kidnapper who kills.

The three distinct goals of a system of deterrent threats are in competition with one another because only a finite range of threatened punishments is available for the entire system. A system that wishes to scare off potential offenders from all criminal conduct wants to threaten substantial amounts of punishment for all offenders. A system that wants to reduce the rate of inherently dangerous felonies wishes to maximize the distinction between the punishment threatened for nonviolent felonies like larceny and the punishment threatened for more violent potential alternative felonies like robbery. But the higher the penalty threatened for larceny, the harder it will be to create a highly visible distinction between the punishment threatened for robbery and larceny. Finally, any system that wants to minimize loss of life aims for a sharp distinction between crimes that kill and crimes where lethal violence is avoided.

The criminal law in the Anglo-American world wishes to achieve all three of these goals. But the conflict between these objectives as points of emphasis for a deterrent system usually has been ignored in both scholarly literature and policy debate. The distinction between crime prevention generally and differential deterrence for more serious offenses was discussed in an earlier work on deterrence where so-called "fortress" and "stepladder" threat management strategies were contrasted (Zimring and Hawkins 1973:203–208). Two decades later, an economic theory to the same effect was put forward (Friedman and Sjostrom 1993). There has been no empirical assessment of the relative efficacy of the "fortress" and "stepladder" approaches. Indeed, since the values protected at each juncture are measured in different ways, a unified statement of costs and benefits might be impossible.

But choosing to emphasize the prevention of death and life-threatening violence as the preferred objective of the deterrent system creates a tendency to favor policies that achieve the differential deterrence of violent crime generally and of crimes that kill over a system that devotes a larger amount of effort to deterring all crime. As between the second and third objectives, a preference for saving lives does not generate a preferred strategy unless we know the life-saving magnitude that can be achieved by deterring robberies with guns by increasing the threatened punishment for gun use, as opposed to the magnitude of life saving that would result if the penalty for gun robbery is kept lower, but the gap between the penalty for gun robbery and robbery murder is kept larger. A perspective that emphasizes the prevention of lethal violence gives us a common standard for choosing between these strategies. But it cannot provide the rates of exchange that are involved in a real-world contrast in policy emphasis.

Indeed, discourse about deterrence at this level of specificity is fact-free. This is a shortcoming that embarrasses all but the bravest criminologists, although it has no apparent deterrent effect on economic theorists of law (Friedman and Sjostrom 1993). The type of empirical question that needs to be answered before we can allocate punishment threat resources between crimes that carry a high risk of lethal outcomes and only the sub-class of those crimes that produce a killing is very specific. Would increasing the penalty for robbery with a loaded gun result in a greater saving of lives than keeping the threatened punishment for gun robbery lower so as to maximize the gap between gun robberies that do not result in injury and those that result in injury or death?

There is no a priori answer to a question as specific as that. Moreover, reliable information about the trade-off in lives saved between avoiding gun robbery and avoiding robbery killing may not generalize to other settings. The calculus of lives saved may be quite different for a comparison of additional threatened punishment for gun assaults versus maintaining a maximum gap between gun attacks and gun killings. For example, the fact that gun assaults more frequently produce woundings may make the prevention of assault a more efficient method of savings lives than maximizing the gap between fatal and nonfatal shootings. And this might be the case even if a wider gap between gun robbery and gun robbery killing was more efficacious. The questions generated by the competition between deterrent strategies call for very specific empirical answers.

There are some issues of deterrence policy where the identification of the saving of life as the policy priority has a decisive impact. One example of this is the toy gun conundrum in the definition of armed robbery. There are two reasons why including toy guns in the definition of offenses that call for enhanced punishment can be justified even though toy guns do not risk death and injury to victims. The first is a matter of proof. If the criminal prosecution needs to establish that a gun used in a robbery was in fact capable of discharging bullets, there will be difficulties encountered in the prosection of many armed robberies when evidence is not available about the type of weapons used at the time of trial. If that were the only justification for including toy gun cases, the law could allow for an affirmative defense that the weapon used was not dangerous to life and provide access to the reduced punishment only to those who could prove the innocuousness of the weapon.

The second reason why authorities may regard harsh punishment as necessary for toy gun robberies is that the use of a realistic toy gun is an effective method of achieving success in robbery when the nature of the weapon is undiscovered by the victim (McClintock and Gibson 1961: 25). So prosecutors desiring to punish more effective methods of robbery more severely might consider the use of a convincing toy gun to be an aggravating circumstance. But if saving lives rather than frustrating robbery is the law's primary objective, the robbery defendant should be encouraged to use toy guns in the commission of crime and allowed to prove his use of innocuous methods at trial. The reason for this is clear. Toy guns represent the lowest risk of death or injury that exists—at least for the victim.

The other major conclusion that can be reached on the existing evidence is that the deterrent power of the criminal law should be concentrated on those offenses that carry relatively high risks of victim injury and death. Most property crimes are committed in circumstances where the physical security of the victim is not at risk. Such is the case with the vast majority of all larcenies and automobile thefts. Victim injury and death are also quite rare in burglary. The death risk from the average burglary in the United States is one-fiftieth the death rate from robbery (see Chapter 4).

So, if deterrence is the primary motive of a law enforcement strategy and the saving of lives is a dominant objective, relatively light punishment for nonviolent property offenders might be the preferred outcome on the basis of criteria of qualitatively informed crime prevention. Under such circumstances, however, there may be a conflict between punishment policies for nonviolent crime that should be invoked for deterrent purposes and those that might minimize the number of lives saved through the operation of incapacitation. This type of conflict is discussed in the third part of this chapter.

Incapacitation

One further way in which criminal punishment can reduce life-threatening violence is by restraining persons who are at risk of committing further offenses so that they are incapable of doing so regardless of their intentions. While deterrence strategies are designed to influence the potential offender's will to violate the law, incapacitation strategies are designed to limit an offender's ability to commit crimes. The primary instrument of incapacitation in the American criminal justice system is secure penal confinement. While an individual is locked up in a prison or jail, he or she is unable to commit offenses in the community. There are other methods of incapacitation associated with criminal punishment in the United States that we have discussed elsewhere (Zimring and Hawkins 1995:155–172), but secure confinement is currently the dominant method of restraint directed at the prevention of life-threatening violence.

Three different types of incarceration policy can prevent lethal violence in the community by locking up persons who would otherwise have committed such acts while at liberty. First, a sentencing policy that restricts imprisonment to those individuals who are predicted to be at special risk of committing life-threatening violence, and lengthens the terms of incarceration for such individuals, will reduce violence to the extent that the prediction technology is accurate. This strategy is predictive confinement of individuals.

Second, a sentencing strategy that reserves a substantial share of all imprisonment for those persons who are convicted of crimes of high-risk violence will prevent violent acts that would otherwise have been committed by such offenders. If persons already convicted of violent offenses are more likely than other offenders to engage in life-threatening behavior in the future, then the number of person years of prison devoted to this policy of incapacitation for convicted violent offenders will prevent a relative larger amount of violent crime for each year of imprisonment than a sentencing policy that treats violent and nonviolent offenders alike. But while an imprisonment policy that does not single out violent offenders might be less efficient per each additional year of incarceration in reducing violent crime, a general prison policy that imprisons many more convicted offenders of all types may prevent more total violent crime if it results in much higher levels of imprisonment than more specially targeted policies.

All three types of incapacitation strategy can be found in American sentencing law and practice. The additional confinement of persons believed to be at special risk of future violent behavior has been attempted with clinical prediction of future violence in both civil and criminal confinement settings (see Monahan 1988). The singling out of individual offenders at special risk because of prior personal history has been much discussed as "selective incapacitation" in the United States (Greenwood 1982; Blumstein et al. 1986). Very few of the evaluations of these strategies have been concerned with the prediction of lethal violence. The empirical results of those policies and practices that have been evaluated suggest that those supposed to be at high risk of committing future violent acts are somewhat more likely than other convicted offenders to be violent in the future. But the large number of individuals falsely predicted to be dangerous under such protocols raise serious questions about the justice of any substantial extension of penal confinement that is based on individual predictions (see Morris 1974, 1984).

A general policy that allocates imprisonment to those convicted of acts of life-threatening violence may also provide more incapacitation of violent behavior for every person-year of imprisonment than would a less selective imprisonment policy. An empirical test of this would be the assessment of whether violent offenders are more likely to commit future violent offenses than other offenders. But the most effective method of reducing the volume of life-threatening violent offenses would probably be the incarceration for the longest period of time of the broadest cross-section of offenders that could be identified.

There is, for this reason, an important distinction between the efficiency of incapacitation policies in reducing violence and the effectiveness of incapacitation policies in reducing homicide and life-threatening injuries. The most efficient policies are those policies that are likely to generate the largest amount of prevention for each additional year of confinement. These policies will probably be limited to a relatively small group of individuals and will prevent a total volume of crime of only very modest proportions. Those policies that are least selective in choosing candidates for confinement may be locking up nonlife-threatening offenders ninety times in every hundred trials. But if the additional number they confine is sufficiently large, the total amount of violence avoided by incapacitation will be greater. In terms of gross effectiveness, the unselective policy will prevent the greatest volume of crime.

The contrast between efficiency and effectiveness illustrates a potential distinction between deterrence policies and incapacitation policies with regard to the prevention of violence. In discussing deterrence, we showed how the various different goals of a deterrence policy compete with one another for priority. But the various goals of incapacitation such as preventing violent crime and preventing nonviolent crime are only in a zero-sum competition with one another if the level of resources that can be devoted to penal confinement is fixed or limited. If not, the least selective policies with respect to violence may still produce high levels of gross effectiveness.

Referring to the total volume of lethal violence prevented by various incapacitation policies leads to the question of whether it is possible to estimate the amount of life-threatening violence that is prevented by current incapacitation policy, or that might be prevented by changes in incapacitation policy, as a proportion of the total lethal violence. The proportion of all violent acts prevented by an incapacitation policy will vary with the degree to which that type of act is concentrated in a distinctively "criminal" population of active offenders. Jacqueline Cohen and José Canela-Cacho estimated that the recent expansion of the U.S. prison population was responsible for an incapacitation-saving equivalent to 10 to 15 percent of robbery (Cohen and Canela-Cacho 1994). Zimring, Hawkins, and Ibser found no consistent relationship in the volume of violent offenses associated with a tripling of the imprisonment rate in California during the 1980s, although there was some indication of a decrease in forcible rape (Zimring et al. 1995:4–7).

Making the prevention of life-threatening violence the dominant objective of criminal justice policy need not influence the choice of persons to incapacitate as long as there are no significant limitations on the availability of incapacitation facilities. As long as there is a general policy of preferring prison that locks up many more offenders, it will also tend to increase the amount of violent crime prevented by the use of incapacitation. Locking up burglars and robbers will not interfere with the incapacitation of violent criminals if the additional incapacitation of burglars does not diminish the resources available to restrain those convicted of robbery. If imprisonment is a limited resource, however, a priority concern for the prevention of violence would argue for concentrating on the incarceration of those who are at a greater risk of indulging in life-threatening violence if not restrained.

In the terms introduced earlier in this section, limiting the amount of space available for imprisonment shifts the emphasis from incapacitation policies that maximize the total number of violent crimes prevented regardless of the extent of the imprisonment necessary to achieve it to those policies that maximize the likelihood that each individual year of incarceration will prevent life-threatening violence. If the space available for imprisonment is limited, the best way to increase the *effectiveness* of the system as we have defined it is to increase the *efficiency* of preventive imprisonment. Imposing a limit on total incarceration thus creates competition between violence prevention and other crime prevention goals that an incapacitation policy might serve. As we shall see, however, assuming finite prison space for an incapacitation strategy might reduce the conflict between incapacitation as opposed to deterrence and education as methods of violence prevention.

Conflict Between Purposes and Means

Coherent criminal justice policy must not deal with the purposes of criminal punishment one at a time, but, rather, policies must be selected that maximize the degree to which educative, deterrent, and incapacitative mechanisms interact to maximize the prevention of life-threatening violence. To the extent that resources can be devoted to specialized law enforcement, a violence prevention strategy must also select the mix of targeted offenses and offenders that will yield the maximum prevention of life-threatening violence.

As a general matter, it does not appear that there are any major conflicts between using the educational and moralizing mechanism of the criminal law to reduce life-threatening violence and manipulating deterrent threats to produce the same effect. To most effectively mobilize the educational potential of the criminal law, it would seem necessary to convince audiences that crimes that risk causing death or bodily injury to victims are more reprehensible than other types of crime although less so than actually killing. The hierarchical scaling required for these messages seems similar to that required for maximum deterrent efficacy.

Conflict of purposes may be quite substantial between maximum deterrence and maximum incapacitation if there are no significant limits on the capacity of a society to imprison its citizens. Maximum deterrence might downgrade the punishment of nonviolent crime to create a larger gap between unaggravated crime and life-threatening violence, whereas the best method of increasing the aggregate amount of violence prevented through incapacitation would be to lock up as many offenders as possible for a longer time. The dilemma is this: Using imprisonment more selectively would decrease the total effectiveness of the prison as an incapacitation device, while using the threat of imprisonment indiscriminately would reduce the special salience of the threats attached to the commission of life-threatening felonies and life-threatening injuries.

Ironically, scarcity of penal resources may avoid a conflict between deterrence and incapacitation. As soon as an incapacitation policy must recognize fixed limits on the amount of imprisonment it can impose, it may be much easier to harmonize the deterrent and incapacitative methods of reducing violence. When only limited space is available, an incapacitation policy begins to look for persons with a particularly high likelihood of committing violence and those targets may turn out to be persons who have committed violent offenses previously. As soon as an incapacitation policy is pursuing efficiency, the tendency will be to reserve imprisonment for offenses of violence and the incapacitation and deterrent strategies of maximizing violence prevention can be harmonized. It is only when some nonviolent offenders are at a known high risk of future violence that deterrent and incapacitation agendas will conflict.

Punishing Risk versus Punishing Harm

Because the resources needed to enforce the law and punish offenders are limited, the various different types of harm that criminal laws seek to minimize find themselves involved in a competition for special priority in law enforcement. Securities fraud, automobile theft, rape, and homicide are all prohibited by the criminal law. But which crime should receive special emphasis when extra police and prison cells are to be allocated?

A policy that places special emphasis on the prevention of life-threatening violence helps to resolve some, but by no means all, of the competing claims for law enforcement resources. Placing special emphasis on the prevention of life-threatening violence gives a substantial advantage to homicide when homicide and securities fraud compete for extra law enforcement resources. But what about a competition between extra punishment for robberies that kill, extra punishment for robberies committed with guns, and additional punishment of all robberies? All three strategies are intended to reduce the same kind of life-threatening violence. For that reason, referring to a general preference for reducing lethal violence does not push the conflict between conflicting means to the same end to any obvious conclusion.

One recurrent conflict in using the criminal law as an instrument for the prevention of lethal violence is that between policies targeting extra punishment to the worst-case situation where the maximum harm risked by violent crime occurs and policies that provide extra punishment for behaviors that risk lethal consequences whenever such persons are apprehended for violating the law. The distinction here is between punishment of harm (e.g., additional punishment when the robber kills) and punishment of the risk of harm (e.g., additional punishment for carrying loaded guns or for armed robbery).

Are there general principles that tell us when an emphasis on the punishment of risk makes more sense or when an emphasis on the punishment of harm is superior? Whenever harm is unintended, as in the case of drunk driving, an intuitive preference is for the provision of extra punishment for all drunk drivers rather than the small subsample of drunk drivers involved in cases where death or serious injury result. Punishment of risk rather than of harm seems both more just and more likely to produce deterrence. But where the additional harm prohibited by the criminal law is often intended by the offender, there is no a priori principle that resolves the risk versus harm conflict. Should an extra million dollars' worth of resources go into enforcing gun control laws, punishing those who rob with guns, or punishing those who shoot to wound or kill during a robbery?

Where the risk of death or injury is regarded as an inevitable byproduct of other criminal behaviors, singling out the worst-result cases for more severe punishment does not appear promising. But what about encouraging safe gun robbery when the robber's choices while armed will affect the chances that death or injury may result? The only standard that recommends itself in such cases is pragmatic.

The pragmatic basis for a decision between emphasizing the punishment of risk versus the punishment of harm is a preference for the result that will maximize the saving of life with available resources. If the value of life and physical security is what justifies giving priority to the prevention of life-threatening violence, then the life-saving efficiency of alternative approaches should determine how additional resources are invested. The problem is that data on the differential effectiveness of different combinations of antiviolence strategies are all but nonexistent. Under current conditions, a standard can be suggested but not applied.

Supplements and Alternatives

Just as important choices must be made within criminal law when allocating resources for the prevention of violence, the wide variety of different ways in which a government may seek to reduce violence ultimately require choices between criminal law enforcement and many other kinds of public investment that possess potential for the reduction of life-threatening violence. Our concluding chapter discusses some of the wide variety of methods available for reducing losses from violence. And while many of the methods of controlling the environment involve the criminal justice system, there is a considerable number of strategies of environmental control that rely on public financial incentives and on civil and regulatory legal provisions.

Given the extensive range of the antiviolence action available to government, what should be the criteria for choice? This specific question has not been addressed in any literature we have identified. However, sentiments frequently expressed in crime control debates in the United States suggest two rather different broad decisional frameworks for the selection of weapons in a campaign against lethal violence. On the one hand, there is a pragmatic approach that would make further investment in the criminal law compete on an equal footing with noncriminal law means of violence prevention. This is the result that public health approaches would favor. The sole criterion for determining the winner would be cost-effectiveness.

A pragmatic judgment would involve a straightforward choice as to whether extra resources to combat taxicab robberies should be invested in extra police and prosecutors or whether they should be invested in the acquisition of extra bulletproof safety shields between the driver and passenger compartments. It would favor the strategy that provided the largest measure of life saving for dollars invested. Alternative paths to violence prevention would be chosen without a general preference in favor of or against punishment.

A moralistic approach to violence prevention would prefer recourse to strategies that would maximize punishment of the guilty and minimize the inconvenience to innocent parties. From this moralistic perspective, the suffering of offenders is a public good; while the inconvenience and suffering of persons other than the law violators is a substantial cost. Only if the calculus of cost effectiveness greatly favors a noncriminal approach that inconveniences the innocent will an American moralist prefer it.

Because the moralist and public health position have only been expressed in sound bites of sentiment, it is difficult for us to determine whether those who express those moralist sentiments are in favor of a cost–benefit calculus that carefully measures citizen inconvenience, or whether they would regard a cost–benefit calculation of any kind as an inappropriate basis for decision.

There may be a further dimension to this conflict. Many who express moralistic sentiments would resist choosing evenhandedly between policies that punish risk and policies that punish harm on the ground that intended harm deserves more punishment. Moralistic sentiments are expressed by persons who oppose penal law regulation of risks such as gun control, as in the slogan "Punish criminals, not gun owners." In the case of drunken driving, the moralistic sentiment seems to have changed over time because of the shift in public attitudes toward drunk driving as morally offensive. Now that the drunk driver's risk-generating crime is regarded as more serious, his punishment is less troublesome. So a moralist would prefer investing resources only in the punishment of "real crime."

If moralistic sentiments are taken only to suggest a broader calculus of cost and benefit, there are two points in the moralistic position that deserve serious attention. First, the inconvenience and restricted liberty imposed on law-abiding citizens by governmental regulation in order to reduce lethal violence are costs that should be recognized when a choice must be made between strategies. Second, the suffering experienced by convicted offenders as a result of the official sanctions imposed through the criminal justice process should not be regarded as an unmitigated public harm.

Both lessons of the moralist critique deserve serious consideration. The cost of governmentally required citizen compliance surely is part of the public cost of prevention. And the punishment of the guilty is certainly not equivalent to the punishment of the innocent from a public policy perspective. Yet the suffering imposed by criminal punishment on the offender should also not be ignored in calculating the cost of the criminal law. Even Jeremy Bentham, who believed in the prevention of crime simply by "intimidation or terror of the law," also observed that "all punishment is mischief: all punishment in itself is evil" (Bentham 1841a:83, 1841b:396).

The Perversity of Crime Wars

The analysis in the preceding sections of this chapter provides a theoretical explanation for the failure of generalized anticrime crusades to successfully reduce the risks of lethal violence. The disappointing impact of general crime crackdowns on life-threatening criminal violence recently has been demonstrated. The tripling of California's rate of imprisonment over the 1980s produced a substantial reduction in two of the Federal Bureau of Investigation's seven index crime felonies—burglary and larceny—but no consistent and measurable decrease over the decade in homicide or in any of the violent index offenses (Zimring and Hawkins 1995:117–120; Zimring et al. 1995:5–7).

That sort of outcome produces anger and frustration on the part of those who see the most important mission of the criminal justice system to be the protection of life and physical integrity. One natural reaction to the lack of measurable reduction in lethal violence is to call for larger doses of the same penal countermeasures that have characterized present penal policy. But if general crackdowns on crime are the wrong medicine for the disease of lethal violence, then doubling the dose presented is unlikely to speed the patient's recovery.

Why might a general "get tough" policy be the wrong medicine to bring about the reduction of high lethality violence? To the extent that the prevention of violence is enhanced by a large difference in the punishment of life-threatening and non-life-threatening offenses, any shift in penal policy that fails to widen the gap may not enhance the moralizing and educative message that lethal violence is especially wrong. Further, to the extent that general increases in the severity of penal policy narrow the gap between the punishment for dangerous and nondangerous offenses, the law's educative and moralizing emphasis on violence is actually diminished by across-the-board increases in penal severity. When most of the persons who go to prison are violent offenders, the distinctiveness of that crime category is enhanced. When many more nonviolent offenders are sentenced to prison as well, the distinction between the dangerous and the nondangerous that the difference in imprisonment policy was designed to underscore becomes blurred. So that even if the absolute severity associated with violent offenses increases in a general crime crackdown, the relative severity of the punishments of these offenses may diminish.

This distinction between the absolute and relative severity of punishment for crime is also an important matter in assessing the impact of punishments as deterrents to lethal violence. If the punishments for both robbery and burglary increase, but the punishments for burglary increase more than those for robbery, the gap between the punishment for robbery and the punishment for burglary has actually narrowed. Insofar as a utilitarian calculus animates potential offenders' decisions, this will tend to produce a higher ratio of robberies to burglaries than under the previous and more lenient regime.

There is a further problem of scaling effect that inhibits the ability of general increases in the severity of criminal punishment to produce reductions in lethal violence. To the extent that killing in the course of other criminal conduct is deterred by threatening the maximum punishment for lethal acts and much lesser punishment for nonlethal acts, the incentive to avoid killing is reduced as the severity of the punishment for the nonlethal form of the crime is increased because the gap between the two punishments will be diminished. If the threatened punishment for robbery is two years and that for a robbery killing is fifty years, the difference between those two is a penal incentive to refrain from killing. If the punishment for robbery is increased to eight years, the difference between the two penalties is smaller. And if lethal violence is punished with the law's maximum penalty in the first instance, there can be no recourse to a higher threatened punishment for it. The analogy is to a building where the ceiling's height cannot be increased. Raising the level of the floors in the course of remodeling inevitably decreases the distance between the floor and the ceiling.

The law's emphasis on the special status of life-threatening violence would be compromised even if the resources devoted to increasing penal severity were evenly divided between the most violent crimes and offenses of lesser seriousness. But increasing emphasis on penal severity in a crime crackdown is almost never evenhanded in this fashion. The paradox of crime wars is that the largest increases in punishment resources occur in relation to offenses of lesser seriousness, those on the margin between prison and nonprison sanctions.

The paradox here was mentioned in Chapter 1. Public fear regarding murder and life-threatening assaults produces programs that then invest a disproportionate share of resources on burglars, drug offenders, and automobile thieves. The explanation for this pattern is that the criminal justice system always operates selectively, concentrating most of its resources on what are regarded as the most serious crimes and the most dangerous offenders. The murderer, the life-threatening rapist, and the armed robber will probably go to prison whether available prison spaces are 20,000 or 100,000. Having extra prison space available will make much more difference in the treatment of housebreakers who might escape imprisonment in a 20,000-space environment, but who would constitute much more attractive candidates for imprisonment if the amount of space available in prisons were to expand?

A recent study of imprisonment in California between 1980 and 1991 makes this point dramatically. From 1980 to 1991, the number of prisoners imprisoned for all offenses increased by almost 80,000. The numbers of robbers in prison in California grew by 104 percent during the decade, or less than one-third of the general increase in prison population. The number of burglars in the California prison system grew at a rate just equal to prisoners generally—a rate of 335 percent. The number of persons in prison convicted of larceny expanded by 565 percent; and the number of people in prison after conviction for drug offenses expanded fifteen-fold (Zimring and Hawkins 1992:32).

The explanation for the peculiar pattern is not that California prosecutors and judges regard drug users and burglars as more dangerous than robbers. Indeed, the rate of prison commitment for each 100 convictions is much higher for murderers and armed robbers than it is for those convicted of larceny or motor vehicle theft. But the high seriousness with which the offense of murder is regarded means that the murderer will already be in prison before a crime crackdown and the bulk of the additional resources invested in prison expansion will go to offenses of less seriousness. In this special sense, cracking down on crime because of concern about violence can prove to be self-defeating.

When crime crackdowns generate across-the-board increases in penal severity, there does not appear to be any tendency for the criminal justice system to self-correct in the face of disappointing results and to reassess the special importance of life-threatening violence. In California, for example, the infamous kidnapping and murder of twelve-year-old Polly Klaas in 1993 produced a groundswell of public demands for the extension of the mandatory prison sentences for repeat violent offenders to as much as twenty-five years to life imprisonment when two prior convictions existed.

Most of the proposals in California restricted "three strikes" treatment to persons with a conviction for violent crime. But the ultimately successful version of the law included burglary as one of the special crimes eligible for three-strikes treatment. In doing so, it tripled the scope of the law and extended these long mandatory sentences to a population that experts estimate would consist of two-thirds nonviolent offenders (Zimring 1994; Rand Corporation 1995).

Did public opinion include burglary in three-strikes treatment because the average citizen is equally afraid of threats to his life and threats to his property? Our earlier discussion of the fear of crime and the process of categorical contagion suggests a more plausible explanation. The repeat offender that California citizens thought of in considering three strikes was a composite character made up of elements derived from offenders described in mass media accounts of a variety of crimes.

Categories like kidnapping, burglary, and robbery probably do not conjure up discrete images of specialized offenders in citizens' perceptions. The burglar that citizens think of when developing sentiments about minimum punishments is likely to be the worst case of life-threatening home invader. Under these circumstances, fears of crime inspired by accounts of life-threatening violence can inspire policies that systematically undermine the special treatment of violent offenders in American criminal law. If so, the generalized fear of violence will often disserve the interests of those most fearful. The political economy of punishment might well systematically lead to perverse results.

Conclusion

Assigning an explicit priority to physical security and the protection of human life will not have a revolutionary impact on the criminal law because for the most part it merely restates the implicit goals of the present system. But establishing this central aim and repeatedly testing policies against it both clarifies many current practices and suggests some promising new ways in which the criminal law might serve as an instrument of loss prevention.

Because so little is known about the operation of deterrent and incapacitative processes at the margin, merely clarifying the goals of penal policy is not a sufficient basis for detailed policy guidelines. Whether it would be better to widen the gap in penalties between gun robberies and gun robberies where the victim is shot or to increase the base penalty for gun robbery cannot be decided at present. For we lack any direct measurement of the aggregate death rate produced by these two different policies. To use an earlier analogy, we have decided on a common currency, but have not evaluated the rates of exchange that different policies will imply in lives saved.

There is also some ambiguity about why life-threatening violence deserves special priority, which can influence the way resources should be directed in the criminal law. One justification for a priority is that this is the aspect of crime that is most feared by the public. A second reason lethal violence is special is that human life is more important than the other interests protected by the law.

If the first justification is paramount, then resources should flow to those life-threatening behaviors the public most fears. If the second justifi-

cation is controlling, then resources should go where the lifesaving benefits are greatest. The largest lifesaving benefits in the criminal law would
probably result if additional resources were invested in traffic safety, while
the largest public concerns are with intentional violence.

It seems to us that the degree of public fear associated with behavior
should modify allocations of resources from what would obtain on a strictly
"lives saved" criterion. The cost of violence thus broadly reflects subjective
fear as well as more palpable disabilities, and life-threatening violence receives a higher priority in governmental response than its rank as a cause of
death and injury. For the same reason, crimes like rape and assault that generate harms the state cannot insure against or compensate and that produce
public fear should receive a high priority in criminal law enforcement.

Some current policies do not seem coherent even on the basis of the
limited data currently available. Assigning equivalent punishment to robbers with toy guns and robbers with real ones makes sense only if property
interests are more important than human bodily integrity. Across-the-
board increases in penal sanctions blur the distinction between life-threatening and other offenses. Incomplete as current information may be, the
prevention of life-threatening violence is yet another aspect of the criminal justice system where we know better than we do.

11

Strategies of Prevention

THIS FINAL CHAPTER of our study differs in two respects from the discussion of the criminal law in the previous chapter. First, while Chapter 10 dealt only with the penal law, this analysis concerns the entire spectrum of government policy that can influence lethal violence. Second, the previous chapter used the current structure of the criminal law as a starting point for considering changes that a greater priority for personal safety might require. This chapter considers the ways in which a variety of different policy tools might reduce the death rate from interpersonal violence and concerns variations on the theme of loss prevention. Once the central purpose of social controls related to intentional injury becomes reducing the loss of life and serious injury, what structures should be established to guide and coordinate policy?

The first section of this chapter introduces five contrasts that help to illuminate the special nature of loss prevention as a policy goal. The second part of the chapter discusses some necessary elements in a balanced agenda of loss reduction. The final part of this chapter discusses the relationship between social tolerance of the problem of lethal violence and the priority of violence as a social problem. We argue that the larger salience of lethal violence in recent years is, to some extent, evidence of salutary social developments.

Five Questions

The uncertainty and conflict about the appropriate way to think and talk about lethal violence in the United States of the 1990s provides evidence of the potential for change in attitudes toward violence. What kind of problem is violence? How important is it? How should it be controlled? These are significant questions without obvious answers. Under these circumstances, it is advisable to address some fundamental issues about how to think about lethal violence as an American problem. This section addresses five basic issues.

Lethal Violence: Disease or Disorder?

One of the major changes in public discourse about violence in the United States since the mid-1980s has been the claim by a new set of researchers and policy advocates that violence should be viewed as a public health problem. The impact of this new perspective has been almost wholly positive, bringing new scientific talent in to an understudied field and providing valuable new perspectives on the control of violent behavior.

But the emergence of violence as a public health concern has also generated some confusion about whether the intentional injury of persons should be regarded as the result of a disease process similar to problems resulting from contaminated drinking water. We think not.

There is, in fact, no necessary connection between the value of public health approaches and the propensity of a problem to fit a disease model in its etiology and control. Public health approaches have value for a wide variety of socially costly phenomena, including drunk driving, drug taking, and tobacco use, which do not closely conform to a disease model of etiology, transmission, or control. Thus public health approaches to intentional lethal violence can be entirely appropriate, but that does not mean that lethal violence should be regarded as a type of physical disease. There are three reasons why the disease analogy is inappropriate. The first problem is that there are a number of dissimilarities between most diseases and lethal violence. There is no germ or other single cause of lethal violence, as there is with a contagious disease. Instead, lethal violence is a single result that can be produced by a wide variety of different agencies. The closest analogy in physical medicine is to a category such as traumatic death.

A second major distinction between disease and lethal violence concerns the focus in disease on the vulnerability of potential victims. For violence, the major risk factors for its incidence are often found in the propensities and conduct of potential perpetrators rather than of likely victims. Another major difference between violent death and disease is that a violent death may be desired by the person who causes it.

A further reason the disease analogy is inappropriate for violence is because the label itself is ambiguous. There are many different forms and types of disease with different characteristics: chronic and acute, contagious and noncontagious. Calling lethal violence a disease will generate confusion about what characteristics of a disease are implied by the label. While the connotations conveyed by the disease label are substantial, there is surprisingly little that use of this term denotes to a careful listener. Disease in what sense?

A final argument against labeling lethal violence as a disease is that no such label is needed. One of the hallmarks of public health as a discipline is that its applications have value outside the usual boundaries of physical disease. The most appropriate precedent for the value of public health approaches to loss prevention in lethal violence is the work on traffic safety that revolutionized the public policy approach to the deaths and injuries caused by automobile crashes.

Prior to the 1960s, public policy for thinking about the social costs of automobile crashes concentrated on single causes and, more particularly, on the fault of drivers, in explaining the 50,000 road fatalities a year in the United States. The National Safety Council was as close to an official organ of the traffic safety establishment as existed in the United States of the 1950s, and the orthodoxy preached by that automobile industry-sponsored group was that "the most dangerous part in an automobile is the nut behind the wheel."

What followed in the early 1960s was the identification and analysis of particular risk factors associated with serious and fatal accidental injuries and a series of countermeasures to reduce accident costs. Seat belts, padded steering wheels, air bags and anti-lock brakes, changes in highway design, and special emphasis on drunken driving are only a partial list of the government-mandated changes that comprehensive traffic-accident loss prevention generated in the United States. This change from emphasis only on driver behavior was the most dramatic shift to a public health perspective that occurred in the United States in the second half of the century.

The analogy between traffic accident loss reduction and reducing the losses from life-threatening violence is almost perfect. The only important distinguishing feature between violence and automobile crashes is that a lethal outcome is often desired by those who launch violent assaults. Yet the role of single-minded intention in American lethal violence is not that dominant. Most frequently, attackers are prepared to risk lethal consequences, but will not doggedly pursue them (Zimring 1968). While the violent attacker's attitude toward harm is still distinct from that of drivers in traffic crashes, the distinction does not seem to be crucial from a policy perspective. The eclectic campaign by the American government against traffic fatality is the most appropriate model currently available for an effective program to reduce lethal violence in the United States.

The role of public health perspectives in the earlier traffic campaign was never in doubt. The architect of the National Highway Safety Program was a medical doctor, William Haddon (Haddon et al. 1964). Yet there was never serious consideration of a disease label for the manifold disorders that produced deaths in traffic. Labeling lethal violence a disease is thus neither necessary nor constructive. Lethal violence is the undesirable outcome of a wide variety of socially determined causes. It is a symptom of dangerous dysfunction in some social relations; a disorder rather than a disease.

Loss Prevention versus Crime Prevention

A strategy of loss prevention attempts to reduce the amount of death and life-threatening injury associated with intentional attacks. There are two fundamental differences between this type of loss prevention and the more commonly encountered concept of crime prevention. The loss-prevention strategy is both much narrower than crime prevention as a policy and very much broader. A violence loss-prevention strategy is narrower than crime prevention because it is not concerned with all forms of crime or the many different types of costs generated by crime. Fewer than one-fifth of all crimes involve personal force and most of these do not carry the risk of serious personal injury. So a violence loss-prevention strategy will concentrate on a thin layer of risky behavior, perhaps one in twenty official recorded crimes in the United States and an even smaller fraction of the crime found in other countries. What makes these behaviors special is the uniquely threatening harm that they generate, a harm that potential victims cannot insure against, one that creates fear and insecurity in a general population. Loss reduction pays serious attention only to that small fraction of crime that most frightens citizens.

For that narrow band of high-risk behavior, however, the methods of reducing harm that loss prevention will consider are much more numerous than the traditional boundaries of crime prevention. The only positive goal of crime prevention to reduce the number of crimes that occur. A loss-prevention approach will welcome strategies that reduce the volume of dangerous crimes, to be sure, but will also seek other ways to insure that those crimes that do take place are less dangerous to their victims. This broader agenda multiplies the strategies available to meet the policy goal.

In the highway safety case history just discussed, it is instructive to consider how many of the accepted methods of traffic-accident loss prevention would be irrelevant to a policy that wished only to reduce the number of highway crashes, the proper analogy to crime prevention. Among the safety strategies excluded by such a narrow focus would be air bags, seat belts, padded dashboards and steering wheels, crashworthy car bodies, and improvements in emergency medical services. None of these reduce the volume of crashes. Even speed limits would be excluded from consideration to the extent that they save lives not by reducing the number of crashes, but rather by reducing the injuries generated by collisions at higher speeds. Traffic safety tools for crash reduction include law enforcement, road design, and automotive improvements such as antilock brakes but these probably account for fewer than half of the important improvements in traffic safety that decades of comprehensive loss-reduction planning have produced.

The wider spectrum of loss-reduction tools available for interpersonal violence is also substantially greater than the range of methods available to prevent attacks. In addition to reducing assaults, policy interventions can try to make assaults less dangerous to victims by controlling the harm done in attacks and by reducing the number of crimes that involve personal violence. As silly as it might sound to adopt a policy of making American crime safer, it is more foolish still to ignore important methods of reducing death and injury from violence on the argument that such methods would not also reduce the crime rate.

Newly emphasized strategies of crime prevention can help make the United States a safer country (Clarke 1995). There is hope here for strategies such as cash control to reduce incentives for robbery and defensible space design features to deter personal attacks. Like crash prevention in the case of highway safety, strategies designed to reduce the amount of violent crime are an important part of loss prevention, yet loss-reduction efforts should never be confined to crime prevention.

The Compound Benefits of Multiple Intervention

The United States is a nation where many conditions exacerbate rates of lethal violence. Chapter 7 suggested that the simultaneous escalation of two risk factors—gun availability and the propensity to attack—can generate exponential growth in lethal violence rates. In essence, two separate exacerbating problems can more than double the negative impact they cause jointly. There is a bright side to this logic of compound impact and that is that the compound effects of changes for the better in the risk conditions associated with lethal violence can also produce an amplified effect in a positive direction. Reducing the rate of assault without substituting less lethal weapons in the attacks that occur will produce fewer deaths from violence. Lessening the lethality of weapons used in assault will save lives even if the rate of attack remains constant. But the most dramatic progress will come if both risk factors are abated simultaneously.

This point is worth emphasizing because of its implications for loss-prevention planning. Often, the search for optimum loss prevention becomes a search for the single most dramatic tool of leverage on death rates. In the current medical cliche, this is a quest for the single "silver bullet" in loss prevention. But the optimum harm-reduction strategy is more likely to be the pursuit of multiple loss-reducing interventions, with each individual contribution to safety being amplified by other reductions in the rate or seriousness of assaults.

If the program to reduce the losses from automobile crashes is the correct precedent, that experience certainly teaches the virtues of multiple interventions. Better road design, crashworthy vehicle construction, and more attentive vehicle operators have never been regarded as alternative ways of reducing the hazards of traffic, but rather as supplements to each other in a program of multiple interventions (Haddon et al. 1964).

There is one other important reason why multiple interventions may be necessary in a program of risk reduction for violence. The public need for safety may require lower levels of risk than can be produced by interventions dealing with only one set of risk factors. The larger the ambitions of a public safety program, the more likely that the benefits required can be achieved only through multiple interventions. If the tolerance for risk is low—and this seems to be the case for many forms of lethal violence—then acceptable levels of risk cannot be achieved by any single intervention strategy. Assume, for example, that stringent gun control might produce reduction in some forms of lethal violence by as much as half. These would be huge gains by almost any standard, but they would still leave U.S. rates of killings by strangers at more than five times the level obtaining in many European cities (see, e.g., Figure 3.6). If larger risk reductions than that are necessary, programs to reduce risk must have multiple targets.

Yet the necessity for multiple interventions runs counter to an ideological propensity in the United States to search for single solutions to crime or violence. The typical policy debate about crime and public safety is about which single countermeasure will produce acceptable levels of public safety, be it higher criminal penalties or gun controls or greater economic opportunities. This search for singular solutions reflects a need for solutions to the problems of crime or violence that sound morally right to an audience because the countermeasures deal with those forces that the audience regards as basic causes. If the basic cause of murder is human evil, then observers might assume that only programs that will incapacitate evildoers can control murder. If one believes that violent crime is caused by injustice, then it might seem that only remedies to injustice can reduce violent crime. Chapter 6 has already pointed out that the conflating of causes and prevention is usually mistaken. The important point we make here is different: Single-solution interventions may doom any loss-prevention program to failure because demands for public safety require more than any single intervention can achieve.

For this reason, one necessary element in a climate of effective loss prevention is to change expectations in the United States from single- to multiple-solution sets. Until there is public tolerance of a diversified portfolio of countermeasures to lethal violence, acceptable levels of safety may be impossible to achieve. The substantial barriers to effecting that change are discussed in the second part of this chapter.

Economies of Scale in the Prevention of Lethal Violence

There is one sense in which it is literally true that high rates of lethal violence are good news for programs of loss prevention. The rate at which a society suffers lethal violence defines the maximum tangible benefits that countermeasures to violence can produce. If the rate of bus robbery is high, the potential benefits of cashless buses are substantial. If the risk of bus robbery is low, the potential benefits in reducing robbery are that much lower. The analogy that comes to mind is the benefits of scale in the economics of production. Those social systems with high rates of violence have the most to gain from measures of prevention.

The higher potential benefits of prevention are an offset to the higher costs that face antiviolence countermeasures when rates of violence are high. It is an axiom of public policy that easy problems are easier to solve than hard problems. The costs of maintaining effective gun control in Great Britain, where as reported in Chapter 3 half the gun crime is from pellet guns and air rifles, are orders of magnitude lower than the costs of bringing 50 million American handguns under control. Violence prevention is an enterprise involving higher stakes in both cost and benefit in settings where rates of lethal violence are high.

There are two significant qualifications to the notion that a society's rate of violence defines the benefits that violence prevention can produce. One is that it is the potential harm from violence rather than just the current death toll that might be taken into account in calculating the potential benefits of prevention programs. Even settings with low rates of lethal violence may place a high value on avoiding more serious problems. If the potential for violence is considered large, then the benefits from prevention will also carry a high value, higher than a modest current rate of violence would suggest. So airports without any history of terrorist attacks might still regard investment in weapon-screening systems as well worth making.

A second qualification of the notion that benefits for loss prevention are greatest in high-violence environments is that the social value of reducing losses from violence is usually higher in societies where the rate of violence is low. If the value of avoiding an intentional killing is three times as great in one country as in another, a program of loss prevention will be valued more highly by the citizenry of that state, even if the volume of lives preserved is only half as great as it would have been in a nation that places a lower value on avoiding violent death. To the extent that rates of lethal violence accurately track social tolerance of the risk of violence, the number of lives to be saved might be a limited measure of the benefits of loss-prevention programs.

The Interplay of Public and Private Countermeasures

Government authorities do not act in isolation when making policy about violence. Individuals who worry about their safety and the physical security of those they care about will invest time and resources in defending against the threat of violence. There is an enormous and varied private sector response to the threat of violence that public policy must comprehend and regulate.

The conduct of persons responding to the threat of violence ranges from violently harmful to publicly constructive. At the negative extreme are those who respond to the real or perceived threat of violence by using force themselves, often before there is a manifest attack to defend against. Most wars are violent exchanges where the combatants on both sides sincerely believe that they are using deadly force only in self-defense. That mindset carries over to the violent exchanges between youth gangs on city streets. The joint product of two armed youth groups caught in violent conflict is horrible human waste. But each side describes its violence as the necessary response to an immediate and unlawful threat from the enemy camp. As discussed in the last chapter, the more disordered the social setting, the more likely it is that the law will be forced to regard a large proportion of all such violent acts as justifiable or excusable.

At the individual level, we encounter potentially problematic claims of self-defense in ordinary survey research on crime. On some surveys, persons report using guns to discourage attackers in a large number of instances. The insoluble problem for such a survey is evaluating the plausibility of this claim when the survey team is hearing only one side of the story. After all, Catherine de Medici probably thought she was defending herself against the Huguenots with her infamous preemptive strike in 1572.

Violent attacks are only the most direct form of private sector response that disserve the public interest in reducing violence: Loaded guns, badly trained attack dogs, and the undisciplined use of tear gas generate what economists call externalities that make life harder for many innocent citizens.

At the other extreme are private acts defending against the threat of violence that are altruistic, and private acts of self-defense that benefit not only the actor but others. Creating good lighting where poor lighting generated a risk of robbery and assault benefits the citizen who provides the lights and many others as well. When two students walk together down a college campus path, each is safer in the company of the other. The interests of each individual are served and a public interest in reducing violence is also advanced. The same kind of interactive benefit can occur when the presence of a large number of people in a street reduces the risk of violent assault because it is difficult to avoid notice and detection.

What are the proper roles of government in regulating the ways in which private citizens defend themselves from the threat of violence? The first need for government is to provide minimum standards that must be met before antiviolence measures are allowed. Wherever positive harm is a known or likely outcome of particular antiviolence measures, few would deny to government the power to prohibit the conduct. Even where particular types of self-defense are viewed as positive individual rights they must be rights qualified by the interests of other members of the community and balanced against those other rights.

Should government also prohibit private behavior that is innocuous but ineffective in protecting against violence? If all that is lost when citizens elect ineffectual self-defense is the resources invested, the case against prohibition is a strong one. The government's central role in relation to violence is security for persons from physical harm, not consumer protection. Only if reliance on ineffectual means of prevention actually increases the hazard of violence to the consumer would the prohibition of the ineffectual come within the core concerns of government.

But prohibiting conduct is only one of many tools available to government that can shape private sector behavior to better serve public ends. Public education and governmental encouragement seem appropriate for antiviolence behavior that generates what economists would call positive externalities. Public subsidies of private behavior would also seem appropriate when large groups are benefited by the resulting antiviolence effects or where the subsidy can be made widely and equally available. Helping people help themselves is a conspicuously attractive form of antiviolence government policy as long as conditions of access to the publicly supported benefits are carefully monitored.

So there is much that government can do to shape and encourage constructive private sector efforts to reduce the losses from violence. Are there also dangers of overreaching when the government becomes the chief cheerleader for particular forms of antiviolence precautions? There are dangers of silliness, corruption, and mistake in official sponsorship of private antiviolence behavior, but such problems are not as serious as when government mistakenly prohibits citizen behavior in self-defense.

There is, of course, a tendency for government to choose attractive-sounding measures to sponsor, such as educational programs of violence prevention, and not to worry deeply about evaluating the effectiveness of such programs once selected. Political correctness in the selection of antiviolence tactics is inevitable, and it may be dangerous if public authorities put themselves considerably ahead of their data in creating fashions in violence prevention.

Despite the potential problems that public responsibility for loss prevention can produce, there is no viable alternative to a very large governmental role in violence policy. In an age where privatization is a popular reform proposal, what is not being proposed about changing governmental responsibility for loss prevention in violence is eloquent testimony to the importance of safety, security, and order in even the most minimal models of the modern state.

The control of violence has not been an area where criticism of governmental mistakes produces credible calls for removing governmental authority. It is instead an area where the substantial governmental responsibility is assumed across the political spectrum and reform rather than replacement of the governmental role is required.

From Strategies to Programs

The central purpose of this study was to change the subject in American policy debates from the problem of crime to the problem of lethal violence. Our objective is to open a dialogue on policy toward life-threatening violence. A book of this kind would be a terrible place to posit a detailed and comprehensive program of loss prevention from violence on a number of counts.

In the first place, issuing an antiviolence program in a book of this kind would shift the focus of these materials from the proper ends of a governmental program to the proper means for their achievement. Certainly this book's last chapter is the wrong venue for such an abrupt change. Changing the priorities of public policy seems to us an adequate ambition for this volume.

But more than being the wrong place for a detailed program of loss reduction, this volume is also written at the wrong time for producing any comprehensive plans to reduce the societal costs of lethal violence in the United States. Whatever value added can come from sustained discussions about loss reduction from lethal violence is missing now and can only evolve over time out of analytic processes that have not yet begun. This book must do its job before that evolutionary process can start.

This section attempts to contribute, in unsystematic fashion, policy perspectives on the prevention of losses from American lethal violence. What we intend here is the sort of preliminary thinking that usually carries a title like "Notes Toward" in academic journals.

Our particular collection of notes toward loss-prevention policy is organized under three headings: "A Formula for Failure," "On Priority Concerns for American Violence Control," and "Open Questions." If everything in this section is correct beyond question, this chapter still would leave architects of a loss-prevention strategy with far less information than they would require to design programs. But even the fragmentary principles discussed in the following pages may be valuable in organizing the policy-planning process.

A Formula for Failure

Would it be possible even at this early juncture in the history of loss-prevention methods for violence to design a program that was certain to fail? If so, what would the obvious flaws in a success proof campaign teach about the correct way to plan strategies of loss prevention?

Here is our version of a four-point program guaranteed to fail:

- Aim high: announce that the goal of the program is to cure violence in the United States.
- Announce strict time limits on goals and progress.
- Maintain a moving target by not specifying whether the special priority of the program is crime, violence, or lethal violence.
- Emphasize the search for a single central program to deal with the root causes of violence.

The reader may have noticed that the program for guaranteed failure hypothesized above has more than a passing resemblance to current policies toward crime and violence in the United States. In this sense, the failure of such policies is more than a hypothesis; it is a proven failure rooted in the experience of recent decades.

Announcing a program to cure violence in America is to assure failure on at least two grounds. It misrepresents both the qualitative nature of lethal violence and the maximum impact that governmental efforts might produce. This approach misdefines violence as a disease. (How, after all, can one implement a cure for a condition that is not a disease?) And it generates expectations of eradicating violence as if it were a latter-day smallpox germ when in fact some volume of lethal violence is a chronic condition in every industrial nation on earth. Any program planner who starts down this path will soon have created a success proof strategy.

One sure way to make matters worse is to attach strict time limits to the achievement of goals by unknown means. A program of loss reduction for violence in the United States will be a series of trial-and-error experiments. Generating a precise timetable for the achievement of particular qualitative goals is the equivalent of scheduling the time for a train trip to a particular city without knowing either the distance to be traveled or the speed that the train can achieve. Yet shot-in-the-dark time limits are encountered frequently in governmental program plans. This is a legacy of two technical achievements in American history that tempt planners to believe that unknown forces can be domesticated by imposing a timetable. The Manhattan Project was the first such episode, and the John F. Kennedy promise to land an American on the moon by the end of the 1960s was the second.

The imposed calendar imagines that all that stands between a particular problem and its definitive solution is human will and economic resources. On this account, we hear advocates call for a Manhattan Project for our cities, for our sewer problems, and for our schools.

Why not a Manhattan Project for lethal violence? Putting such a timetable on loss prevention misconceives the process in many ways. The need for loss prevention from violence is not a single technical problem requiring a one-time breakthrough; it is an incremental process that achieves its highest effectiveness on a cumulative basis.

The analogy with road safety programs illustrates the importance of cumulative impact. Innovations in automobile and highway designs are absorbed on a gradual basis. If seat belts become a standard in new car production in 1965, ten times as many cars on the highway will benefit from seat belts after a decade of the new standard as will have acquired seat belts at the conclusion of year one. Improvements in road design have their maximum impact years after their first introduction because it takes time for innovations to spread throughout a system. Over time, the aggregate safety benefits will increase because the number of safety improvements introduced in the system will grow larger and the extent to which particular improvements are prevalent in the system will increase. There is, in theory, no saturation point in this cumulative process, no point at which the marginal returns from additional safety innovations become negative. Instead, both the history and theory of traffic safety lead to the Panglossian prognosis of never-ending improvement.

There are good reasons to expect a similar pattern of incremental, progressive, and cumulative impact in loss prevention from violence. And this model of cumulative impact is far removed from crash campaigns of problem-solving that imagine the process has a beginning, a middle, and an end. So the final vice of high-visibility time schedules is that they lead us to expect that a never ending process should come to a conclusion.

Another sure prescription for frustration in program planning is to maintain the lack of clarity now found in current policy about the type of harm that should be the central target of a loss-prevention campaign. It is very difficult to coordinate a campaign of loss prevention without some agreement on the kind of loss to be prevented. It is true that many different symptoms of community disorder coincide. Broken windows and the unrestrained loudness of urban ghetto blaster radios inspire citizen fear of muggings and assaults. As discussed in Chapter 1, there is some evidence that the disorderly urban environments that produce broken windows are associated also with high rates of intimidation and assault. But there is a danger in concluding from such associations that broken windows are the core problem of public safety in the United States. In recent American history, general agreement that crime and violence is a serious problem is not accompanied by agreement about what is particularly problematic.

Operating with an amorphous and undifferentiated problem definition is good politics, but it is a poor basis for the design of loss-prevention programs. The political genius of this strategy is that it invites everyone with concerns about any aspect of crime or violence into a single coalition, a symbolic crusade in which each citizen's concern is entitled to equal weight. The problem with this kind of war is that the grand coalition lacks a common enemy. If every aspect of crime and disorder is worthy of equal concern, priorities cannot be established and choices cannot be made.

One of the sharpest contrasts between road safety initiatives and government policy toward violence concerns the origins of countermeasures that are employed in each campaign. Policy toward violence is in the main *deductive* in that countermeasures are derived from a predominant theory of the causation of violence. Only those measures that fit the theory are in favor. Only political compromise generates a range of antiviolence measures wider than a single ideology of causation. Even then, as in the notorious Crime Control Act debates of 1994 and 1995 in the U.S. Congress, there is hostility and discomfort manifest when programs that were derived from different theories are authorized jointly.

The combination of midnight basketball programs and strict penalties that was engineered through the Congress in 1994 was already under attack by February of 1995 and regarded as an unstable and transient compromise. By contrast, combining midnight basketball and prison construction under a single antiviolence program certainly would not faze a veteran of the traffic safety campaigns of the 1970s and 1980s. The public health tradition is to identify major risk factors and try a variety of different strategies to neutralize major risk elements. In this sense, the traffic campaign was *inductive* because it allowed data to generate the major areas of primary concern and also eclectic in identifying a range of countermeasures to institute and evaluate.

This inductive and eclectic orientation of public health is among the most important lessons that the highway safety experience might teach to the architects of violence policy. But the ideological censorship of violence policy is a longstanding tradition in the United States with a powerful constituency. The need for political correctness in violence policy is a structural problem that threatens to waste opportunities and cost lives.

THE DILEMMA OF POLITICAL VISIBILITY

In considering the prospects for overcoming the limits imposed by deductive models of violence, we encounter something very close to a dilemma about the effects of political visibility on the content of violence control. On the one hand, if the control of violence is not an important political question, there is no compelling reason to push against the traditional boundaries imposed by deductive theories of violence. What politicians call the "comfort level" of ideologically determined programs for the control of crime and violence is substantial. A traditional approach to violence control will tend to remain dominant. So that some outside pressure would seem necessary before politically correct formulas are placed in jeopardy.

But public attention to violence control may come at a high price because the appeal of ideologically driven views of violence is greatest when policy toward violence becomes an important political issue. So there is substantial inertia that insulates political definitions of violence from scrutiny in quiet times, and the public appeal of ideological interpretations of violence render "consciousness raising" a risky tactic for the reversal of ideological influence. Does this situation confer inevitability to substantial political limits on violence control?

In the traffic safety campaign, a successful middle course of political visibility was negotiated. The inertial forces of the traffic safety establishment were effectively countered by an information and propaganda campaign principally directed at elite opinion. The information campaign that produced the Federal Highway Safety Administration was aimed at congressional staffs and the League of Women Voters rather than a broad cross-section of the average congressmen's constituents. The objective of the campaign was to increase the importance of the problem area. There was no major effort to redefine the problem because the programmatic details of a highway safety campaign were not regarded as within the public domain. Highway safety was presented as an important public problem that should be delegated to expert authorities for the design of appropriate governmental response.

The prospects for negotiating a similar public relations result for violence are small. Violence policy has a larger public profile in the United States than traffic safety, a fact that can be confirmed by one night's scrutiny of local television news. It would be more than difficult to tiptoe past the media of popular opinion without notice, while making changes in violence policy. Traffic safety was, by contrast, an area of low public visibility even though the volume of traffic fatalities in the mid-1960s was more than four times the volume of homicide in the United States at that time.

There is a second feature of violence that is related to its high public visibility and creates resistance to pragmatic policy making. The motivational and intentional elements associated with violent assault are closely related to the community's moral sense, so that ideological explanations have a more plausible claim on public attention than ideological interpretations of vehicular accidents. The story of Cain and Abel makes a prominent appearance in the Old Testament. This renders a dispassionate and pragmatic reinterpretation of violence as a public health program into a very difficult task.

A third explanation for public resistance to reinterpreting violence is the lack of credible experts to be the repository of public trust. A crucial maneuver in the transformation of highway safety was the delegation of responsibility to professional experts. But who are the professional experts on violence, the equivalents of traffic safety engineers, who appear the worthy recipients of public trust? Public health professionals are recent arrivals to the field of intentional injury control, with credentials that might be regarded as freshly minted.

The cumulative impediments to the transformation of lethal violence are sufficiently substantial to suggest which horn of the dilemma should first be tested by the advocates of change. The prospects for the success of a low-visibility transformation are so remote that the dangers of public attention must be risked.

On Priority Concerns for American Violence Control

The inductive logic of public health analysis allows the major elements of a general problem to emerge from careful analysis of its distinguishing characteristics. The search is for the characteristics that seem most prominently associated with the problem under study. When fatal car crashes are examined, the analyst discovers abnormal concentrations of driver blood alcohol, a large proportion of crashes where the deceased hit the windshield, and a disproportionate number of high-speed collisions. The identification of particular risk conditions is an important step toward finding remedies to the most pressing problems. If speed makes crashes more likely to kill, speed limits may save lives. If passengers who are thrown out of vehicles are at particular risk, then systems to restrain passengers are likely to reduce fatality risks. By providing a more specific reading of the problems that most need to be addressed, these risk comparisons help to direct the search for specific remedies.

What would a comprehensive survey of incidents of lethal violence tell us about the priority concerns for violence control? There are three conditions prominently associated with lethal violence in the United States that must be addressed by any agenda for the control of life-threatening violence. These are handgun availability and use, high rates of lethal violence among African-Americans, and the high incidence of homicides where victim and offender were previously unacquainted.

GUNS AS SINE QUA NON

The characteristic that most dominates the landscape of American lethal violence is the use of firearms in attacks, particularly the use of handguns. Firearms use predominates in American homicide, accounting for seventy percent of all cases known to the police. Even though handguns are about one-third of all the guns in circulation in the United States, they are used in three-quarters of deaths caused by firearms.

While rates of firearms use are high in many kinds of robbery and assault, the cooccurrence is particularly striking between firearms as a means of attack and death as an outcome of attack. Police in the United States report rates of serious assault with knives and other cutting instruments that are as high as rates of firearms assault, but the deaths from firearms assault are five times as numerous. International comparisons also identify as distinctive the overlap between high rates of assault fatality in the United States and extraordinary concentrations of gun use in assault. The circumstantial indications that implicate gun use as a contributing cause to American lethal violence are overwhelming.

We reiterate some of the statistical evidence discussed in Chapter 7 to underscore the distinctive role of firearms as a priority concern in the prevention of lethal violence. The literal translation of the phrase "sine qua non" is "without which not." The phrase is used in this section to emphasize an important implication of shifting the focus of concern from crime, generally, and from violence, generally, to the special problem of lethal violence. No program for the prevention of lethal violence can possess even superficial credibility without paying sustained attention to guns. Without strategies for the reduction of firearm use in assaults, no policy can be accurately characterized as directed at the reduction of American lethal violence.

The design of appropriate strategies of firearms control involves a mixture of relatively easy choices and very difficult ones. A specific focus on handguns is an easy choice in the sense that it emerges from a profile of the firearms at risk for every major category of lethal violence. With regard to homicide generally, the per unit involvement of handguns is nine times as great as for long guns, and the concentration in particular subsets of lethal violence, such as robbery, is even greater. Handguns are differentially at risk also for suicide and fatal accidents. So effective measures of reducing the handgun share of interpersonal assault seem likely to generate benefits in the prevention of self-destructive violence.

There are also substantial indications in the statistical profile of firearms and violence that reductions in handgun violence do not result in compensatory increases in the use of rifles and shotguns in assault and robbery. There is, first, the disproportionate use of handguns in the United States, which indicates that the portable and concealable handgun is not regarded as interchangeable with long guns by its users.

A second indication of limited substitution is that where handguns are subject to special regulations and restrictions, a major problem in gun use remains illicit handguns rather than more easily available rifles and shotguns. This is overwhelmingly the case in the United States, where illegal handguns are still easily available, and is even evident in foreign countries where special restrictions on handguns succeed in reducing the supply of handguns.

Thus, special regulation of handguns is a rational framework for the United States; but what kind of regulation? The basic choice is between trying to deny handguns to only high-risk groups and attempting to curtail the availability and use of handguns generally. The current system in most of the United States is to deny handguns to the immature, to persons with records of felony conviction, and to other persons regarded as special risks. This system fails in two respects. It does not even attempt to restrict the access to guns of many who will misuse them; and its aim to keep guns out of the reach of the young and the previously criminal is frustrated by the large number of handguns in general circulation.

One pattern of reform advocated for gun control in the United States is to strengthen the mechanisms designed to keep guns from the limited classes currently not eligible to own them. Systems that check the criminal records of prospective handgun purchasers are designed to make it more difficult for the ineligible to obtain guns. Systems that make legal owners accountable for each gun that is owned are a second method of reducing the flow of guns from qualified owners to the unqualified.

The alternative basic approach to handgun regulation is to restrict the availability of such weapons generally. The goal of such a scheme is not to keep handguns from particular groups of citizens who are regarded as dangerous, but to keep guns out of general circulation because they are regarded as dangerous. In the permissive system where all but unqualified owners are permitted access to guns, the target of regulation is dangerous gun users. In restrictive licensing schemes where only limited access to handguns is allowed, the target of the regulations is a class of guns that is regarded as too dangerous for general ownership.

The current system of handgun regulation in most of the United States is permissive and the number of handguns in circulation is quite large, in the range of 50 to 70 million. While some guns have been generally restricted in the United States (machine guns, sawed-off shotguns), no weapon in mass circulation has ever been so curtailed. While other industrial democracies have instituted and maintained restrictive handgun regulations, no such system has ever been instituted after generations of mass availability.

If the basic choice for American handgun control is between a permissive or restrictive strategy, each approach seems subject to a decisive disadvantage. The problem with handgun controls that attempt to restrict the availability of weapons is that they depend on radical changes in citizen behavior. Critics of such restrictions make pointed reference to the lessons of alcohol prohibition in the United States (Kaplan 1985; Jacobs 1986). Using the criminal law to change folkways is always a high-risk venture, and handgun restrictions are certainly no exception to this principle.

The decisive objection to permissive handgun controls is that the level of lethal violence that would persist under even the most effective of these modest controls would be substantial. Unless the lethal assault rate in the United States drops by more that half its 1992 level, homicide rates in the United States will remain at more than double the next highest industrial democracy's level. Anything short of drastic change in gun policy is either an acceptance of very high death rates or a gamble on very sharp reductions in violent assault.

So the choice in handgun control is between two unpalatable alternatives. Gun control in the twenty-first century will either be an expensive, unpopular, and untested attempt at bringing the U.S. handgun policy to the standard of the rest of the developed world, or it will consist of minor adjustments to current regulations that will all but guarantee persisting high rates of death. It is likely that this hard choice will amount to the definitive referendum on lethal violence in the United States.

THE AFRICAN-AMERICAN IMPERATIVE

Even cursory exposure to the data presented in Chapter 5 justifies special attention to loss-reduction programs for African-Americans. The distribution of American lethal violence is highly skewed, much more than is crime, much more than are other forms of violence. African-Americans constitute 13 percent of the U.S. population, but more than 45 percent of all homicide victims, and more than half of all killers.

The impact of this concentration on health statistics is not small. In the early 1990s, homicide was the leading cause of death for young African-American males. The threat of violent death inhibits processes of community organization by undermining trust and a sense of physical security. The prospect of lethal violence is one defining element of coming of age for many young African-American men.

Death rates from violence are substantial, but why an African-American "imperative"? The point we wish to underscore is a statistical rather than a moral obligation. The concentration of lethal violence among African-Americans is so great, that it would not be possible for loss-reduction programs to succeed generally without producing substantial results in this key segment of victims and offenders. The urban neighborhoods where high proportions of African-Americans reside are the laboratories of necessity for efforts to reduce death and injury from violence in the United States.

This emphasis on one population group is not to suggest that the forces that generate lethal violence are any different in African-American neighborhoods than in other neighborhoods, or to imply that different tactics of loss reduction might be appropriate for minority populations. The rationale for emphasis on African-American violence concerns not the content of a treatment program, but only its target population. There is no reason to suppose that the effects of mechanisms for reducing lethal violence vary with the skin color of the population at risk, any more than do the effects of seat belts, speed limits, and air bags.

There is, however, one benefit associated with the high rates of lethal violence among the African-American population, a variation of the point made earlier in this chapter about economies of scale in violence loss prevention. The higher the base rate of lethal violence, the more likely it is that any program that reduces levels of violence will generate benefits greater than the costs of the intervention. The higher the costs currently suffered, the larger the benefits a successful intervention can produce. In this sense, the measurement of programmatic effects in high violent death-rate communities provides a sensitive barometer of the potential value of countermeasures in lower-rate environments.

THE VIOLENCE OF STRANGERS

The case for stranger homicide as a special concern of loss-prevention policy has both objective and subjective dimensions. A statistical profile of stranger homicide in the United States is hard to construct with precision, but American stranger homicide is so much more frequent than rates in comparison countries that precision in measurement may be unnecessary. The best available statistics on the relationship between homicide victim and offender come from the police reports where information of this kind is a direct product of the criminal investigation process. In 1992, the policy reports indicated that some 3000 homicides, or 13.5 percent of all killings, involved a victim and an offender who were previously unacquainted. About half these incidents were robberies and 60 percent of them involved some felony other than assault. When the proper account is made of cases where the relationship between victim and offender is not known, perhaps twenty-eight percent of all homicides in the United States involve strangers (see Chapter 4).

When the rate and proportion of stranger homicides in the United States is compared with patterns of other developed countries, the disproportion in occurrence of this type of homicide is huge. The most dramatic example of this disproportion in Part I of this volume concerned the outcome of robbery and burglary incidents in New York City and London. In New York City, the death rate from aggravated property felonies is over fifty times the fatality rate in London, and that 50-to-1 difference persists when the rate comparison shifts from per 100,000 citizens to a death rate per 1000 crime incidents (see Figure 3.6). Overall, the incidence of stranger homicide in the United States is about thirty times the rate reported in Great Britain, where the stranger homicide rates was 0.1 per 100,000 in 1992 (20 percent of the 0.5 per 100,000 total) (see Home Office 1993:79).

The higher rate of stranger killing in the United States is of particular importance because fear of stranger violence is greater than fear of other forms of lethal attack. The greater fear associated with stranger violence is generally acknowledged, but incompletely understood. Two elements in the difference between acquaintance and stranger violence probably play a role: familiarity and choice. In the first instance, citizens measure their personal risk of acquaintance homicide against the cast of characters that they know personally. The general risk of other people suffering harm at the hands of people that others might know is not relevant to the calculation of personal hazard. Any citizen comfortable in the presence of his own circle of acquaintances need not be concerned about general statistical patterns of acquaintance homicide. People tend to feel safe in the presence of those they choose to associate with in all but wildly dysfunctional circumstances.

But we all have far less power to choose the strangers we meet in the public aspects of our lives. Once a citizen elects to enter a public environment, his power to screen out undesirable social contacts is sharply curtailed. The lack of power to modify risk by means of personal choice makes the emotional hazards of stranger violence harder to neutralize. If one can choose one's friends and lovers, this power of choice carries with it the impression that such choices reduce the risks of acquaintance violence. If one cannot choose the strangers in one's midst, the risks we seem to run from the violence of strangers will be every bit as large as the risks run by our neighbors. The newspaper story about the man shot by his best friend need not trouble us much because we have a different circle of acquaintances. But we have no similar and comforting distinction to interpose against a feeling of personal hazard when other citizens die at the hands of strangers.

The larger fears associated with stranger violence may interact with the much higher rate of this kind of violence in the United States to create special problems. From the standpoint of citizen fear, it may not be the difference in total homicide victimization that is the critical risk comparison between the United States and Britain, but the 30-to-1 difference in rates of stranger homicide. So the case for a priority response to stranger homicide may be stronger even than is suggested by the statistical profile of American violence.

How might a public-health style of analysis be applied to a problem area like stranger homicide? This question is important in its own right and also illustrates the type of analysis that might be expected in other problem areas.

The first response that we would expect from a public health analyst on the question of stranger homicide is skepticism that the label denotes a behavioral category appropriate for a specific analysis. Stranger homicide might be a meaningful criminological classification, but such killings grow out of a wide variety of different behavioral systems so that the category is far too broad for a meaningful preventative analysis. From this perspective, stranger homicide is not one problem but the product of many different problems. The analysts' first task would be to identify the many behavioral systems that generate stranger homicide and then to fashion a variety of countermeasures for each constituent behavioral system.

Armed robbery is by far the most important behavioral category associated with stranger homicide in the United States. In 1992, the Federal Bureau of Investigation reported 2,264 fatalities, approximately half the volume of stranger homicides from all causes. Thus, the design of mechanisms to reduce death and serious injury associated with robbery would be a first priority. And the loss-reduction problem in relation to armed robbery is a textbook example of the value of multiple simultaneous interventions.

One branch of risk reduction for robbery deaths is the reduction of the volume of robberies. To the extent that making particular robbery targets less attractive reduces the total volume of robbery, it should reduce the death rate from robbery as well; even if would-be robbers are channeled into other less life-threatening forms of crime such as burglary or theft. Only if discouragement of the robbery of particular targets results in the substitution of other robbery targets on a one-for-one basis will the diversionary influence of a prevention strategy not save lives. The unpremeditated and opportunistic aura of most armed robbery in the United States makes a one-for-one substitution hypothesis extremely unlikely.

The variety of situational prevention strategies for robbery is almost as wide as the range of potential robbery targets. Removing cash from vulnerable environments removes also the incentive for robbery, and this has produced the phenomenon of the cashless bus discussed earlier. Where the cash available for potential robbers cannot be completely removed, potential robbery targets can institute and announce strategies of cash control to reduce the incentive for armed robbery. Stores announcing that only $50 in cash is available at any time, and signs inside taxis proclaiming "Driver carries only $5.00 in change" are two examples of cash control.

Opportunities to rob can be limited as well as the cash incentives for robbery. If the very late hours of trade are at particular risk of robbery, store proprietors might close earlier or subject their late-night operations to cash control. If low levels of street lighting generate high risks of personal robbery, street lighting can be improved. And the prevention of robbery is only one element in a comprehensive program of robbery violence control. A second direction for policy development is to modify the behavior of potential robbery victims in ways that reduce the risk of their injury and death.

One method of finding new ways to reduce robbery deaths is to analyze the circumstances of robberies that lead to fatalities and isolate factors that seem to present particular risks. To the extent that potential robbery victims can be taught to avoid risk-generating behavior, the deaths from armed robberies can be reduced. For example, a comparison of armed robberies that produce death with other robberies in Chicago showed that robberies where the victim actively resists are many times more likely to result in death than nonresistance robberies (Zimring and Zuehl 1986). The behavioral theory to explain this pattern is that once a victim defies a robber, the relationship has become an active conflict in which the robber may feel lethal force is necessary to maintain his standing as the dominant actor in the relationship (Katz 1988).

The significance of this insight is not complicated. Persons at high risk of armed robbery should be instructed to be as cooperative as is possible, and to behave in ways that do not put the robber's feelings of dominance at risk. While the hazards associated with armed robbery might be more effectively combatted if robbers as well as potential victims could be trained, teaching victims the proper response to robbery is an important tool in saving lives.

The list of robbery interventions in this discussion is incomplete. Reducing gun availability would reduce the rate of robbery of commercial locations, for example, because firearms are by far the most effective weapon available for the intimidation necessary to engineer a store robbery. Hidden cameras and other announced technologies can serve both as deterrents to robbery and as aids to identification.

Further, robbery killings are only one of the significant subtypes of stranger-homicide that need to be addressed. But this survey does provide insights into the promise of risk reduction strategies and a sample of the specific flavor of safety engineering as violence control.

Open Questions

Discussions of public health approaches to the prevention of lethal violence run the danger of creating a false impression about our current ability to save lives. The false impression is that violence prevention is simply a matter of filling in the blanks; applying a fully developed technology to a new program area. Some progress in loss reduction can be produced by modest extension of current knowledge, the sort of applied behavioral science methods described in the last section's analysis of robbery deaths. But constructing comprehensive programs that reduce the risk of lethal violence is not simply a matter of filling in the details on a policy map where strategic matters are already known. There is much that we do not know about methods of controlling lethal violence. Many of the gaps in current knowledge concern basic questions. And entire subfields of potential importance in violence prevention are presently terra incognita.

This section pays our respects to two of the more prominent gaps in current knowledge about violence control. We first outline what is not known about the potential value of programs to reduce violence through attitude change. We then discuss some of the problems that surround quantifying an ultimate goal for a program of lethal violence prevention in the United States.

VIOLENCE AND VALUES

Reducing the death rate from armed robbery by teaching potential victims of robbery new ways to behave seems both indirect and inefficient. The victims are not the problem. Would it not be much more efficient to alter the values and preferences of potential robbers? This is the most direct approach to robbery reduction because it does not depend on altering specific incentives. This is also an efficient prevention strategy in the sense that it can save lives without altering environmental elements like weapons control and the robbery response of retail clerks. Changing the values and preferences of potential attackers also carries the moral benefit of making the potential wrongdoer the target of the intervention. The public relations value of this was discussed in Chapter 10.

There is no question that values and preferences are of fundamental importance in determining rates of lethal violence. Further, basic processes of socialization are the major mechanism of violence prevention in any functioning society. The lessons that citizens learn early about the wrongfulness of violent behavior produce patterns of nonviolent compliance to social norms in the great majority of citizens in the great majority of circumstances. So the "software" of violence prevention through the socialization process is of larger importance for explaining compliance than safety engineering and gun control.

Why not then consider deficiencies in the software design of the socialization process as the primary cause of problematic lethal violence, and concentrate social resources on the redesign of socialization processes as the primary agency of additional prevention? There has been serious interest in creating value based violence education and conflict avoidance programs directed at children and youth. There have also been numerous efforts to implement reprogramming treatments for identified adult target populations such as domestic partner abusers. This strategy of violence prevention is close to psychological therapeutic intervention and has created a constituency of supporters among psychologists and educations in the United States.

The usual strategy of value-based violence prevention programs is an attempt to undermine undesirable positive evaluations of violence and to generate antipathy in a target audience about using personal force to maintain social standing. It should be noted that the personal benefits offered by programs of violence prevention are less palpable than the disease avoidance advertised by standard health education campaigns (Webster 1993). It is not avoiding lung cancer or a heart attack that provides the motivational force of the antiviolence campaign. Just as the motivations for violent conduct are social in origin, so too are the motivations to avoid violent behavior that value education programs seek to generate.

The value of violence education programs is for us an empirical question. There is no basis in our analysis for giving value-based programs a preferred position relative to other methods of loss prevention from violence. Neither is there any reason to disfavor value-based approaches to violence prevention. Our current conclusion about the value of violence prevention programs is a retreat to that recurrent academic anticlimax: insufficient data to form a judgment. It is not known whether, or to what extent, particular programs change social judgments and personal behavior.

The ability to make generalizations about particular prevention programs is likely to remain deficient for some time. The most that the proponents of value-based programs can hope for is a mixed pattern of evaluation outcome in which some treatment methodologies produce behavioral change among particular targeted audiences. If there is good news from such program evaluations it is likely to come in small packages, so that evidence for the general effectiveness of value-based interventions will accumulate slowly if at all. Any news about value-based educational programs that comes in large packages is likely to be bad news because a consistent pattern of negative results might plausibly support doubts about the efficacy of the general approach being implemented. If value-based programs work in some settings, we can spend decades sorting out the programmatic and subject characteristics that generate success. If such approaches never work the evidence is easier to uncover and interpret.

One distinction between the focus of most violence prevention programs currently in use and the special emphasis of this study should be noted. Most violence prevention is directed at the general category of physical force rather than the subcategory of lethal violence. It may be that a distinct emphasis on lethal violence would make no difference to the efficacy of a prevention program. But this too is an empirical question that cannot be answered on available evidence.

It is not clear how the propaganda of violence prevention might most efficiently target lethal violence. Putting social stigma on the instruments of lethal violence—guns and knives—and on their use in societal conflict is one attractive alternative. Portraying those who use dangerous weapons in fights as cowardly might be promising, but special emphasis on lethal violence is inconsistent to some extent with the rhetoric of violence avoidance. To stigmatize the knife attacker as a coward may involve implicitly a set of machismo values about manly virtues in unarmed self-defense that violence prevention advocates would oppose. The rhetorical high ground in violence prevention may leave little room for distinguishing between types of violence.

If we were pushed to guess about the efficacy of value-based prevention programs, we would place more stock in very general socialization processes at one end of the social spectrum and intensive behavior-changing therapies at the other end, rather than on the classroom violence prevention programs that are instituted as part of the public education programs for adolescents. Value-based attempts to stigmatize the unjustified use of lethal force are more appropriately launched through general media of communication and absorbed by general audiences than reserved for classroom presentation. General social attitudes toward lethal force may be changeable, but not, we suspect, through formal educational processes. We would emphasize, however, that our theories on prevention programs have no special value on a topic where the only hard currency is empirical evidence.

ULTIMATE GOALS AND MOVING TARGETS

The appropriate way to begin this discussion is by asking an important question that we cannot answer: What level of intentional homicide should be the ultimate goal of an American violence prevention program? We will explore the difficulty encountered in setting ultimate goals by contrasting three methods of determining appropriate goals for American violence prevention; what we call political, comparative, and economic methodologies.

The political approach to goal setting rests on popular opinion. What level of intentional homicide would public opinion desire in the United States of a generation hence? The rhetorical high ground in any political discussion is the total abolition of homicide. Since any intentional taking of human life is abhorrent, a zero-homicide society would be the program goal that one would expect to emerge from a political process. A zero-homicide society is also an unobtainable fantasy that dangerously misconceives the capacity of governmental intervention to change social behavior. There has never been a post-tribal human society where deaths from intentional injury did not occur. In an open society like the United States, freedom of individual action is produced by attenuating the capacity of government and society to monitor and control individual behavior. A big city without homicide could only exist in a society without privacy and choice. The danger of zero-homicide rhetoric lies in creating a goal that could be approached only by totalitarian means.

We have earlier referred to the low visibility of traffic safety in the political process. One benefit of low political visibility was that the goal of a zero-fatality national highway system never entered the public dialogue about traffic safety. The only way to make highways that safe is to prohibit travel.

A far more practical-sounding method of establishing goals for American violence prevention is to analyze behavior in comparable social systems and use the lowest homicide rate in such societies as the goal for an American program. Taking as an example the homicide rates found in the G7 nations, two of those seven countries report homicide rates about 7 percent of the U.S. total, and the median and modal homicide rates cluster around one per 100,000 per year. Why not take the British rate of 0.6 per 100,000 per year, or the French and German levels of 1.0 per 100,000 and establish them as the ultimate targets of American violence prevention efforts?

The use of such statistics as comparative benchmarks is of substantial value, but the experience of other countries should not be regarded as definitive in setting goals for American violence prevention. Selecting a target homicide rate from the current experience of industrial nations is more realistic than conjuring up a zero-homicide goal, but it is still an arbitrary process and one that puts too much expectational pressure on loss-prevention policy. The divergent homicide experience of different nations is produced by far more than the range of their public policies. Different histories, populations, and social and economic conditions will also influence death rates from acts of intentional violence. As soon as it is recognized that homicide experience is derived from a wide range of social and policy variables, the arbitrariness of comparative benchmarks is exposed. Selecting the English rate of 0.6 per 100,000 in 1992 as a target for U.S. homicide is not the equivalent of saying: "Let us adopt Great Britain's violence loss-prevention policies." It is instead saying: "Let's be Great Britain."

While the primary dangers of using comparative benchmarks to set goals lie in overestimating the potential of prevention policies to influence homicide rates, there is one sense in which limiting policy targets to currently observed outcomes may understate the opportunities for violence reduction. In the late 1970s, homicide rates in Great Britain averaged around 1.0 per 100,000 population. These levels are enormously attractive by American standards. Homicide rates then fell by 40 percent, a larger percentage decrease than can be found anywhere in the post-World War II experience of the United States. There was still room for improvement in the homicide rates of the 1970s.

Comparative statistical benchmarks can provide Americans with important data about levels of violence that are possible in other countries. But these do not directly translate into appropriate targets for American policy. Comparative study is of enormous value in assessing both the etiology and control of lethal violence. But it is an exercise that must be administered with caution.

Economic conceptions of appropriate levels of loss prevention may be an alternative to the indeterminacy of the previous analysis. Economists would start with the notion that there exists an optimal number of homicides at any given time in the United States that can be determined as a matter of cost and benefit. On this view, the government should invest in loss prevention until the marginal cost of saving an additional life exceeds the economic value of the life that would be saved. This conception of an optimal number of homicides is a rhetorical disaster in the sense that it suggests that there are intentional killings the existence of which should be preferred to the cost of programs to prevent them. Is it nonetheless an analytic guide to the appropriate expenditure on violence loss prevention?

There are a number of practical problems that limit the ability to calculate costs and benefits, and some of these reflect larger difficulties in the conception of cost and benefit. One problem in the computation of cost and benefit is distinguishing between social and individual loss. If a thirty-year-old construction worker, with a lifetime income expectation of $1.1 million, is the victim of robbery homicide where death could be prevented by additional investment in loss prevention, we have one set of accounting principles in civil law to compute the economic cost to his family of his removal as a source of support. But how many of these individual costs are social costs as well? And under what contingencies? If the prospective victim were both unemployed and unemployable, would that diminish the public costs of a robbery killing or make them disappear? There are fundamental questions as to what the government is about that lurk behind computational issues in the calculation of public cost (see Zimring and Hawkins 1995).

A second problem relates to the computation of program costs and benefits. If loss-prevention initiatives for violence occurred one at a time, and each had measurably discrete individual impacts and temporarily limited effectiveness, the computation of programmatic benefits could be more easily achieved. But when the effects of policy are cumulative over time and involve the interaction of several different program initiatives, the computation of discrete program costs per life saved is a complex process where different plausible assumptions can lead to wildly different cost benefit conclusions.

A third problem in relation to the valuation of lives saved from violence is that the public benefits of decreased fear are not reflected in the usual economic methods of valuing lives. If our hypothetical construction worker is killed in a street robbery, millions of people may feel less secure in using public streets. This may be the primary difference in economic impact between a robbery killing and a death in traffic or one resulting from chronic disease. Failure to account for the economic impact of feelings of safety and risk could produce catastrophic errors in calculations of cost and benefit.

An illustration from a related problem of political economy may clarify this issue. One of our colleagues, the late Walter Blum of the University of Chicago, used to point out that the investment for safety on commercial airlines in the United States had clearly proceeded well beyond the standards of efficiency as these are usually measured. We seem to be willing to invest $2 million or even $5 million to save our hypothetical construction worker from becoming an airline passenger fatality when his individual economic value would never be that large and where investment of far less in public funds could save a life in traffic accidents or from cardiac arrest. Why is this?

One answer to Blum's paradox may be that low death rates from commercial airline traffic produce feelings of safety that are public goods of great significance to airline travelers; and that making the commercial airline system appear safe produces economic benefits larger than those associated with saving an additional life from highway accidents or even from private plane crashes. The potential analogy here to violence is that some reductions in homicide rates may produce special value in feelings of public safety that are indivisible public dividends enjoyed by persons who walk the streets when the rates of robbery homicide, or homicide associated with stranger rape, can be kept low.

How Large a Problem?

The final task of this book is to incorporate some of the perspectives discussed in this chapter into a reconsideration of a fundamental question: How large a problem is lethal violence in the United States of the late 1990s?

The earlier analysis in this chapter would deny that objective data about death and injury can provide a reliable measure of the social cost of intentional injury because the anxiety associated with lethal violence creates fear of public social life for many citizens. The ripple effects of such fear are considerable. Many of the victims of violence in American society have received no physical injuries; instead the boundaries of their public opportunities are narrowed, and fear of public environments diminishes the quality of personal life. Under these circumstances, the lives lost and injuries sustained from violence may provide some rough measure of the magnitude of the problem at one time as compared with another, or when different places are being compared. But the costs imposed by lethal violence are far higher than any body count would indicate.

There can be no doubt that subjective evaluations by the public are an important element in defining the magnitude of lethal violence as a social problem. This does not mean, however, that government policy must slavishly follow public fears in allocating resources for safety. Even if large segments of the public imagine that visitors from outer space are a clear and present urban danger, this should not generate a governmental responsibility to invest resources in the detection of space invaders. If the public fear is sincere, there is a responsibility generated for a government response, but the appropriate government response may be public education when particular fears do not reflect reality. The public Roads and Traffic Authority informs visitors to Sydney, Australia, that pedestrian road accidents caused 500 times as many deaths in Australia as shark attacks over the eleven years between 1983 and 1993 (Roads and Traffic Authority 1995). This is a perfectly appropriate effort to bring public appreciation of risks into a more accurate relation to objective facts. However, the effect of presenting such statistics is likely to be more fear of pedestrian risks rather than greater public comfort about the prospect of shark attacks. With only one death a year in a country of 18 million, public authorities in Australia would still be well advised to maintain the shark nets surrounding their public beaches.

The point of the shark example is not to assert that lethal violence is a one in 18 million problem in the United States. Instead, the shark story suggests a model of governmental response to public fear in which the public importance of a problem generates the obligation either to alter public priorities through an educational process or to respect those priorities in the allocation of prevention resources.

Even widespread fear does not require exhausting the public treasury in shark nets while preventable pedestrian fatalities pile up on Sydney streets. Still, spending more money per life saved on shark precautions may make good sense if a feeling of safety from sharks on beaches is an indivisible public good of special value, in the same sense that additional expenditures for commercial airline safety can be justified as an important benefit to airline passengers and the public at large. The same notion may justify spending larger resources on reducing the risk of lethal violence if the public cost of current feelings of insecurity is sufficiently substantial.

On these grounds alone, the degree of public fear of lethal violence in the United States becomes an important element in determining the appropriate governmental response. What do we know about the magnitude of lethal violence as a societal problem in the United States of the

1990s? What can this tell us about the appropriate priority of loss prevention from lethal violence in the competition for scarce resources?

By most measurements of public opinion, lethal violence is a major problem in the United States of the mid-1990s, a problem that seems more important in current circumstances than was evident in 1980 when the death toll from violence was somewhat higher. There are two reasons why subjective measurements of violence as a problem might have increased while the objective manifestations of violence have not. In the first place, the number of serious problems pressing for public attention in the United States was somewhat larger in 1980 than in 1997. In 1980, epic inflation in the United States and acute Cold War tensions abroad may have diverted attention from annual homicide rates, then at their highest point in the twentieth century. This comparative perspective on societal problems suggests that the same general level of lethal violence may generate more public anxiety in good times than in bad times when the population has so many other things to worry about. The current heightened concern about life-threatening violence in the streets may thus be a byproduct of peace and prosperity.

The peace and prosperity analysis above would predict a cyclical pattern to concern about lethal violence, a pattern where the relative standing of violence as a societal problem can be expected to decline in the next economic recession. But there is a second possibility, that social tolerance of lethal violence is declining over time in the United States so that the same number of killings can be expected to produce a larger problem response steadily over time. On this interpretation, the increased worry about violence in the United States will not abate in the next recession. Instead, a volume of violence equal to current rates can be expected to provoke more public reaction with the passing of time.

Has the tolerance for lethal violence in American society changed in recent years? Should one describe the social tolerance for lethal violence as high or low in the United States? A sophisticated student of American social history might argue that Americans have historically displayed high levels of tolerance for some forms of lethal violence and low levels of toleration for other types of lethal violence; that little notice was taken of assault-generated homicide involving minority male victims and offenders in urban ghetto locations, while killing of higher social status persons, particularly violent attacks that crossed social and geographic boundaries into America's nicer neighborhoods, have always generated high levels of fear and low social toleration.

This two-track pattern of social toleration of violence continues in the United States, and huge differences continue in rates of victimization by race, class, and location. But the two tracks of social concern may be moving closer together because the perceived distance between the usual scenes of killing and woundings in the United States and the physical and social locations where most citizens live has declined. Part of this may be due to mass media, as television has brought citizens in more proximate contact with local violence. Part of this diminishing distance reflects increasing social integration of the American workplace and some schools. Many more Americans know and care about people who are at high risk of lethal violence than in the past.

The lesson here again is that increasing public fear and anxiety about lethal violence can frequently be a product of social progress. Social changes that lower tolerance for lethal violence produce higher levels of public discomfort with the same amount of violence. But if increasing discomfort is the consequence of rising social expectations, it can stand as a positive sign of public health. Indeed, a society that was untroubled by current American rates of lethal violence would represent a significant retrogression in social development.

One Problem or Many?

Since the degree of social concern about lethal violence varies with the type of violence, should not the various subtypes of American lethal violence be kept in separate categories, rather than as part of an aggregate, competing for public attention and preventive resources? If the public fears robbery killing more than lethal barroom brawls, why lump these two categories together instead of separately determining appropriate budgets for prevention of each? To some extent, this kind of subdivision of lethal violence makes sense as a matter of public health policy as well as of democratic politics. The separate analysis of robbery homicide in the previous section of this chapter stands as an example of a behavioral category where prevention priorities and strategies can be calculated separately.

But the robbery example also demonstrates that many of the important responses to lethal violence must be applied broadly in a social environment and will tend to diminish lethal violence everywhere as they become effective anywhere. Any policy that makes handguns scarce for armed robbers also reduces the proportion of altercations between acquaintances that will generate shootings. Often, countermeasures to lethal violence cannot be fine tuned so that they are dedicated to specific behavioral subcategories. A general social priority on the prevention of lethal violence will be necessary, and public fear about particular subcategories will produce programs of loss prevention that will be widely effective if they are beneficial at all.

Two Questions of Priority

What can be concluded about the importance of the control of lethal violence in the United States? Two different questions can be asked about the priority of lethal violence: First, how great should be the priority of lethal violence among all the concerns relating to crime and violence in the United States? Second, more generally, how great should be the priority of lethal violence among all the social and governmental concerns of the United States? The first question is easy for us to answer. The second question is impossible to address within the confines of this study. Happily, the path to appropriate policy can be found by answering only the first question.

Lethal violence is obviously the most important problem related to crime and criminal justice in the United States, and its control should be the highest priority of the system. If one could separate out the fear of lethal violence from the rest of American crime, the economic and social damage attributable to crime would be rather modest. High levels of general prosperity in the United States make the property losses from crime easier to spread throughout the economy and to absorb than is true in nations with equivalent crime rates and smaller economic resources. It is the prospect of encountering violent strangers that makes Americans anxious at home and fearful in public. Remove the threat of lethal violence from American crime and what is now terrifying would be regarded as inconvenient and irritating. The majority of the many billions of dollars budgeted on crime and justice in the United States would be best spent in the control of lethal violence.

It is much more difficult to assess the relative importance of lethal violence when compared with some of the other major claims on public attention and governmental resources at the turn of a new American century. How does lethal violence rate against research and treatment for AIDS, or the need for improved schools, or the threat of environmental pollution in the United States? Assessing the dimensions of social problems across categories involves apples-to-oranges comparisons that ultimately depend on subjective value judgments. Entering into dialogue on what should be considered our very largest governmental needs involves arbitrary evaluations well worth avoiding.

Arbitrary choices of this sort can be painlessly avoided. It turns out that it is unnecessary to rank lethal violence against air pollution or education in order to commit the public resources necessary to bring effective violence loss prevention to the United States. The programs best suited to loss prevention are incremental and cumulative, not good candidates for trillion-dollar Manhattan Projects for violence. Giving the control of life-threatening violence a high priority in spending the money that we currently devote to crime and criminal justice will provide ample material and human resources to establish effective control programs. In this important sense, the control of lethal violence is not competing with good schools or clean water for financial support.

Sufficient money is already spent on the control of crime and violence in the United States to generate significant long-term improvements in public safety. Just as crime is not the principal problem that threatens public safety, the absence of money is not the principal impediment to a rational and effective policy of social defense from lethal violence. We need not prejudice either the education or the environment of our children to assure that they will live in a safer society.

Appendix 1

Explaining Distributions of Violence versus Levels of Violence

It is essential to distinguish between theories that attempt to explain the amount of life-threatening violence in a society and theories that try to account for the total distribution of violence among various social groups. One would investigate different *amounts* of violence in different social systems by asking, for example, why does the United States have eighteen times as much homicide as Great Britain per capita? One investigates the *distribution* of violence in the United States by asking which groups in the United States have the highest rates of life-threatening violence.

It must be first understood that explaining the *distribution* of violence within a social system may involve factors that are not important in explaining the different *amounts* of violence one finds in one social setting when compared with others. And factors that are not important in explaining the distribution of violence may have significant impact on the amount of violence. In all Western nations, gender and age are among the most powerful factors affecting the distribution of violence. In Great Britain, men are five times as likely to kill or intentionally injure as are women, and late adolescents and young adults are many times more likely than senior citizens and young children to attack and kill. But these distributional characteristics may tell us next to nothing about why some societies have much more violence than others. British men may be just as overrepresented relative to British women in the homicide statistics as are U.S. men, but they are less than one-tenth as likely as U.S. men to kill. Further, variations in age structure and gender are not an important part of the explanation of the great difference in rates of lethal violence between nations. This is obvious because the proportions of men and young adults do not vary greatly between developed nations.

There is one further distributional characteristic of violence that may not explain the high rates of violence when the United States is compared with other countries. It is known that rates of violence are higher among persons who commit nonviolent crimes than among noncriminal citizens. Involvement in crime is thus a significant variable in explaining the distribution of violence among a population. But does it also explain why levels of violence vary over time or across national borders? There are two important reasons to doubt that variations in amounts of criminality predict parallel differences in life-threatening violence.

The first reason for caution is the logical point that there is no necessary linkage between factors that are important in the distribution of violence in a particular population and those factors that explain the total level of violence in a community.

The second reason for doubt is the evidence now accumulating that levels of crime do not vary as much as do levels of violence in developed nations. Just as the proportion of males and young adults do not vary much between Great Britain and the United States, there are indications that the volume of property crime in London is quite close to the level of property crime in New York City (see Chapters 1 and 3). If the number of criminals in the two environments is nearly equal, there is no hope of explaining large differences in lethal violence as the result of different levels of crime.

The logical point of importance here is that explaining differences in distribution of behavior may not be relevant to explaining differences in rates. Chapter 2 contains one example of this distinction. At any given time, low socioeconomic status groups have higher rates of officially noted theft than higher socioeconomic status groups (see Wolfgang et al. 1972). But the explosive growth of theft in G7 nations over the 1960–1990 period came as general levels of income did not drop. This phenomenon of "crime amidst plenty" has been called a paradox (Wilson 1975). In fact, it is no by no means clear that expanding gross national product should be associated with reductions in levels of theft.

The methodological point we would emphasize is that most sociological research has been on the distribution of crime in particular populations. The issues of what factors influence overall rates of lethal violence in a society have been understudied. Generalizations from distributional findings may not be justified.

/

Appendix 2

Assault in New York City and London

The heterogeneity of assault reported by official statistics is discussed in Chapters 3 and 4. While this requires caution in the interpretation of such statistics, a London–New York City comparison of assault and assaultive homicide may still prove of value.

Table A2.1 begins an analysis of assault in London and New York City with data on London assault and homicide cases by weapon for 1992. The data for Table A2.1 come from assault and homicide incidents broken down by weapon. Excluded are explosives cases, weapons-unknown cases, and a category of cases where a firearm was present but not fired.

The weapons breakdown for London confirms what the national-level data on England suggested about assault in Great Britain: that the official statistics are dominated by attacks with relatively low death rates. Eighty-two percent of all reported assaults involved the use of personal force, and fewer than one in 500 of these attacks causes a death. Still, the assault-to-killing ratio for London, at 192 to 1, is half that for England as a whole, as reported in Chapter 3.

Table A2.2 (see p. 220) presents data on aggravated assault and killings resulting from assault in New York City.

Table A2.1

Fatal and Nonfatal Assaults by Weapon Type, London, 1992

	Total cases	Percentage of all attacks	Percentage of all attacks, excluding personal force	Fatalities	Death rate (%)
Firearms	429	1	6	23	5.4
Knife, sharp instrument	2,391	6	35	68	2.8
Other weapon	4,096	11	59	58	1.4
Personal force	30,403	82	–	45	0.15
Total	37,319	100	100	194	

Not tabulated in this table are cases where no firearm was fired, cases where the weapon was unknown (including one fatality), and forty-three cases where explosives were used (including six fatalities). Source: Data provided by Performance Information Bureau, London Metropolitan Police Service.

Table A2.2

Fatal and Nonfatal Assaults by Weapon Type, New York City, 1992

	Total cases	Percentage of all attacks	Fatalities	Death rate (%)
Firearms	17,034	26	1,702	10.0
Knife, sharp instrument	17,752	27	217	1.2
Other weapon	22,537	34	145	0.6
Personal force	8,358	13	88	1.1
Total	65,681	100	2,152	3.28

Source: New York City Division of Criminal Justice Services, Uniform Crime Reporting Section.

The volume of attacks, the mix of weapons, and the case fatality rates for each weapon type are quite different in New York City and London. How much of the elevenfold difference in death is the result of each of these factors? The number of assaults reported is 76 percent higher in New York City than in London. The independent contribution of this factor might be estimated by asking what volume of homicide would result in New York City if the death rate per 100 reported attacks remained constant, but the volume of assault dropped from 65,681 to 37,319. The number of New York City homicides under this condition would have been 1,223, a homicide total 43 percent under the actual 1992 level, but still more than six times the volume of homicides that occurred in London.

How might one estimate the influence of weapon mix on the death rate from assault in these two cities? One method would be to ask what number of homicides would be expected in New York City if the case fatality rates experienced in New York City for each weapon remained as they were in 1992, but the mix of weapons used in attack was that found in London. For this computation, we take London's percentage distribution of weapons for 1992 and multiply the death rate noted for each weapon and the assault volume in New York City. If knives are involved in 6 percent of London attacks, we multiply 0.06 times the 65,681 New York City attacks to estimate 2,365 knife assaults. Adding all categories give us the data in Table A2.3.

Changing only the weapons distribution of New York City assaults would produce an expected volume of homicides of 743 for 1992, slightly more than one-

Table A2.3

Hypothetical Homicides, New York City

Projected assaults	London percentage		New York City assault volume		Estimated attacks	New York City death rate	Total deaths
Firearms	.012	x	65,681	=	788	.10	79
Knife, sharp instrument	.06	x	65,681	=	2,365	.012	28
Other weapon	.11	x	65,681	=	7,225	.006	43
Personal force	.82	x	65,681	=	53,859	.011	593
Total							743

third of the actual volume of deaths from assault (2,152), and more than three times the volume of homicide in London.

To what extent is this radical downsizing of an expected homicide total the result of the 82 percent dominance in London of assaults with no weapon other than personal force? To test this effect, we excluded all personal force cases and redistributed the 65,681 New York City attacks among firearms, knives, and other weapons in the 0.06, 0.35, 0.59 percentages shown in the third column of Table A2.1. The estimated deaths by guns, knives, and other weapons distributed in that fashion are 394, 276, and 233, for a grand total of 903 expected deaths—still fewer than half the deaths recorded in 1992. The shift away from guns accounts for the entire reduction in their distribution.

One final note concerns the different case fatality rates reported by the two cities for specific weapons. The rate of death for all knife and "other weapon" attacks is higher in London than in New York City, which may reflect a greater proportion of attacks in earnest using weapons other than guns. But the death rate from firearms is just over half the New York City rate even though the London cases are only those where the firearm has been discharged. Are London offenders poor marksmen?

The answer to this puzzle underscores the need for greater detail in the cases used for statistical comparison than current statistics allow. It turns out that the "firearms" category in England includes air rifles and pellet guns, weapons with very low death rates (Home Office 1993:59–60). Indeed, about half the firearms used in crime are reported to be these low-lethality weapons, so that the types of instruments covered by the firearms category vary between the two cities.

The huge difference in death from assault between London and New York City is produced by a pattern of interaction, just as was noted for deaths from property felony. A higher rate of assault would elevate homicides in New York City even without more dangerous weapons used. But the combination of a much larger involvement of deadly weapons and a high rate of assault multiplies the death rate.

More than the availability of weapons is involved in the different patterns of weapon use. Knives and other cutting instruments are widely available in London, but are used in only 6 percent of assaults. This means they are not commonly carried and used. But even at 6 percent, knives are six times as frequently used in London assault as are guns, compared with a gun-to-knife ratio of 1 to 1 in New York City. If the difference between 6-to-1 and 1-to-1 knife ratios is the result of tighter controls on gun availability in London, these data suggest the impact of controls on death rates is substantial. If the 34,786 gun and knife assaults in New York City and been distributed 6-to-1 knife to gun, 855 deaths would have resulted for 1992 gun and knife assault death rates. That is less than half the number of deaths that resulted from the actual mix of knife and gun cases in New York City (1,919).

Appendix 3

Patterns of Three Violent Crimes in the United States

The three nonfatal offenses of violence linked to homicide outcomes are aggravated assault, robbery, and rape. This appendix discusses patterns of each of these offenses.

Aggravated Assault

The official police statistics in the United States divide criminal assaults into aggravated assault and simple assault. Aggravated assaults include attacks using deadly weapons as well as attacks intended to produce great bodily harm (U.S. Department of Justice, Federal Bureau of Investigation, 1994a). For this reason, almost all attacks likely to threaten life are reported in the aggravated category.

The official definition of aggravated assault is quite broad, and the attacks within the category range from extremely life-threatening to weapon-brandishing with no intent to injure. The first column in Table A3.1 shows the distribution of aggravated assaults by weapon in the United States in 1992.

The different classes of weapon give some indication of the seriousness of assaults, with gun attacks being more deadly than knife attacks and knife attacks being more likely to kill than attack with other weapons. But within each weapon category, the range of intention and injury is substantial.

With this range of intention and injury, no offense of violence is more heterogenous than assault, and no offense of violence is as difficult to classify, measure, and compare over time or between different areas. Whenever physical force is used or threatened, there is a prima facie behavioral basis for finding that an assault has taken place. Police statistics in the United States traditionally require that behavior be both unjustified and more than minimally serious to be classified

Table A3.1

U.S. Aggravated Assaults and Robberies by Weapon, 1992

	Assaults	Robberies
Knives and cutting instruments	17.6	10.6
Firearms	25.1	40.3
Other weapons	31.0	9.5
Personal force	26.3	39.6

Source: U.S. Department of Justice, Federal Bureau of Investigation, 1992.

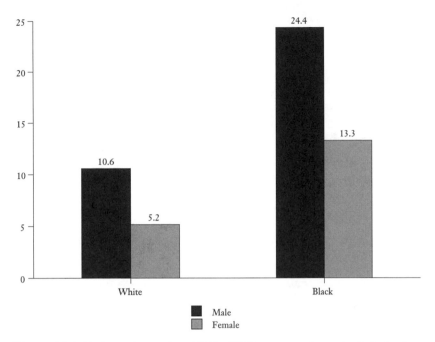

Figure A3.1. Estimated rates (per 1000) of U.S. aggravated assault victimization by race and sex, 1992. *Source:* U.S. Department of Justice, Bureau of Justice Statistics, 1993.

as an assault; and then draw a further distinction between what is called simple assault and assault offenses that are called aggravated either because extensive injury is inflicted or intended or because a dangerous weapon is used in the attack.

The National Crime Victimization Survey also divides reported assaultive behavior into simple and aggravated events, with the intent of defining each category in parallel with the police classification. Figure A3.1 reports estimated rates of aggravated assault victimization by race and sex for the National Crime Victimization Survey for 1992.

There are significant differences in victimization risks for both gender and race. Males of both races are twice as likely as females to report becoming victims of assault and blacks of both sexes are two and a half times as likely as whites to do so. The male-female differences are of the same magnitude as noted in robbery, but the noted concentration of aggravated assault is less pronounced among blacks than for robbery.

The most noteworthy statistical contrast is between the incidence of aggravated assault—the offense covering the most serious violent attacks that do not kill—and homicide—the offense category used when serious assault results in death. The homicide risk for men is more than three times as large as for women, while the aggravated assault risk for males is only double that for females. The homicide risk for blacks is five times as great as for whites, while the racial concentration for blacks in reported aggravated assaults is only about half as great.

The simple explanation for this contrast is that aggravated assault is a mixture of lethal attacks—which are concentrated in the same pattern as homicide—and less deadly assaults—which are spread more evenly throughout the population. The inclusion of less life-threatening forms of attack in the category of aggravated assault will then tend to dilute the predominance of the highest risk groups of crime victimization.

When comparing the racial concentrations for homicide and aggravated assault, the difference in concentration is not evidence that the distribution for either category must be wrong or mistaken. Each category has a separate significance. If one is interested in the overall distribution of serious attacks, then the all-inclusive reports in the assault category are probably appropriate. If, on the other hand, one is interested in the racial distribution of attacks likely to kill, the risk ratios found in the homicide statistics will furnish better guidance on that question.

There are a substantial number of statistical indications that aggravated assault is the most heterogeneous offense category of the three major violent crimes. In addition to the less dramatic concentration of assault victimization among males and blacks, the concentration of aggravated assault in major cities is much less than the concentration of either robbery or homicide. Only 23.2 percent of all aggravated assault reported to the Federal Bureau of Investigation in 1992 occurred in the twenty largest cities compared with the 11.5 percentage of total U.S. population that lives in those cities. This 2-to-1 ratio is much smaller than the concentration noted for homicide (3 to 1) and robbery (4 to 1).

Because homicides are more concentrated in large cities than aggravated assaults, the apparent death rate per 100 aggravated assaults varies dramatically when cities are compared with suburbs. The simple explanation for the geographical variation is that the less severe forms of aggravated assault are spread more evenly across the different types of community in the United States, while the most life-threatening forms of assault tend to be more concentrated in the major cities. This "heterogeneity" interpretation of the geographical difference is consistent with the explanation we offered above about the smaller concentration of victimization among blacks and males in the aggravated assault category.

Data on the concentration of arrests for aggravated assault give further support to the nomination of aggravated assault as the most heterogeneous of the violent offenses. The concentration of violence arrests among men in the Federal Bureau of Investigation statistics in 1992 was pronounced: 9.7 percent of all persons arrested for homicide and only 8.5 percent of all persons arrested for robbery were female. By contrast, 14.5 percent of all persons arrested for aggravated assault were women.

The data on racial concentration are even more dramatic. More than 60 percent of all persons arrested for robbery in 1992 were black, and the parallel figure for homicide was 55 percent. By contrast, fewer than 40 percent of all those arrested for aggravated assault were black. Is this evidence that males and blacks are better shots than women and whites when involved in violent assaults and thus are more concentrated in assaults that kill? More likely, it reflects the fact that aggravated assault is an admixture of different types of assault with significantly different death rates and that the less serious forms of aggravated assault are not as intensely concentrated among males and blacks as the most serious forms of attack.

Robbery

Robbery is committed when an offender attempts to take property from the person of another by the use or threat of force. As with assault, the extent to which robberies are life-threatening varies widely. Among the important elements associated with the risk of death from robbery are the type of target attacked and the type of weapon used.

In general, robberies on the street are less likely to produce a fatality than robberies in business and residential settings, which tend to last longer and produce more use of deadly weapons (Zimring and Zuehl 1986). The distribution of robberies by weapon differs from the weapon distribution of assault, as shown in Table A3.1. About four out of ten robberies are committed with guns, and fewer robberies than assaults involve knives and other cutting instruments.

For robbery the concentration of that offense in big-city environs is even more marked than for homicide. According to the Uniform Crime Report, 41 percent of all reported 1992 robberies were reported in the twenty largest cities, which together made up 11.5 percent of the U.S. population. The police statistics on robbery also indicate a strong concentration of robbery offenders are male (92 percent) and black (61 percent).

Figure A3.2 provides data from the National Crime Victimization Survey's estimate of the rate of robbery victimization per 1000 in the United States during 1992.

The categories reported parallel the analysis of homicide presented in Figure 4.7, but the robbery victimization estimates are based on survey results projected on the U.S. population, while the homicide rate comes from a comprehensive count of killings. The estimated robbery rate in Figure A3.2 is a rate per 1000 citizens rather than the rate for 100,000 citizens reported for homicide. This compen-

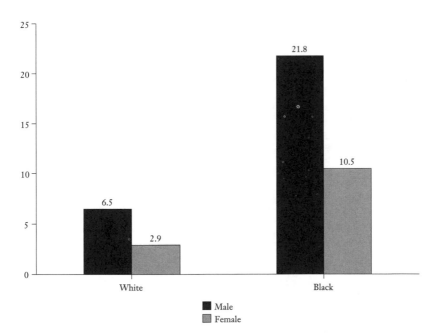

Figure A3.2. Estimated rates (per 1000) of U.S. robbery victimization by race and sex, 1992. *Source:* U.S. Department of Justice, Bureau of Justice Statistics, 1993.

sates for the fact that rates of robbery are approximately two orders of magnitude larger than rates of homicide.

The general pattern documented in Figure A3.2 is similar to the demography of homicide in two respects. Both gender and race are associated with significant variation in the risk of becoming a robbery victim in 1992. With respect to gender, men are twice as likely to be robbery victims as women and the magnitude of this difference is the same for whites (6.5 vs. 2.9) as for blacks (21.8 vs. 10.5). The robbery victimization rate for blacks is approximately three times that for whites and the threefold difference exists both for males (21.8 vs. 6.5) and females (10.5 vs. 2.9).

A fourth parallel with the data presented on homicide is that the size of the difference associated with race is larger than the size of the difference associated with gender. There are two respects, however, in which the data on robbery victimization differs from the information on homicide. First, the concentration of victimization in males and blacks is less pronounced for robbery than for homicide. Blacks are victims of homicide five times as frequently as whites, compared with a 3-to-1 robbery differential. A similar diminished concentration is found in respect of gender.

This diminished concentration in the robbery category is probably the result of the great range of different types of robbery reported, together with the tendency of racial and gender concentration to be greater for most serious and life-threatening forms of violence. Larger numbers of less serious forms of conduct in the count will tend to dilute the stark concentration of males and racial minorities found in the homicide statistics.

The second major difference between the patterns of homicide and robbery concerns the very different demography of the victims and offenders in robbery. While the victimization rate among blacks is three times that of whites in the general population, this still means that two-thirds of all robberies reported to the National Crime Victimization Survey have white victims. But Federal Bureau of Investigation data on the race of those arrested for robbery reveal that 61 percent of all robbery arrests are of blacks. If the racial distribution of robbery arrests accurately reflects the racial distribution of robbery offending—and there is no reason to believe the contrary—then a very significant proportion of all robbery incidents involve a victim and offender of different races. This is in marked contrast to homicide, where perhaps 10 percent of all killings involve a victim and offender of different race.

Rape

Rape is defined by the compilers of criminal statistics as sexual intercourse compelled by force or the threat of force. It is usually confined to female victims although parallel provisions in the criminal law of most jurisdictions also forbid forcible sexual contact with males. Attempts are counted as rapes in surveys and police statistics. All legal systems have defined sexual contact with children as serious crime and not infrequently as a form of rape. Rape is both a sex crime and a crime of violence. For this reason, one would expect to find different victim and offender profiles and different patterns of offense than are found for robbery and assault.

Little is known with confidence about the demographic distribution of rape victimization in American society, but the contrasting statistical profiles that are fueling the debate about the prevalence and distribution of rape victimization are an important illustration of the significant shift we have noted in the case of robbery and assault in the concentration of victimization when definitions of violence are broadened. There are no clear physical markers for when a rape occurs to parallel the occurrence of a death and the indications of intentional agency that usually accompany homicide. There is also no separate statistical agency responsible for rape statistics as there is for homicide.

Traditionally what was reported about rape victimization in the United States was a product of police statistics on rapes reported to the police where the police assessment agreed with the victim's characterization of the event. There are two substantial problems with using such a database to compile a demographic description of the incidence of forcible rape. First, the reputation of city police forces for insensitivity and the social stigma of being a victim of a forced sexual encounter generated substantial incentives for women *not* to report rape episodes to the police. This pattern extended even to sexual predation by strangers, but was probably more pronounced in situations where the victim and the offender had some prior social relationship.

Under these circumstances, the proportion of rapes reported to the police could vary over time, increasing during periods when the police appeared to be trustworthy and decreasing when the authorities seemed less sympathetic to rape victims. Ironically, this pattern tends to increase apparent crime rates as citizen–police relationships improve and to decrease the recorded rape rate as the social reputation of the police declines.

But not all rape reports to the police are recorded by the authorities as rape. Further, the propensity of the police authorities to "unfound" a substantial proportion of the rapes reported to them has often seemed both to understate the incidence of rape and to distort the demographic pattern by more frequently recording a rape when the victim came from a social group more trusted by the police.

The victim survey is the usual antidote to untrustworthy criminal statistics. But sample surveys of victims of rape have themselves enormous variations in profiles of the incidence of rape and of persons most at risk of encountering it. The National Crime Victimization Survey is the most reliable and frequently administered instrument for determining survey-based estimates of the incidence of violent crime. For rape, however, the smallness of the number of rapes reported represents a substantial handicap when observers try to use the data to supply detail on the incidence of rape and demographic patterns of rape victimization. Moreover, there is some evidence that the survey method is prone to inaccurate measurement of rape victimization, particularly those involving nonstrangers (Law Enforcement Assistance Administration 1972; Gottfredson and Gottfredson 1980).

The range of estimates of rape rates is wide. The Uniform Crime Reports show a rate of 42.8 per 100,000 citizens for 1992. The National Crime Victimization Survey usually produces estimates of about 100 per 100,000. This rate would generate relatively low odds that a woman would be raped either in a particular year or over a longer period of time. By contrast, the sociologist Diana Russell reported a rate of rape among 930 women randomly selected in San Francisco that totaled 2.8 rapes per woman surveyed, or 1.7 rapes per survey subject aged eighteen and older when rapes by spouses were deleted. The prevalence rate of rape among this sample and the annual rate estimates from these lifetime questions are not provided in the Russell report, but a career-to-date victimization rate of 170,000 per 100,000 is 1700 times the annual rate for the National Crime Victimization Study (Russell 1982:27–41, 65).

The rape demography that emerges from the study of cases known to the police is of an offense concentrated among young women victims, with rates of victimization considerably higher for black than for white women. Detailed analyses based on police records for Philadelphia, Los Angeles, and Boston put the victimization rate of black females as between four to six times the rate of white females, although there is a substantial interaction between age and race in victim differentials (see Amir 1971:43–50; Chappell et al. 1977).

Sample surveys generally find less substantial differences in victimization by race, and the more broadly the offenses is defined, and the more heterogeneity is introduced into the category, the less substantial the racial concentrations that are noted. The 1972 Law Enforcement Assistance Administration's victimization survey reported the racial concentration of rape and attempted rape incidents and showed that black rates of total victimization were approximately one-third higher than white rates, a far cry from the victimization risk of multiples of four to six based on police statistics. Yet detailed analysis of the early victim survey results provide an important case study of the impact of offense heterogeneity on conclusions about victimization risk.

Less than one-third of rape incidents reported in that Law Enforcement Assistance Administration study involved "completed" rapes, that is, incidents where sexual penetration occurred (Hindelang and Davis 1977:92). Black women were more than twice as likely to report completed rape victimization as were white women. For the 70 percent of all rape incidents that were classified as attempts, the black rate exceeded the white rate by only 13 percent. Although the 2-to-1 black–white ratio for completed rapes is also still measurably below the rape differential estimated from police records, it is starkly different from the evenness of pattern by race found in the case of rape attempts.

Finding that sharp a distinction in the demography of attempted and completed rape should be a clear warning against aggregating the data together as if the two components were similar in other ways. Further, the distinction within the census survey points up once more the clear relationship between broader behavioral categories and concentrations of experience among discrete minority populations. In general, later surveys, some involving even broader definitions than the census survey, tend to find near parity in the distribution of rape victimization by race.

The racial distribution of rape offenders follows the general pattern that we identified earlier: The racial concentration found in the case of offenders will generally reflect the pattern of racial concentration of victims, only more pronouncedly. But the impact of this is strikingly different depending on whether narrow police statistics or broad survey estimates are the basis of the analysis. The concentration of rape offenses among blacks is stark in the police statistics, mirroring and magnifying the differences found in the race of victims. But the concentration of offenses among blacks is much less pronounced when those reporting rape incidents are asked about the race of their assailants.

If police statistics are used as the measure of rape incidence, the risk of death resulting from a rape incident is 1.4 per 1000 rapes, less than half the death risk for police-reported robbery. Shifting to victim survey estimates of rape incidence would cut that death risk by more than half. In any event, the risk to life for female victims of robbery is more than twice as great as for rape victims.

The racial profile of women killed in police-reported rape episodes more closely resembles the police statistics portrait of rape than that presented in the National Crime Victimization Survey. Black women made up 32 percent of the rape victim homicide total in 1992, a rate of homicide from rape 3.4 times that of women from other ethnic groups (U.S. Department of Justice, Federal Bureau of Investigation, 1994b). So those varieties of rape reported to the police seem most closely connected to the risk of fatality that is classified as rape-related.

Other Crimes

There are at least two behavioral systems that produce more homicides than felonies like burglary and arson, but are not separately reported by police agencies: domestic assault and child abuse. Domestic assault, however, defines a major part of police work in the United States and every other developed nation. Nonfatal cases number in the hundreds of thousands and fatalities comprise about 10 percent of all homicides.

Child abuse is a second category of assault not separately reported by the police. While injuries from adult maltreatment of children are not uncommon at all ages, child abuse deaths are clustered in infancy and early childhood when the victims are physically more vulnerable and dropping and beating can more easily cause death. The rates of fatality reported in the American health statistics (0.1 per 100,000 children) are somewhat higher than comparative estimates from other industrial nations. But the differences in suspicious child death rates are nowhere near the differentials noted for the homicide of older victims.

Any transnational comparison of suspicious childhood deaths should be accompanied by a series of warnings about the quality of the available statistics. The line between accident and abuse is a judgment call that may vary over time and also cross-sectionally. Jurisdictions that focus on the possibility of child abuse in child fatality cases may produce statistics where suspicious deaths are high even though the nation's children are no more at risk than in countries where more casual attitudes toward determining responsibility in ambiguous death cases obtain. Further, death caused by intentional abuse may be undercounted in all jurisdictions because the benefit of doubt is still extended in questionable cases.

But the biases and uncertainties associated with child abuse death statistics are relatively minor compared with the perplexities encountered when examining the civil and administrative statistics on nonfatal instances of child abuse. The passage of mandatory child abuse reporting legislation in most of the United States has been associated with an explosion in reported instances of custodial maltreatment during periods when no significant changes were occurring in the rate of suspicious deaths. It is very difficult to determine the proper interpretation of child abuse reporting data as an index of the violent risks faced by youngsters when changes in administrative rules may have such a tremendous impact on reporting. These problems are compounded by a lack of follow-up investigation to determine the existence and extent of abuse in many cases.

While the rate of fatal child abuse in the United States may not be much greater than that reported in other industrial countries, the rate of domestic homicide in the United States is at least twice that of any other G7 country. The killing of spouses and sexual intimates comprises a smaller fraction of American homicide than that of the homicide experienced in Canada and Western Europe, and trends in domestic killing have been flat to diminishing over the last twenty years. Nevertheless, the differentials in spousal homicide, while smaller than for homicide, generally exceed those found for child abuse.

Age Distribution of Offenders

Figure A3.3 provides a summary picture of the age distribution of offenders for three types of violent crime by separately estimating the relative concentration of arrests for homicide, aggravated assault, and robbery for eleven different age groups from the population. For each age group, we attempt to normalize the age-specific arrest rates by comparing the percentage of all arrests for a crime that occurs in a specific age group with the percentage of that age group in the general population (e.g., if a particular age group contains 10 percent of the general population but 20 percent of all persons arrested for aggravated assault, the value of that age group for aggravated assault on the chart will be (2/10) x 100=200. If the age group is 10 percent of the population but only 5 percent of those arrested for aggravated assault, the value will be 0.5 x 100=50. The straight line drawn at 100 in Figure A3.3 is where an arrest rate would be entered if a particular age group represented the same proportion of persons arrested for a crime as it did of the general population.

There are three ways in which those arrested for robbery tend to be more youthful than those arrested for other violent offenses. First, the youngest age group at which relative proportion of that age group in the arrest pool exceeds the

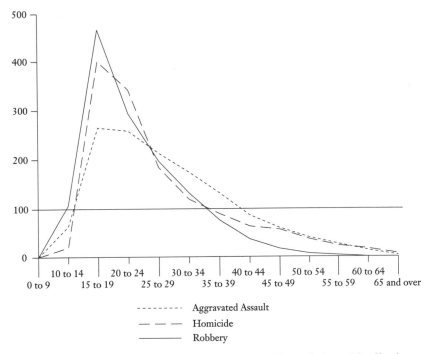

Figure A3.3. Comparison of age distribution: general population with offenders.
Source: Data provided by U.S. Department of Justice, Federal Bureau of Investigation, Uniform Crime Reporting section.

proportion in the general population is ten to fourteen for robbery—five years younger than the first age when the percentage of persons arrested for aggravated assault and homicide exceeds the percentage of that age group in the population.

The second way in which robbery is a more youthful offense than homicide and aggravated assault is that arrests are more intensely concentrated in the population under twenty-four for robbery than for homicide and aggravated assault. Robbery is also a distinctively youthful crime in that arrest rates drop off more pronouncedly in the older age groups for robbery than for the other crimes. The last age group in which the percentage of robbery arrests exceeds the percentage of the general population is thirty to thirty-four, and robbery arrests after fifty are less than one-tenth the size that would be predicted if they had been distributed randomly across age groups. By contrast, there are substantially larger concentrations of homicide and aggravated assault arrests in the age groups above forty, and the concentration of homicide arrests relative to population does not dip as low as the 8.7 rating that robbery achieves at ages fifty to fifty-four until after age sixty-five.

The age curve for homicide arrests shares one similarity with robbery and two similarities with the aggravated assault pattern. The similarity to robbery derives from the fact that homicide arrests spike at 400 (or four times the share of general population) on the chart at ages fifteen to nineteen which is where robbery arrests spike at 468. The two respects in which homicide most resembles aggravated assault are: the much smaller likelihood that very young persons (in the ten-to-fourteen age group) will be arrested; and the relatively substantial number of arrests that involve offenders in their forties, fifties, and sixties.

Aggravated assault is singular in the flatness of its distribution of arrests by age. There is no age group where the share of aggravated assault arrests outnumbers the share of population by as much as 3 to 1. And there is no single age group much more likely than any other to contain a high concentration of aggravated assault arrests. The average deviation from the 100 percent baseline for aggravated assault is significantly smaller than a similar frequency for robbery and homicide.

The most economical explanation that we can think of for this phenomenon is that aggravated assault rates vary less over ascending age groups than do other rates of violent crime, and frequently involve the participation of members of age groups that are rarely arrested for other violent crimes. The use of arrest statistics to compile this distribution necessarily means that the spike associated with youthful offenders overestimates the number of homicides, aggravated assaults, and robberies that young offenders are responsible for committing because they tend to commit crimes in groups far more often than older offenders and thus to be arrested more frequently in groups (Zimring 1981). If four juveniles are arrested for one robbery and one adult for a solo robbery, a comparison of the arrest statistics might be misinterpreted to mean that 80 percent of all robberies were attributable to juveniles, whereas the correct figure in regard to responsibility for crime would be nearer to 50 percent.

The somewhat different distribution of arrests for homicide and aggravated assault also provides further evidence of the extreme heterogeneity of aggravated assault. Figure A3.4 (see p. 232) shows the ratio of homicide arrest rates for each age to aggravated assault arrest rates for the respective ages through the teen years as shown in the Uniform Crime Reports for 1992.

The ratio of homicide arrests to assault arrests is a simple way of measuring how deadly the aggravated assaults attributed to each age group tend to be. In the

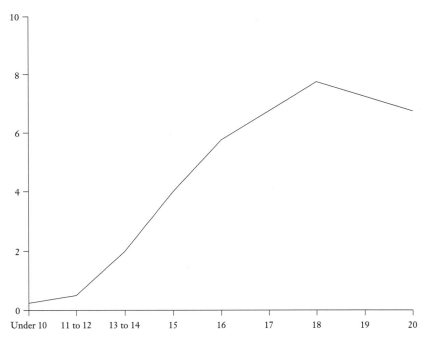

Figure A3.4. Homicide arrests per 100 aggravated assault arrests by age group of offender, 1992. *Source:* U.S. Department of Justice, Federal Bureau of Investigation, 1993.

youngest age group, for every homicide arrest, there are more than 300 aggravated assault arrests—a very low death rate. The number of assault arrests for each homicide arrest drops steadily—showing that the attacks are more dangerous—for each increase in the age category through age eighteen, by which time the ratio of homicide arrests to aggravated assault arrests is more than twenty-five times higher than among the youngest group.

What this shows is the large extent of heterogeneity found in the aggravated assault category. If twelve-year-olds can engage in conduct that meets the criteria of the aggravated assault category but that generates one-tenth the death rate of aggravated assaults committed by sixteen-year-olds, then the types of violence covered in the category are diverse indeed. All the more so because one can also expect that same diversity of dangerousness within each age group.

Appendix 4

Race and Lethal Violence: A Five-City Comparison

This appendix uses a sample of arrest data from five large U.S. cities to compare black and nonblack offense rates in order to hold constant the variations in population area that can produce confusion in racial comparisons at the national level. The cities selected include the three largest cities in the United States—New York City, Los Angeles, and Chicago—and two southern cities in the top ten for population—Dallas and Houston.

The appendix begins with an illustration of how variations in population area reporting standards can masquerade as racial differences. The appendix then considers offense-specific arrest ratios by race at the city level.

A striking example of the confusion of city-size effects and racial difference concerns the very large difference in the ratio of aggravated assault arrests to homicide arrests that was displayed in Figure 5.2. For blacks in the United States, there was one homicide arrest for every sixteen aggravated assault arrests during 1992, an implicit fatality rate of about 6 percent. For whites, we found only one homicide arrest for every thirty-one aggravated assault arrests, a ratio of aggravated assault to homicide about twice as high as that found for blacks. The implicit estimated death rate for aggravated assault by whites was about 3.2 percent.

Data from the five-city arrest sample demonstrate that most of the difference noted between the two aggregated racial categories is not really a racial difference by providing disaggregated data on aggravated assault to homicide arrest ratios. Table A4.1 (see p. 234) compares aggravated assault to homicide arrest ratios for blacks and all other offenders both in the overall arrest totals reported by the Federal Bureau of Investigation and for the five large cites for which we obtained arrest statistics by race.

The difference in aggravated assault-to-homicide ratios shrinks dramatically when controls are introduced to make sure that racial detail is obtained for comparable areas. The ratio of nonfatal to fatal arrests is only 20 percent greater for whites than blacks in the five-city sample as compared with a 94 percent gap when the comparison is made between blacks and whites for the United States as a whole. So, more than three-quarters of the apparent difference between the races disappears when a demographic control is introduced.

Moreover, the data in Table A4.1 are suggestive of a reason for the difference. The ratio of nonfatal to fatal attack arrests for blacks in the five large cities is 15 to 1, almost identical to the 16-to-1 ratio that is the overall statistic for blacks nation-

Table A4.1

Aggravated-Assault Arrests Compared with Homicide Arrests, United States, 1992

	United States aggregate	Five cities (New York City, Los Angeles, Chicago, Dallas, Houston)
Black assault to homicide arrest ratio	16	15.1
White assault to homicide arrest ratio	31	18.1
Percentage difference	+94%	+20%

Source: U.S. Department of Justice, Federal Bureau of Investigation, 1992 (U.S. aggregate); data provided by U.S. Department of Justice, Federal Bureau of Investigation, Uniform Crime Reporting Section (five cities).

wide. But the ratio of nonfatal to fatal arrests is much lower in the five big cities for nonblacks (18 to 1) than the nationwide aggravated assault to homicide ratio of 31 to 1. Obviously, the national-level nonblack totals have been flooded with arrest data from towns and suburbs with different standards for aggravated assault arrests and with only small black populations.

Finding this artifact is consistent with the use of Figure 5.2 (see Chapter 5). We argued there that the very different aggravated assault to homicide ratios for the two races suggested that black offenders were involved in life-threatening assaults more often than white offenders, and that the official 4.3-to-1 black-to-white ratio probably understated the real concentration of life-threatening aggravated assault among blacks.

Crime-Specific Arrest Ratios

The main purpose of a five-city sample of arrests is to test the concentration of arrests by race that were discussed in Chapter 5 against a set of black versus non-black comparisons restricted to large cities. Figure A4.1 shows two different black versus nonblack arrest ratios for four crimes of violence and for burglary. One set of estimates comes from the national-level data reported by the Federal Bureau of Investigation and displayed in Figure 5.1. The second measure of differential arrest ratios was obtained by adding differential arrest rate measures for all of the five cities together and dividing the total by five. This produced a mean value for racial concentration in the five cities that does not give each city any differential weight because of its population size.

Restricting the arrest rate comparison to big city populations produces a substantial reduction in the degree to which blacks are more likely than nonblacks to be arrested for homicide. The aggregate U.S. difference by race was 8.43 to 1, while the black to nonblack ratio found in the five-city sample was approximately half that at 4.29 to 1. There are two plausible reasons why our five-city sample could be expected to produce smaller differences than the national aggregate. The comparison is made only between residents of large cities, a setting associated with higher homicide rates and also one that contains a larger proportion of the nation's black population. Eliminating suburban and small-town nonblack populations

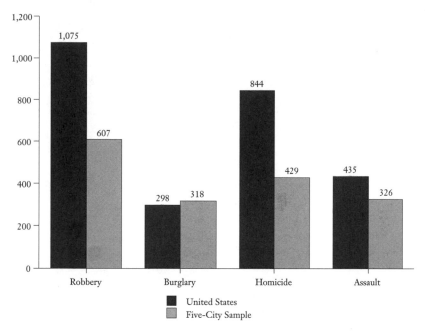

Figure A4.1. Comparison of two black versus nonblack arrest ratios, 1992.
Source: U.S. Department of Justice, Federal Bureau of Investigation, 1992 (United States); data provided by U.S. Department of Justice, Federal Bureau of Investigation, Uniform Crime Reporting Section (five cities).

would be expected both to increase the rate per 100,000 of offenses for all the urban nonblack population and to decrease the gap between the African-American and non-African-American rates.

The second reason the ratio of black to nonblack arrest rates should shrink when the comparison is restricted to large cities is that the nonblack population in our largest cities is itself demographically quite different from the nonblack population of the United States as a whole. The nonblack population of large cities like New York City and Los Angeles contains much higher concentrations of other ethnic minorities. And some of these ethnic minorities have rather high rates of arrest for homicide. This different composition of the residual nonblack population would be expected to increase the rate of nonblack homicide and therefore to decrease the black to nonblack arrest ratio.

The use of a nonblack population with a large concentration of other ethnic minorities seems an appropriate method of testing how much the distinctiveness in rates of black violence can be regarded as reflecting a differential tendency on the part of blacks. Moreover, the substantial decrease in racial concentration that is obtained when the residual nonblack population is restricted to those living in big cities should focus our attention on the importance of the specific demographic mix of the population that is used in a comparison with largely urban African-American populations.

The better than 10-to-1 black to nonblack ratio of robbery arrests drops by over 40 percent when the comparison is restricted to the five-city sample: from 10.75 to 6.07. But even with that shrinkage, the robbery arrest ratio is larger than for any other crime. So restricting the comparison population to big city residents reduced the black to nonblack arrest ratio by controlling for the fact that robberies are predominantly big-city crimes. For aggravated assault, the effect of restricting the racial comparison to the residents of the five big cities is to reduce the racial concentration by approximately 25 percent. For burglary, the arrest ratio is 3.18 to 1, equivalent to the U.S. aggregate differential of 2.98.

Appendix 5

Studies of Mass Communications and Homicide

The vast majority of studies of mass communication effects deal with mild forms of aggressive behavior that are difficult to link directly to life-threatening violence. But there are exceptions to that pattern, and while such studies are few in number and methodologically flawed, efforts to tie the content of mass communications to variations in homicidal and suicidal behavior are of particular relevance to the larger enterprise of the book.

This appendix examines two lines of published research that claim to find that stimulus by media produced measurable changes in the death rate from violence. These mortality studies are a small and unrepresentative sample of the social explorations of mass media effects. Neither line of research is experimental, obviously, although many of the assessments of short-term response to violence cues have come from controlled experiments. These mortality studies do not gather data at the individual level on populations exposed to mass communications, but seek to infer audience reactions from general social statistics. Further, they are not the work of experimental psychologists.

But the potential importance of mortality studies in the analysis of lethal violence is obvious. No one can say on the basis of existing research what the link is between hitting a Bobo doll (see Chapter 8) and the potential to inflict life-threatening injury. But if claims of direct influence on mortality experience stand up to sustained scrutiny, there is a direct link established between mass communications and lethal violence. As we will demonstrate, however, the claims that have been made to the effect that mass media events have a measurable influence on mortality cannot be confirmed.

The Lethality of Television Ownership

The most ambitious claims made about television's effect on lethal violence were published by Brandon Centerwall, an American physician and epidemiologist (see Centerwall 1989a,b, and 1992). Dr. Centerwall compared annual data on television set ownership in four countries with annual rates of aggregate homicide in those countries. The center of this analysis was a comparison of homicide trends in Canada and among whites in the United States, where television set ownership expanded enormously in the decades following World War II, and homicide rates among South African whites, where the advent of television was delayed until the mid-1970s. Dr. Centerwall concluded:

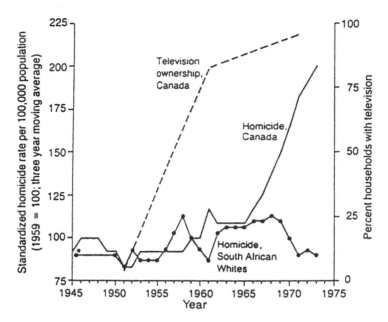

Figure A5.1. Trends in homicide and television ownership, Canada and South Africa (homicide—whites only). *Source:* Centerwall 1989b, Fig 1.

> Comparisons of South Africa with Canada and the United States indicated that the introduction of television into Canada and the United States caused a subsequent doubling of their respective homicide rates. . . . (Centerwall 1989b:44)

The causal attribution of increases in homicide over time in Dr. Centerwall's study comes from the use of data on South Africa's homicide as a quasi-control. Figures A5.1 and A5.2 reproduced from the Centerwall study show television set ownership and percentage fluctuations in homicide rates for Canada (Fig. A5.1) and the United States (Fig. A5.2). (Both of the figures have been photographed from the original source to avoid inaccuracy in reporting the underlying data from the study.)

In each figure, South African homicide-rate fluctuations over the period 1945–1975 are included as a quasi-control and the reader is invited to conclude, for example, that the differences between the homicide trends in Canada and South Africa are attributable to the television set ownership changes in Canada. Using this *post hoc ergo propter hoc* interpretation, television set ownership increases are reflected in similarly steep increases in homicide that begin about fifteen years later and continue throughout the period pictured in the graph. In the longer research report (Centerwall 1989a), the comparison over time is made additionally for England and Finland, and a series of subanalyses by region and city size in the United States is presented. The inference to be drawn from these statistical materials is described in the following terms:

> The more general theory—that exposure of susceptible populations to television causes a major percentage increase in rates of violence—has been tested here against eleven falsifiable hypotheses. All eleven hypotheses have been empirically validated,

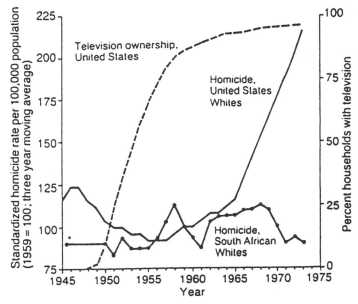

Figure A5.2. Trends in homicide and television ownership, United States and South Africa (homicide—whites only). *Source:* Centerwall 1989b, Fig. 2.

supporting the theory of a causal relationship between exposure of populations to television and a major percentage increase in rates of serious violence. (Centerwall 1989a:44)

There are a number of problems associated with the basic post-hoc methodology employed in the Centerwall study. Particularly troublesome is the use of television set ownership as a measure of presumed provocative television communication and the assumption that white homicide rates in South Africa can function as an appropriate control for the United States and Canada, when the white residents of South Africa account for fewer than 5 percent of all homicide victims in that country. But these theoretical problems need not concern us here because the general theory that the expansion of television exposure produced increases in lethal violence can be tested and refuted by an overwhelming number of examples counter to those used in the Centerwall analysis.

In the first instance, homicide trends in the nations singled out by Dr. Centerwall do not fluctuate in the pattern predicted by his hypothesis in subsequent years. The post-1974 trends are provided in Figure A5.3 (see p. 240).

Rates of homicide dropped in the mid-1970s in the United States, rose again to a peak in 1980, and then dropped substantially through 1985. In England and Wales, the homicide rate dropped by more than one-half from 1978 through 1982, and then stabilized at a rate as low as the pre-television levels cited by Dr. Centerwall. The exposure of children and adults to television never decreased in the United States, Canada, or England. Why did homicide rates decline?

A second set of counterexamples relates to homicide rates in industrial nations where television set ownership expanded quite sharply at approximately the same time as in the United States and Canada, but where the homicide trends over time

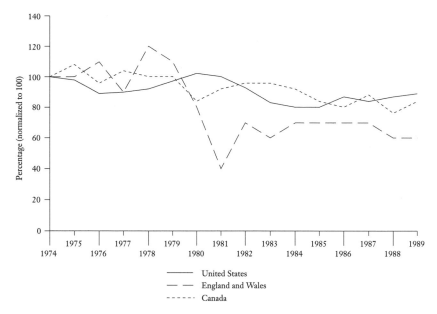

Figure A5.3. Trends in homicide in the United States, England and Wales, and Canada, 1974–1989. *Source:* World Health Organization 1974–1989.

were quite different. Figure A5.4 shows trends in television sets and homicide over forty years, 1950–1990, for the four other G7 nations—France, Germany, Japan, and Italy—where television set ownership expanded roughly contemporaneously with the English-speaking G7 group.

There is considerable heterogeneity in trends over time in the homicide rates in developed countries, as we showed in Chapter 2. These four different countries display four quite different patterns of homicide over the same long term. But there is no sustained increase in the noted homicide rates anywhere near the fifteen-year time lag from expanding television ownership that can be found in any of these four countries' otherwise divergent homicide trends.

The increase in television ownership in the four non-English-speaking G7 nations is substantial in every year after 1955. Dr. Centerwall is not specific about whether the sharpest proportionate increase in ownership or the move past majority ownership should trigger the fifteen-year latency for a homicide epidemic, but this sort of detail is irrelevant given the actual homicide trends observed. In Germany, the homicide rate declined after 1970 when any television effects would have to be noted. In France, homicide rates more than doubled in the late 1950s, drop back precipitously in the early 1960s, and fluctuate in the fifteen years after 1975. Italy is characterized by narrow-band fluctuation throughout the thirty-five years after 1955, with decreases in the first decade, increases in the 1970s, decreases in the mid-1980s, and increases after that. The long-term trend is flat. And recent Japanese history inverts the hypothesized relationship between television ownership and homicide. The former is up all through the period, while the homicide trends are steadily and consistently down. The aggregate pattern for television over time is up. The aggregate pattern for homicide is trendless in three

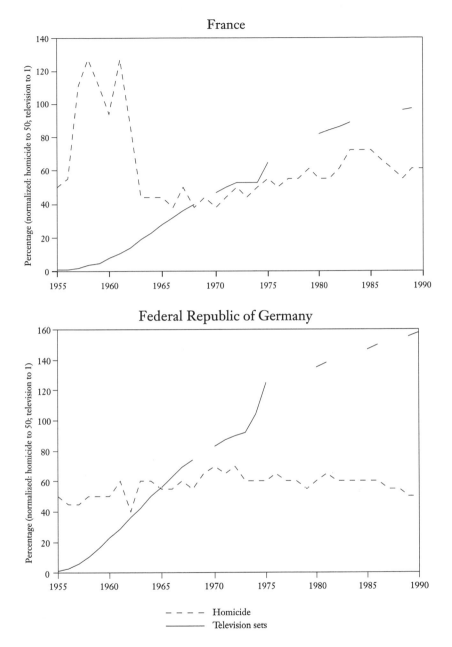

Figure A5.4. Trends in homicide and television Sets, four G7 nations,
1955–1989. *Source:* United Nations 1955–1989 (television); World Health Organization,
1955–1989 (homicide).

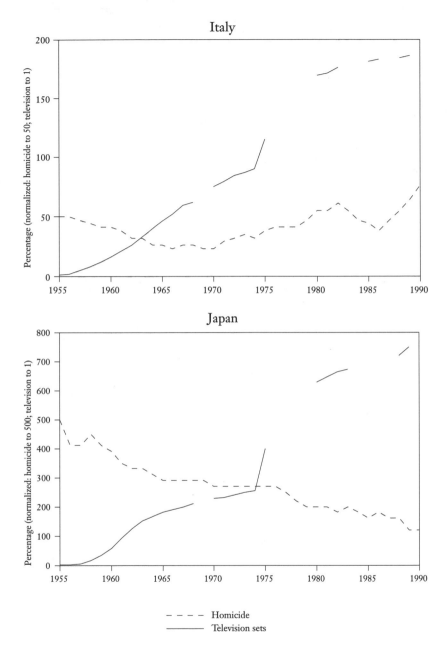

Figure A5.4. (*continued*)

nations and down in a fourth. The safe conclusion is that homicide rates in these nations vary independently of television ownership.

The two different types of counterexample carry different implications. The fluctuations after 1975 in the United States, Canada, England, and Wales show that television expansion was clearly not the dominant influence on homicide rates after 1975 and support our skepticism about the suggestion that trends in television set ownership played the dominant role attributed to them in the decade before 1975. The additional cases added to create a full G7 sample go further: They *disconfirm* the causal linkage between television set ownership and lethal violence for the period 1945–1975. It may be that television interacted with other circumstances peculiar to the United States to increase homicide at one historical period. That cannot be disproved. But the general hypothesis that television produces homicide is a victim of expanding the trend analysis to all G7 nations.

There is, however, some methodological good news that emerges from the wealth of counterexamples just reviewed. The resort to comparative statistics from a broad sample of developed nations can provide a fairly rigorous test of causal claims that are made on the basis of national-level statistics.

Prize Fights and Homicide

The second sequence of studies connecting the mass media to lethal violence concerned the impact of discrete historical events, which were publicized by the mass media, on homicide rates and suicide rates in the immediate aftermath of the publicized event. The most multifaceted and elaborate of these studies was published by David Phillips of the University of California at San Diego in the *American Sociological Review* under the title "The Impact of Mass Media Violence on U.S. Homicides" (Phillips 1983:560–568). Professor Phillips is also the sole or senior author of many other studies using homicide or suicide as a dependent variable.

The independent variable in the Phillips study was a heavyweight championship prize fight occurring anywhere in the world between the years 1973 and 1978. The dependent variable was his calculation of the difference between the expected and actual homicide volume by day from the day before the prize fight to ten days after the fight in the United States. Expected homicides by day for the United States were derived from a formula that emphasized the historic homicide rate during the same month and day of the week. The statistical finding was that the number of homicides experienced in the third and fourth day after a heavyweight title fight exceeded the number of homicides to be expected during the same day of the week and month, with the largest effect noted for the third day after the fight (Phillips 1983).

Two further subanalyses of the data were reported to support the inference that media communication about the fight generated the delayed reaction increase in homicide. In the first instance, Phillips reports that the most extensively publicized fights produced the greatest excesses of observed homicide over expected homicide in his statistical analysis (Phillips 1983:563). In the second place, there was a peculiar type of race matching reported that links the race of the losing fighter to trends in homicide victimization rates. Homicide rates of young white male victims increased on the day that a white boxer lost the title fight and two days after a white boxer lost a title fight.

While "black-loser" fights are not associated with any statistically significant elevation in white-victim homicides, black-victim homicides increase substantially four or five days after a black boxer loses a heavyweight title fight. There is no statistically significant increase in black victimization after whites lose heavyweight title fights, although the average increase in black-victim homicide three days after a white loses a title fight is as great as any increase noted after a black loses a title fight (Phillips 1983:565–66).

The claimed significance of this study is as a demonstration of a direct link between mass media stimuli and lethal real-world outcomes. Professor Phillips concludes:

> The data presented in this paper indicate that mass media violence *does* provoke aggression in the real world as well as in the laboratory. In contrast to laboratory studies, the present investigation assesses the effect of mass media violence in a natural context. Unlike laboratory studies, the present study examines a type of violence which is of serious concern to policy makers. (Phillips 1983:567)

There are, however, several problems that arise when trying to make the evidence adduced in this study part of a direct indictment of the media as a cause of homicide. In the first place, this is not a study of any specific communication or stimuli that can be tied to the mass media. Most of the heavyweight fights that were the occasion for the Phillips study were not broadcast on commercial television in the United States, but rather were broadcast live only to persons who paid for admission to a theater location where a closed-circuit broadcast was received. We researched the contemporary newspapers around each fight for information on coverage. Data were readily available for fifteen of eighteen fights, and 53 percent of these were only available in theaters. The four biggest effects found in the study were from nontelevised fights.* While news of a fight's outcome was communicated by radio, television, and newspapers, the only *live* coverage that is typical of these heavyweight championship fights in the United States is round-by-round summaries on some radio stations. This is of importance because there is really no "mass media violence" to assess in most of the events covered in the Phillips study, notwithstanding the title of his article.

The second problem with noting an effect on the incidence of homicide that is strongest three or four days after a particular stimulus is the lack of any plausible psychological mechanism that might be expected to generate a peak effect after that kind of delay. The reader will recall that our summary of effects derived from a review of the psychological literature in Chapter 8 was divided into "short-term" responses, such as excitation and imitation, and "long-term" effects that build or cumulate over time, such as reinforcement or desensitization.

Yet the responses found here conform to neither pattern. The short-term effects of the psychological laboratory are same-day phenomena. But Phillips finds no significant same-day or next-day effects in his analysis. And finding a delayed peak after three or four days that then quickly dissipates does not mesh with any psychological construct of long-term effect. The author describes his finding as "heavyweight prize fights provoke a brief, sharp increase in homicides" (Phillips 1983:567). He concedes that: "At present, we do not know the precise psychologi-

---

*Muhammad Ali vs. Joe Frazier, Ali vs. Joe Bugner, Ali vs. George Foreman, and George Foreman-Joe Frazier. See Phillips 1983: 563; Sam Kamin did the archival research.

cal mechanisms producing the third day lag . . ." (Phillips 1983:562–563). But, in fact, the article never mentions any mechanism from the psychological literature as a candidate for causal responsibility.

The absence of theory to account for the delayed homicide reaction to prize fights was not viewed as a great disadvantage by Professor Phillips because a similar delay was found in other studies that he had published:

> It is interesting to note that this "third-day peak" appears not only in the present study but also, repeatedly, in several earlier investigations: California auto fatalities peak on the third day after publicized suicide stories (Phillips 1979), as do Detroit auto fatalities (Bollen and Phillips 1981) and U.S. noncommercial airplane crashes (Phillips 1978, 1980).(Phillips 1983:562)

Yet there are two ways in which the evidence cited by Phillips can be regarded as particularly vulnerable to counterexample. First, the empirical data stand isolated from any specific theory of human behavior; a series of intriguing but mysterious outcomes. Because of this isolation and the absence of any other plausible explanation, the statistical pattern documented is the *only* basis for accepting Professor Phillips' explanation. The second problem is that all the "third-day peak" studies were conducted by the same investigator, using the same methodology of statistically projecting an expected level of homicide or suicide and comparing the actual homicides or suicides after the event to the projections from the model. If there is anything wrong with the common method, it would be expected to invalidate all of the "third-day peak" findings. So the multiple findings of delayed response are more fragile than would be the case if different methods of study had confirmed the same pattern.

An alternative rival hypothesis was soon published by James Baron and Peter Reiss in the *American Sociological Review*. They illustrated their critique of the models that generated expected homicide volumes in the Phillips research by using the same methods to produce estimates of the homicides to be expected on the same day of the week as the prize fights almost exactly one year later. Even though there was no heavyweight championship fight in the one-year-later base period, Baron and Reiss demonstrated a statistically significant increase in homicide on the third day after the fight anniversary. Their conclusion was that the delayed reaction peak in both homicide and suicide was an artifact of a flawed methodology for predicting the expected homicide rate (Baron and Reiss 1985:347–363). Professor Phillips and an associate, Kenneth Bollen, responded to this critique by arguing that the bogus third-day effects produced by Baron and Reiss were smaller than the ones generated by Phillips's work and by reminding readers that there were other indications in the data such as the larger effects produced by the more publicized fights and the peculiar pattern of racial match in which homicide victimization rates increase more for whites when a white boxer loses and increase more for blacks when a black boxer loses. Phillips and Bollen also assert that there would not have been a statistically significant bogus effect if their critics had selected the year before rather than the year after the fight as an anniversary base point (Phillips and Bollen 1985).

While this response uncovered some fascinating statistical loose ends, it cannot function as a rehabilitation of the Phillips methodology because it does not account for the significant homicide increase finding produced by Baron and Reiss three days after their selected anniversary. Unless this sort of accident could occur frequently without any artifactual problems in the methodology, the unexplained three-day peak in the Phillips research now has a plausible rival explanation.

It is of some importance to contrast the verdict we reach on prize fights and homicide with our conclusion in the previous section on the relationship between television set ownership and rates of intentional homicide. We consider the correct conclusion on the Phillips research to be "not proven." It is plausible to suppose that external events communicated by the mass media might have some influence on homicide and suicide rates. But the statistical evidence so far presented does not persuade us that any such effects have been detected in the U.S. homicide statistics.

In contrast to the "not proven" verdict regarding heavyweight title fights, we think that a mechanical relationship between television ownership and viewing and subsequent homicide rates has been *disproved* by extending the time-series data in the United States and Great Britain and by showing patterns of homicide inconsistent with such an effect in four other G7 nations.

One difference between unproved and disproved theories is that the former invite further empirical research while the latter would discourage it. We would hope that further research will be encouraged particularly on copycat patterns of homicide and suicide. The interest in copycat phenomena has a longer pedigree in criminology than many media studies acknowledge. It is interesting to note that neither Dr. Centerwall nor Professor Phillips mention the work of Gabriel Tarde, who they might have regarded as a forerunner or precursor, although his approach was both more subtle and more complex than their own. Sandra Ball-Rokeach and Louis De Fleur have in fact described the work of David Phillips, which we have examined in this chapter, as an attempt "to revive the nineteenth-century contagion theories of Gabriel Tarde by arguing that members of the audience imitate powerful media suggestions" (De Fleur and Ball-Rokeach 1975:1024). And it is true that Tarde wrote both about what he called "suggesto-imitative" crime and also about what he referred to as "the pernicious influence of general news [in] the newspapers" (Tarde 1912:340).

Tarde's examples of the copycat hypothesis concerned newspaper coverage:

> The newspapers were filled with the exploits of Jack the Ripper, and, in less than a year, as many as eight absolutely identical crimes were committed in various crowded streets of the great city. This is not all; there followed a repetition of these same deeds outside of the capital and very soon there was even a spreading of them abroad. At Southampton, attempt to mutilate a child; at Bradford, horrible mutilation of another child; at Hamburg, murder accompanied by disemboweling of a little girl; in the United States, disemboweling of four negroes [Birmingham], disemboweling and mutilation of a colored woman [Milville]; in Honduras, disemboweling, . . . etc. The Gouffe case had its almost immediate counterpart in Copenhagen. . . . Infectious epidemics spread with the air or the wind; epidemics of crime follow the line of the telegraph. (Tarde 1912:340–341)

Yet Tarde was considerably more sophisticated than that passage taken alone might suggest. The truth is that he was often more rationalist than empiricist and would, like many of his contemporaries, be nowadays regarded as sometimes guilty of dogmatic assertion. As, for example, when he refers to "criminality" as "*always being,* in its characteristic form and its realization in fact, *a phenomenon of imitative propagation*" (Tarde 1912:362; emphasis added). But as far as he was concerned, this followed logically from the fact that imitation, which he referred to as "this characteristic force of the social world . . . by means of which we account for all the phenomena of society," inevitably "applied to crime as well as to every other aspect of societies" (Tarde 1912:322 and 326).

In a world without television, "the force and forms of imitation" were transmitted through "the increase in the relations established by correspondence or by printing, of intellectual communications of all kinds between fellow citizens scattered over the vast territory [which] has the effect of diminishing in this sense the distance between them" (Tarde 1912:326–327). It was, he asserted, as a result of what he called "imitative contagion" that, for example, there had been in Paris recently "an increase in the number of crimes of a bloodthirsty nature" (Tarde 1912:350). This has remained a plausible, but untested hypothesis throughout the twentieth century.

The statistical misadventures of Professor Phillips should not discourage further research on copycat homicide and suicide, but the experience should influence the way in which research is designed. The uncertainties of any formula modeling expected aggregate homicide rates suggest to us that statistical studies of the aggregate volume of homicide or suicide will be unlikely to produce definitive conclusions. However, specifying in advance qualitative dimensions regarding the kinds of homicide or suicide to be expected could strengthen research designs and make research results more credible. Specific theories about the behavior that media cues should generate can be formulated in advance. *Romeo and Juliet* can be expected to have more influence on suicide rates among adolescents than among the elderly, and more impact on those adolescents who are depressed or upset about a romantic involvement. Prize fights, on the other hand, should have more behavioral impact on people who watch them and/or care about them. One could do a prospective case control study comparing persons arrested for homicide prior to prize fights, in the immediate aftermath of prize fights, and perhaps of persons arrested for homicide one year later. If a larger number of fight fans are in the post-fight homicide sample, a case for causality can be made.

Even more specific assessments that search for the imitation of particular means of homicide or suicide or other types of violence could, for example, examine whether movies about bank robbers generate a larger-than-expected number of similar bank robberies. One reason why the Phillips studies are less-than-compelling evidence of the psychology of imitative violence is the lack of a specifically testable qualitative aspect of behavior that we could search for in the aftermath of particular cases.

Appendix 6

Drugs and Homicide in the
District of Columbia: A Research Note

This appendix is a report on a research sounding on drugs and lethal violence in Washington, D.C. The Office of Criminal Justice Planning and Analysis of the District of Columbia produces an annual report that provides data on the yearly number of homicides and the percentage of those homicides that the police classify as drug-involved. There is no subclassification into types of drug-related homicide. But the fluctuations over time in both the number of District of Columbia homicides and the proportion of those homicides that are thought to be drug-related have been substantial.

In Washington, D.C., overall homicide expanded dramatically from 1986 to 1991: from 194 in 1986 to 489 in 1991. During the first part of this time period, the number of killings listed as drug-related expanded more quickly than all other homicides and reached a peak of 53 percent in 1988. The growth in nondrug homicide exceeded that of drug-related homicide over the period between 1989 and 1993. There is no method of auditing the police classification in this data set to determine how faithfully drug involvement is recorded or the degree to which there is consistency in the criteria that are used to indicate drug involvement in homicide cases.

If crack cocaine is the driving force in the rapid expansion of Washington, D.C., homicide, there are some indications that the larger role of drug conflict in homicide may change the profile of homicide victims as it also increases the rate of violent death. A concentration of homicide among drug users and sellers tends to increase the proportionate share of all homicide victims who match the characteristics of the young, low-status males most at risk for retail street sales of hard narcotics.

Certainly the increased concentration of District of Columbia homicide among local minority males fits this pattern. As the number of killings expanded by 150 percent, the concentration of homicide among young black males increased substantially. Eighty-five percent of all homicide victims in the District of Columbia in 1986 were black and 70 percent of all 1986 homicide victims were black males. Of the additional homicides added by 1991, however, black males were the victims in 86 percent of all cases, and black males and females together constituted 97 percent of the increased homicide victims.

The impact of changes in homicide risk was just as pronounced among other ethnic groups. In 1986, 21 of 194 homicides had white victims, a little under 10 percent. Five years later when the volume of homicide was two and a half times the

1986 rate, the number of white victims in the District of Columbia actually dropped from twenty-one to eighteen. This pattern of risk distribution is not a normal one and may be related to the explosive increase in systemic drug-related homicide. Normally the pressures that produce higher rates of killing in poor neighborhoods spill over and produce smaller increases in death outside the highest risk groups: Robbery and robbery-related killings are a common way in which increasing violence extends outside the geographic and demographic boundaries of the urban ghetto (Block and Zimring 1973).

Perhaps the diversion of energy into the illegal drug trade may have helped reduce the homicide risks of whites in Washington. If the opportunity to sell drugs diverts a large number of violence-prone persons from robbery, the number of white robbery victims killed might decline. If crack and heroin sales are concentrated among younger, ghetto-dwelling blacks, the same vectors that increased homicide rates in a drug-impacted urban area may reduce the risks of robbery and robbery-killing of merchants and pedestrians.

Both the increase in total homicide and the pattern of that increase in Washington are consistent with a shift of homicide vulnerability that increases the load on the highest-risk group. But the available data on the relationship between drug-related killings and other homicide risks are fragmentary. For all of the speculation about the impact of drug markets on urban violence, there is a paucity of systematic research either over time in single cities or cross-sectionally among several cities, to test the influence of different measures of drug use and different drug market conditions on the rate and character of urban homicide.

To further investigate the possibility that robbery homicide rates declined in Washington, D.C., we obtained data from the individual offenses reported to the Federal Bureau of Investigation by the Washington, D.C., police to determine the volume of suspected robbery murders by year in the District of Columbia from 1979 to 1992. The results are shown in Figure A6.1 (see p. 250).

The decline in robbery killings recorded after 1982 was as sharp and substantial as any we have observed. But so too was the subsequent increase recorded in the first three years of the 1990s. Police-nominated robbery killings averaged fifty per year from 1980 to 1982—about 25 percent of all District of Columbia homicides. The rate of reported robbery killings fell by more than one half in one year, 1983, and went as low as seven—about 4 percent of Washington homicides for 1986.

By 1989, as the homicide rate more than doubled, the volume of robbery killings stayed at about 4 percent of total homicide. And the absolute number of robbery killings in 1989 was about one-third of the 1980–1982 average. Then just as suddenly as robbery homicide had decreased, the rate of lethal robbery tripled again to average forty-eight per year from 1990 through 1992. Unless this time series is a product of two quite sharp changes in police recording practices, the statistics on robbery homicide in Washington, D.C., are documenting shifts in behavior that merit serious study. An inspection of the data for all reporting areas in the program showed declining rates of robbery killing during the early 1980s, but nothing like the pronounced recession documented in the District of Columbia.

If the sharp decrease in police-nominated robbery killings is genuine, these data provide important new evidence that what is called the "economic–compulsive" motive for drug-related violence is not as important as the systemic violence that drug markets may produce (Goldstein 1985). If economic–compulsive motivation was very important, the expansion of illicit drug markets would be associated with

Figure A6.1. Trends in robbery-related homicide, Washington, D.C., 1979–1992. *Source:* U.S. Department of Justice, Federal Bureau of Investigation, 1994.

a steady if not rising proportion of all homicide cases being attributable to robberies. If the number of such cases drops while illegal drug use expands in an urban area, that would provide some good evidence that systemic drug-related killing is much more important than economic–compulsive violence. Robbery is by no means the most important way in which drug-hungry persons can obtain money for drugs (see Johnson et al. 1985). But the spectacle of robbery killings declining markedly while illegal drug markets boom would be regarded as surprising by most analysts with a strong stake in economic–compulsive theories of drug-related violence. The data in Figure A6.1 suggest that just such a surprising development may have occurred.

There are a variety of different ways in which the relationship between illegal drugs and lethal violence can be explored. If good data were available on the extent of illegal drug use, either over time or cross-sectionally, the correlation between patterns of drug use and total rates of criminal homicide could be obtained. One measure of the activity of illicit drug markets might be the number of homicide cases that the police believe involved illicit narcotics.

Figure A6.2 provides data on the total number of cases of homicide in Washington, D.C., for each year between 1985 and 1992 and the number of cases in which the police believe that drugs played a significant role. These data came from a reanalysis of the Supplementary Homicide Reports provided on each case by the police to the Federal Bureau of Investigation over this eight-year period. There is a substantial gap between the number of cases in which a drug involvement is suggested in the criminal justice reports from individual cities we mentioned earlier and the number of case summaries with indications of narcotic involvement. In

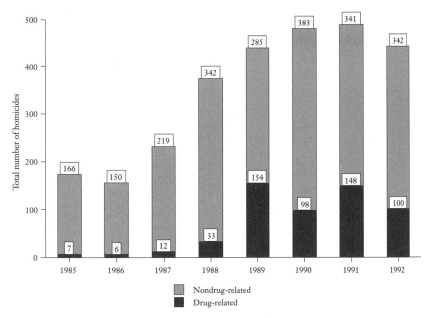

Figure A6.2. Trends in drug-related homicide, Washington, D.C., 1985–1992.
Source: U.S. Department of Justice, Federal Bureau of Investigation, 1994.

1989, for example, when the Office of Criminal Justice Planning estimated 53 percent drug involvement, only 35 percent of the Supplementary Homicide Report cases gave an indication of drug involvement. So the data reported in Figure A6.2 are the more conservative of the two drug estimates.

The figure shows a clear relationship between the growth in drug-related homicide and the growth in homicide generally. The appropriate way to analyze these data is not to compare the number of drug homicides with the total number of homicides in any one year because that would be the part–whole correlation that we criticized in Chapter 7 while discussing guns. But the figure also shows that the four years when drug-related killings represent the greatest proportion of Washington homicides were also the four years with the highest volume of total homicides; and that is not an artifact of the part–whole correlation phenomenon. The only exception to this pattern is 1990, when the second highest homicide rate in Washington, D.C.'s history coincided with only the fourth highest proportion of all homicides involving drugs.

What the data in Figure A6.2 add to estimates of the proportion of homicides that involve drugs is evidence that increases in drug-related homicides are associated with increasing general rates of violent killing. But there are two significant limits to these data as a basis for an inference about drugs and lethal violence. First, the number of drug-related killings is not a well-documented index of either the prevalence of illicit drug use generally or of trends in drug use. Second, the District of Columbia is just one American city among many. Each of these limits suggests the need for substantial supplementary empirical exploration.

References

Amir, Menachem. 1971. *Patterns in Forcible Rape*. Chicago: University of Chicago Press.

Andenaes, Johannes. 1974. *Punishment and Deterrence*. Ann Arbor: University of Michigan Press.

Archer, Dane, and Rosemary Gartner. 1984. *Violence and Crime in Cross-National Perspective*. New Haven, Conn.: Yale University Press.

Baron, James N., and Peter C. Reiss. 1985. "Same Time, Next Year: Aggregate Analyses of the Mass Media and Violent Behavior." *American Sociological Review* 50:347–363.

Benson, Bruce L. 1984. "Guns for Protection and Other Private Sector Responses to the Fear of Rising Crime." In *Firearms and Violence: Issues of Public Policy*, ed. Don B. Kates, Jr. Cambridge, Mass.: Ballinger.

Bentham, Jeremy. 1841a. "Introduction to the Principles of Morals and Legislation [1789]." In *The Works of Jeremy Bentham*, ed. J. Bowring, Vol. 1, pp. 1–54. London: Simpkin, Marshall.

———. 1841b. "Principles of Penal Law [1802]." In *The Works of Jeremy Bentham*, ed. J. Bowring, Vol. 1, pp. 365–580. London: Simpkin, Marshall.

Block, Richard. 1977. *Violent Crime: Environment, Interaction, and Death*. Lexington, MA: Lexington Books.

Block, Richard, and Franklin E. Zimring. 1973. "Homicide in Chicago, 1965–1970." *Journal of Research in Crime and Delinquency* 10:1–12.

Blumstein, Alfred, Jacqueline Cohen, Jeffrey A. Roth, and Christy A. Visher, eds. 1986. *Criminal Careers and "Career Criminals."* Washington, D.C.: National Academy Press.

Bollen, Kenneth A., and David P. Phillips. 1981. "Suicidal Motor Vehicle Fatalities in Detroit: A Replication." *American Journal of Sociology* 87:404–412.

———. 1982. "Imitative Suicides: A National Study of the Effects of Television News Stories." *American Sociological Review* 47:802–809.

Bonger, W.A. 1943. *Race and Crime*. Trans. Margaret M. Hordk, New York: Columbia University Press.

Broder, John M. 1995. "Dole Castigates Hollywood for Debasing U.S. Culture." *Los Angeles Times*, June 1, p. A1.

Butterfield, Fox. 1997. "Number of Slain Police Officers Is Lowest Since 1960." *New York Times*, January 1, Section 1, p.12

Centerwall, Brandon S. 1989a. "Exposure to Television as a Risk Factor for Violence." *Public Communication and Behavior* 2:1–58.

———. 1989b. "Exposure to Television as a Cause of Violence." *American Journal of Epidemiology* 129:643–652.

———. 1992. "Television and Violence: The Scale and the Problem and Where to Go from Here." *Journal of the American Medical Association* 267:3059–3063.

Chappell, Duncan, Gilbert Geis, Stephen Schafer, and Larry Siegel. 1977. "A Comparative Study of Forcible Rape Offenses Known to the Police in Boston and Los Angeles." In *Forcible Rape: The Crime, the Victim, and the Offender*, ed. Duncan Chappell, Robley Geis, and Gilbert Geis, pp. 227–244. New York: Columbia University Press.

Clarke, Ronald V. 1995. "Situational Crime Prevention." In *Crime and Justice: A Review of Research*, ed. Michael Tonry and David P. Farrington, Vol. 19, p. 91. Chicago: University of Chicago Press.

Clarke, Ronald V., and Pat Mayhew. 1988. "The British Gas Suicide Story and Its Criminological Implications." In *Crime and Justice: A Review of Research*, ed. Michael Tonry and Norval Morris, Vol. 10, p. 107. Chicago: University of Chicago Press.

Cohen, Albert K. 1983. "Sociological Theories." In *Encyclopedia of Crime and Justice*, ed. Stanford H. Kadish, Vol. 1, pp. 342–353. New York: Free Press.

Cohen, Jacqueline, and José Canela-Cacho. 1994. "Incapacitation and Violent Crime." In *Understanding and Preventing Violence*, ed. Albert J. Reiss, Jr. and Jeffrey A. Roth, Vol. 4, pp. 296–388. Washington, D.C.: National Academy of Sciences.

Comer, Joseph P. 1985. "Black Violence and Public Policy." In *American Violence and Public Policy*, ed. Lynn A. Curtis, pp. 63–86. New Haven, Conn.: Yale University Press.

Cook, Philip J. 1991. "The Technology of Personal Violence." In *Crime and Justice: A Review of Research*, ed. Michael Tonry. Chicago: University of Chicago Press.

Corman, Hope, Theodore Joyce, and Naci Mocan. 1991. "Homicide and Crack in New York City." In *Searching for Alternatives: Drug-Control Policy in the United States*, ed. Melvyn B. Krauss and Edward P. Lazear, pp. 112–137. Stanford, Calif.: Hoover Institution Press.

De Fleur, Melvin L., and Sandra Ball-Rokeach. 1975. *Theories of Mass Communication*, 3rd edition. New York: David McKay Company.

DiIulio, John. 1994. "The Question of Black Crime." *The Public Interest*, Fall, p. 3.

Eliany, Marc, ed. 1989. *Licit and Illicit Drugs in Canada*. Canada: Ministry of Supply and Services.

Eron, L.D. 1972. "Parent-Child Interaction, Television Violence, and Aggression in Children." *American Psychologist* 37:197–211.

Fagan, Jeffrey. 1990. "Intoxication and Aggression." In *Crime and Justice*, ed. Michael Tonry and James Q. Wilson, Vol. 13, pp. 241–320. Chicago: University of Chicago Press.

Federal Highway Administration (1990). *Highway Statistics*. Washington, D.C.: U.S. Government Printing Office.

Feshbach, Seymour, and Robert D. Singer. 1971. *Television and Aggression*. San Francisco: Josey-Bass.

Freedman, Jonathan L. 1984. "Effect of Television Violence on Aggressiveness." *Psychological Bulletin* 96:227–246.

Friedman, David, and William Sjostrom. 1993. "Hanged for a Sheep. The Economics of Marginal Deterrence." *Journal of Legal Studies* 22:345–366.

Friedman, Milton. 1991. "The War We Are Losing." In *Searching for Alternatives: Drug Control Policy in the United States*, ed. Melvyn B. Krauss and Edward P. Lazear, pp. 53–67. Stanford, Calif.: Hoover Institution Press.

Gastil, Raymond D. 1971. "Homicide and a Regional Culture of Violence." *American Sociological Review* 36:412–427.

Goldstein, Michael J., and Harold S. Kent. 1974. *Pornography and Sexual Deviation*. Berkeley: University of California Press.

Goldstein, Paul J. 1985. "The Drugs/Violence Nexus: A Tripartite Conceptual Framework." *Journal of Drug Issues* 15:493–506.

Goldstein, Paul J., Henry H. Brownstein, Patrick J. Ryan, and Patricia A. Bellucci. 1990. "Crack and Homicide in New York City, 1988: A Conceptually Based Event Analysis." *Contemporary Drug Problems* 16:651–687.

Gottfredson, Don H., and Michael R. Gottfredson, 1980. "Data for Criminal Justice Evaluation: Some Resources and Pitfalls." In *Handbook of Criminal Justice Evaluation*, ed. Malcolm W. Klein and Katherine S. Teilmann. Beverly Hills/London: Sage Publications.

Greenwood, Peter W., with Allan Abrahamse. 1982. *Selective Incapacitation*, Report R-2815-NIJ. Santa Monica, Calif.: Rand Corporation.

Hackney, Sheldon. 1969. "Southern Violence." *American Historical Review* 74:906–925.

Haddon, William, Edward A. Suchman, and David Klein. 1964. *Accident Research: Methods and Approaches*. New York: Harper and Row.

Handgun Control Inc. 1995. *Carrying Concealed Weapons: Questions and Answers*. Washington, D.C.: Handgun Control Inc.

Hartnoll, Richard. 1994. *Multi-City Study: Drug Misuse Trends in Thirteen European Cities*. Strasbourg, France: Council of Europe Press.

Hindelang, Michael J., and Bruce L. Davis. 1977. "Forcible Rape in the United States. A Statistical Profile." In *Forcible Rape: The Crime, the Victim, and the Offender*, ed. Duncan Chappell, Robley Geis, and Gilbert Geis, pp. 87–114. New York: Columbia University Press.

Home Office (1961, 1991–1993). *Criminal Statistics in England and Wales*. London: Her Majesty's Stationery Office.

———. 1984. *Statistics of the Misuse of Drugs, United Kingdom, 1983*. Home Office Statistical Bulletin 18/84. London: Her Majesty's Stationery Office.

———. 1987. *Statistics of the Misuse of Drugs, United Kingdom, 1986*. Home Office Statistical Bulletin 28/87. London: Her Majesty's Stationery Office.

———. 1988. *Statistics of the Misuse of Drugs, United Kingdom, 1987*. Home Office Statistical Bulletin 25/88. London: Her Majesty's Stationery Office.

———. 1995. Personal correspondence from P.H. White, Research and Statistics Department, to Franklin E. Zimring, July 24, 1995.

Hoover, J. Edgar. 1938. *Persons in Hiding*. Boston: Little, Brown.

Information Please Almanac, Atlas, and Yearbook. 1995. Boston: Houghton Mifflin.

Istituto Nazionale di Statistica. 1961, 1991. *Annuario Statistico Italiano 1991*. Rome: Istituto Nazionale di Statistica.

Jacobs, James. 1986. "Exceptions to a General Prohibition on Handgun Possession: Do They Swallow Up the Rule?" *Law and Contemporary Problems* 49;5.

Johnson, Bruce. D., Paul J. Goldstein, Edward Preble, James Schmeidler, Douglas S. Lipton, Barry Spunt, and Thomas Miller. 1985. *Taking Care of Business: The Economics of Crime by Heroin Abusers.* Lexington, Mass.: Lexington Books.

Kaplan, John. 1985. "The Wisdom of Gun Prohibition." *Annals* 455:11.

Katz, Jack. 1988. *The Seductions of Crime.* New York: Basic Books.

Kellerman, Arthur L., and Donald T. Reay 1986. "An Analysis of Firearms-Related Deaths in the Home." *New England Journal of Medicine* 314:1557.

Kleck, Gary. 1991. *Point Blank: Guns and Violence in America.* New York: Aldine.

Kristof, Nicholas. 1996. "In Japan, Nothing to Fear but Fear Itself." *New York Times*, May 19, Section 4, p. 4.

Kropotkin, Peter. 1887. *In Russian and French Prisons.* Reprint. 1971. New York: Schocken Books.

Laurence, Michael, John Snortum, and Franklin E. Zimring, eds. 1988. *Social Control of the Drinking Driver.* Chicago: University of Chicago Press.

Law Enforcement Assistance Administration (1972). *San Jose Methods Test of Known Crime Victims*, Statistics Technical Report No. 1. Washington, D.C.: U.S. Government Printing Office.

Leuw, Ed. 1991. "Drugs and Drug Policy in the Netherlands." In *Crime and Justice: A Review of Research*, ed. Michael Tonry, Vol. 14, pp. 229–276. Chicago: University of Chicago Press.

Loftin, Colin, and Robert H. Hill. 1974. "Regional Subculture and Homicide." *American Sociological Review* 39:714–724.

London Research Centre, Demographic and Statistical Studies Department. 1993. *Annual Abstract of Greater London Statistics.* London: London Research Centre.

McClintock, F. Y., and Evelyn Gibson. 1961. *Robbery in London.* London: Macmillan.

McDowall, David, and Brian Wiersema. 1994. "The Incidence of Defensive Firearm Use by U.S. Crime Victims, 1987–1990." *American Journal of Public Health* 84:1982.

McLuhan, Marshall. 1964. *Understanding Media: The Extensions of Man.* New York: McGraw-Hill.

Milavsky, J. R., H. H. Stipp, R. C. Kessler, and W. S. Rubens. 1982. *Television and Aggression: A Panel Study.* New York: Academic Press.

Ministere de L'Economie et Des Finances. 1961, 1991. *Annuaire Statistique de la France 1991.* Paris: Imprimerie Nationale.

Monahan, John. 1988. "Risk Assessment of Violence Among the Mentally Disordered: Generating Useful Knowledge." *International Journal of Law and Psychiatry* 11:249–257.

Morris, Norval. 1974. *The Future of Imprisonment.* Chicago: University of Chicago Press.

———. 1984. "On 'Dangerousness' in the Judicial Process." *Rec. A.B. City N.Y.* 39:102–128.

Morris, Norval, and Gordon Hawkins. 1971. *Letter to the President on Crime Control.* Chicago: University of Chicago Press.

Morris, Norval, and Michael H. Tonry. 1984. "Black Crime, Black Victims." In

The Pursuit of Criminal Justice. ed. Gordon Hawkins and Franklin E. Zimring. Chicago: University of Chicago Press.

Mukherjee, Satyanshu. 1981. *Crime Trends in Twentieth-Century Australia.* Sydney: Australian Institute of Criminology.

Nixon, Richard M. 1973. Radio Address on Law Enforcement and Drug Abuse Prevention. *Weekly Compendium of Presidential Documents* 9:246. Washington, D.C.: U.S. Government Printing Office.

Office of Criminal Justice Plans and Analysis. 1991. *Homicide in the District of Columbia.* Washington, D.C.: U.S. Government Printing Office.

Office of National Drug Control Policy. 1989. *National Drug Control Strategy.* Washington, D.C.: U.S. Government Printing Office.

Pearson, Geoffrey. 1991. "Drug Control Policies in Britain." In *Crime and Justice: A Review of Research*, ed. Michael Tonry, Vol. 14, pp. 167–227. Chicago: University of Chicago Press.

Phillips, David P. 1978. "Airplane Accident Fatalities Increase Just After Stories About Murder and Suicide." *Science* 201:148–150.

———. 1979. "Suicide, Motor Vehicle Fatalities, and Mass Media: Evidence Toward a Theory of Suggestion." *American Journal of Sociology* 84:1150–1174.

———. 1980. "Airplane Accidents, Murder, and the Mass Media: Towards a Theory of Imitation and Suggestion." *Social Forces* 58:1001–1024.

———. 1983. "The Impact of Mass Media Violence on U.S. Homicides." *American Sociological Review* 48:560–568.

Phillips, David P., and Kenneth A. Bollen. 1985. "Same Time, Last Year: Selective Data Dredging for Negative Findings." *American Sociological Review* 50:364–371.

Rand Corporation. 1995. "'Three Strikes': Serious Flaws and a Huge Price Tag." *Rand Research Review* 19:1–2.

Reiss, Albert J., Jr., and Jeffery A. Roth, eds. 1993. *Understanding and Preventing Violence.* Washington, D.C.: National Academy Press.

Roads and Traffic Authority. 1995. *Sydney's Best Map.* Sydney: Roads and Traffic Authority.

Ruggiero, Vincenzo, and Anthony A. Vass. 1992. "Heroin Use and the Formal Economy: Illicit Drugs and Licit Economies in Italy." *British Journal of Criminology* 92:273–291.

Russell, Diana E.H. 1982. *Rape in Marriage.* New York: Macmillan.

Sarvesvaran, R., and C. H. S. Jayewardene. 1985. "The Role of the Weapon in the Homicide Drama." *Medicine and Law* 4:315.

Seitz, Steven Thomas. 1972. "Firearms Homicide and Gun Control Effectiveness." *Law and Society Development Magazine*, p. 595.

Silberman, Charles E. 1978. *Criminal Violence, Criminal Justice.* New York: Random House.

Statistics Bureau, Management and Coordination Agency. 1961, 1991. *Japan Statistical Yearbook.* Tokyo: Japan Statistical Association.

Statistics Canada, Communications Division. 1961, 1991. *Canada Year Book.* Manitoba: D.W. Friesen & Sons.

Statistisches Bundesamt. 1962, 1991. *Statistisches Jahrbuch für die Bundesrepublik Deutschland.* Wiesbaden: Metzler Poeschel.

Tarde, Gabriel. 1890. *Penal Philosophy.* Trans. R. Howell. Reprint. 1912. Boston: Little, Brown and Company.

Tennenbaum, Abraham N. 1994. "The Influence of the Garner Decision on Police Use of Deadly Force." *Journal of Criminal Law and Criminology* 85:241.

United Nations. 1955–1989. *Statistical Yearbook*. New York: United Nations.

———. 1991. *Demographic Yearbook*. New York: United Nations.

U.S. Department of Commerce, Bureau of the Census. 1976. *Historical Statistics of the United States: Colonial Times to 1970*. Washington, D.C.: U.S. Government Printing Office.

———. 1990. *Current Population Reports*. Washington, D.C.: U.S. Government Printing Office.

———. 1990. *Statistical Abstract of the United States*, 112th edition. Washington, D.C.: U.S. Government Printing Office.

U.S. Department of Health and Human Services. 1991. *Vital Statistics of the United States, Volume II—Mortality*. Hyattsville, Md.: U.S. Department of Heath and Human Services.

U.S. Department of Justice, Bureau of Justice Statistics. 1992. *A National Report: Drugs, Crime, and the Justice System*. Washington, D.C.: U.S. Government Printing Office.

———. 1993. *Criminal Victimization in the United States*. Washington, D.C.: U.S. Government Printing Office.

U.S. Department of Justice, Federal Bureau of Investigation. 1947–1958, 1961–1980, 1990–1993, 1994a. *Crime in the United States*. Washington, D.C.: U.S. Government Printing Office.

———. 1994b. *Uniform Crime Reports: Supplementary Homicide Reports, 1976–1992*. 1st ICPSR version.

U.S. Department of Justice, National Institute of Justice. 1990. *Research in Action, March 1990*. Washington, D.C.: U.S. Government Printing Office.

U.S. National Commission on the Causes and Prevention of Violence. 1969a. Mass Media and Violence, Staff Report, Vol. XI. Washington, D.C.: U.S. Government Printing Office.

———. 1969b. *To Establish Justice, to Insure Domestic Tranquility. Final Report*. Washington, D.C.: U.S. Government Printing Office.

van den Haag, Ernest. 1975. *Punishing Criminals*. New York: Basic Books.

van Dijk, Jan, and Pat Mayhew. 1992. *Criminal Victimization in the Industrial World*. The Hague: Ministry of Justice.

———. 1993. "Criminal Victimization in the Industrialized World: Key Findings of the 1989 and 1992 International Crime Surveys." In *Understanding Crime: Experiences of Crime and Crime Control*, ed. Anna Alvazzi del Frate, Ugljesa Zvekic, and Jan van Dijk. Rome: United Nations Interregional Crime and Justice Research Institute.

Vinson, Tony. 1974. "Gun and Knife Attacks." *Australian Journal of Forensic Science* 7:76.

Walinsky, Adam. 1995. The Crisis of Public Order. *The Atlantic Monthly* (July): 39.

Webster, Daniel. 1993. "The Unconvincing Case for School-Based Conflict Resolution Programs for Adolescents." *Health Affairs* 12:126.

Wintemute, Garen J. 1995. *Trauma in Transition: Trends in Deaths from Firearm and Motor Vehicle Injuries*. Sacramento, Calif.: Violence Prevention Research Program.

Wilson, James Q. 1975. *Thinking About Crime*. New York: Vintage Books.

Wilson, James Q., and Richard J. Herrnstein. 1985. *Crime and Human Nature*. New York: Simon and Schuster.

Wilson, James Q., and George L. Kelling. 1982. "Broken Windows." *Atlantic Monthly*, March, pp. 29–38.

Wolfgang, Marvin. 1958. *Patterns in Criminal Homicide*. Philadelphia: University of Pennsylvania Press.

Wolfgang, Marvin E., and Bernard Cohen. 1970. *Crime and Race: Conceptions and Misconceptions*. New York: Institute of Human Relations Press, American Jewish Committee.

Wolfgang, Marvin, Robert Figlio, and Thorsten Sellin. 1972. *Delinquency in the Birth Cohort*. Chicago: University of Chicago Press.

World Health Organization. 1955–1993. *World Health Statistics Annual*. Geneva: World Health Organization.

Zimring, Franklin E. 1968. "Is Gun Control Likely to Reduce Violent Killings?" *University of Chicago Law Review* 35:721–737.

———. 1972. "The Medium Is the Message: Firearms Caliber as a Determinant of Death from Assault." *Journal of Legal Studies* 1:97–123.

———. 1981. "Kids, Groups, and Crime: Some Implications of a Well-Known Secret." *Journal of Criminal Law and Criminology* 72:867–885.

———. 1988. "Law, Society, and the Drinking Driver: Some Concluding Reflections." In *Social Control of the Drinking Driver*, ed. Michael Laurence, John Snortum, and Franklin Zimring. Chicago: University of Chicago Press.

———. 1994. "'Three Strikes' Law Is Political Fool's Gold." *Christian Science Monitor*, April 11, p. 23.

———. 1996. "Kids, Guns, and Homicide: Policy Notes on an Age-Specific Epidemic." *Law and Contemporary Problems* 59:25–37.

Zimring, Franklin E., and Gordon Hawkins. 1970. "The Legal Threat as an Instrument of Social Change." *Journal of Social Issues* 27:33–48.

———. 1973. *Deterrence: The Legal Threat in Crime Control*. Chicago: University of Chicago Press.

———. 1991. *The Scale of Imprisonment*. Chicago: University of Chicago Press.

———. 1992. *Prison Population and Criminal Justice Policy in California*. Berkeley, Calif.: Institute of Governmental Studies.

———. 1992b. *The Search for Rational Drug Control*. New York: Cambridge University Press.

———. 1995. *Incapacitation: Penal Confinement and the Restraint of Crime*. New York: Oxford University Press.

Zimring, Franklin E., Gordon Hawkins, and Hank Ibser. 1995. "Estimating the Effects of Increased Incarceration on Crime in California." *California Policy Seminar Brief*, Vol. 7, July, pp. 1–12. Berkeley: California Policy Seminar.

Zimring, Franklin E., and James Zuehl. 1986. "Victim Injury and Death in Urban Robbery: A Chicago Study." *Journal of Legal Studies* 15:1–40.

Index

―――

Please remember that this is a library book,
and that it belongs only temporarily to each
person who uses it. Be considerate. Do
not write in this, or any, library book.